AND I TURNED
TO SEE THE VOICE

STUDIES *in* THEOLOGICAL INTERPRETATION

AND I TURNED TO SEE THE VOICE

The Rhetoric of Vision in the New Testament

EDITH M. HUMPHREY

*To Steve,
with gratitude for
your expert &
friendship.
Edith.*

Baker Academic
Grand Rapids, Michigan

Published by Baker Academic
a division of Baker Publishing Group
P.O. Box 6287, Grand Rapids, MI 49516-6287
www.bakeracademic.com

Printed in the United States of America

Library of Congress Cataloging-in-Publication Data
Humphrey, Edith McEwan.
    And I turned to see the voice : the rhetoric of vision in the New Testament / Edith M. Humphrey.
        p.   cm. — (Studies in theological interpretation)
    Includes bibliographical references (p.   ) and indexes..
    ISBN 10: 0-8010-3157-5 (pbk.)
    ISBN 978-0-8010-3157-1 (pbk.)
    1. Bible. N.T.—Criticism, interpretation, etc. 2. Visions. 3. Vision—Religious aspects—Christianity. I. Title.
BS2361.3.H86 2007
225.6—dc22   2007018840

To Debra and Fr. Sean,
who have helped me to see more.

CONTENTS

SERIES PREFACE

As a discipline, formal biblical studies is in a period of reassessment and upheaval. Concern with historical origins and the development of the biblical materials has in many places been replaced by an emphasis on the reader and the meanings supplied by present contexts and communities. The Studies in Theological Interpretation series will seek to appreciate the constructive theological contribution made by Scripture when it is read in its canonical richness. Of necessity, this includes historical evaluation while remaining open to renewed inquiry into what is meant by history and historical study in relation to Christian Scripture. This also means that the history of the reception of biblical texts—a discipline frequently neglected or rejected altogether—will receive fresh attention and respect. In sum, the series is dedicated to the pursuit of constructive theological interpretation of the church's inheritance of prophets and apostles in a manner that is open to reconnection with the long history of theological reading in the church. The primary emphasis is on the constructive theological contribution of the biblical texts themselves.

New commentary series have sprung up to address these and similar concerns. It is important to complement this development with brief, focused, and closely argued studies that evaluate the hermeneutical, historical, and theological dimensions of scriptural reading and interpretation for our times. In the light of shifting and often divergent methodologies, the series will encourage studies in theological interpretation that model clear and consistent methods in the pursuit of theologically engaging readings.

An earlier day saw the publication of a series of short monographs and compact treatments in the area of biblical theology that went by the name Studies in Biblical Theology. The length and focus of the contributions were salutary features and worthy of emulation. Today, however, we find no consensus regarding the nature of biblical theology, and this is a good reason to explore anew what competent theological reflection on Christian Scripture might look like in our day. To this end, the present series, Studies in Theological Interpretation, is dedicated.

PREFACE

This book brings together several long-standing interests: a fascination for vision-reports in various kinds of ancient literature, a concern for different approaches in the literary and rhetorical study of texts, and a dawning awareness of the transformative embrace of the Scriptures. In the first case, I am a bit of a voyeur, having never had an unambiguous vision of my own to report (or do luminous dreams count?). In the second, I have been involved for decades, from undergraduate years in discussion with other Victoria College students immediately following the stimulating lectures of Northrop Frye, through to my recent interchanges with Society of Biblical Literature and Canadian Society of Biblical Studies colleagues involved in literary, sociological, and rhetorical analyses of the Scriptures. Finally, I have been drawn by a deepening attachment to the Great Tradition of the church, and emboldened by the growing acceptance of engaged reading and a renewed biblical theology in the academy.

My quest for a fruitful way of reading vision-reports has extended over the past thirteen years, and has been matched by a parallel pilgrimage in the "nonacademic" areas of my life. Some portions of this book have thus appeared in other forms, as I have worked through an approach to reading that seeks to do justice to the literary, rhetorical, and theological aspects of these numinous (and luminous) texts. Other passages are reworked forms of unpublished papers that I have offered in various venues, and newly written analyses done specifically for this monograph based on the insights that have emerged during this time of inquiry. The commentary on the transfiguration episodes, developed from my popular study *Ecstasy and Intimacy,* is marked by the hermeneutic recommended by Georges Florovsky and Theodore G. Stylianopoulos to "integrate 'what is new and what is old'" (Matt. 13:52).[1] Section one and section three contain reconsidered and reframed material on Paul, on Stephen, and on Jesus' vision of Satan's fall drawn from my first foray into this arena published in the 1993 issue of *ARC: The Journal of the Faculty of Religious Studies, McGill University.*[2] Section two includes a revised form of an essay on Acts 10–11 that appeared two years later in *Semeia*[3] at the encouragement of my colleagues Robert Culley and Ian Henderson. I am particularly grateful for conversations with Ian Henderson in these early stages of inquiry. Section four includes and expands the entire argument from the 1999 essay included in the groundbreaking volume *Vision and Persuasion.*[4] I have received permission to reprint this latter piece, for which I give thanks to Chalice Press as well as to the meticulous editing of Greg Bloomquist and Greg Carey, whose work was invaluable in the first appearance of that essay. My thanks are also due to my generous colleagues

1. The plea for a "neopatristic synthesis" was first made by Florovsky in "The Ethos of the Orthodox Church," in *Orthodoxy: A Faith and Order Dialogue,* ed. Keith R. Bridston (Geneva: World Council of Churches, 1960), 36–51. Though Florovsky was describing the strengths of Orthodoxy in particular, Stylianopoulos follows the spirit of his recommendations in calling this an "ecumenical hermeneutical proposal" and detailing it in *The New Testament: An Orthodox Perspective,* vol. 1, *Scripture, Tradition, Hermeneutics* (Brookline, MA: Holy Cross Orthodox Press, 1999), 187–283.

2. "'I Saw Satan Fall . . .'—The Rhetoric of Vision," *ARC: The Journal of the Faculty of Religious Studies, McGill University* 21 (1993): 75–88.

3. "Collision of Modes?—Vision and Determining Argument in Acts 10:1–11:18," *Semeia* 71 (1995): 65–84.

4. "In Search of a Voice: Rhetoric through Sight and Sound in Revelation 11:15–12:17," in *Vision and Persuasion: Rhetorical Dimensions of Apocalyptic Discourse,* ed. Greg Carey and L. Gregory Bloomquist (St. Louis: Chalice, 1999), 141–60.

Dale Allison and Steven Tuell, who read a draft of this book and offered invaluable suggestions.

While I have spent many beguiling and invigorating hours with colleagues who concentrate on the field of rhetorical studies, I do not consider myself a specialist in this area, but one whose main interests, literary and theological, have been greatly enriched by it. Those immersed in classical rhetoric will be all too aware of my novitiate status in their field, but they may be interested in what emerges from a cross-fertilization of strategies and disciplines in the course of the following study. I offer these readings and reflections largely with the New Testament student and analyst in mind, in hope that my findings concerning the literary and rhetorical subtleties of the biblical vision-report will engage them just as I have been engrossed by the issues emerging from these texts. I have tried, where at all possible, to define and explain technical terms to aid the nonspecialist. Likewise, all Greek is translated. For the most part, where the New Testament is cited, I have done my own translation, although occasionally I have used the older RSV, since its formal quality seems more suited to the hieratic quality of vision than the NRSV.

What I have written here is also offered in hope of encouraging a conversation that is increasingly choate and that must be fostered, though with care. It concerns how we can negotiate scholarly discussion and debate in an academic environment that is at once more pluralist and less dispassionate than what was the norm in an earlier generation. My plea for a hermeneutics of receptivity comes from my own passion for reading and especially for the Scriptures. It is clear that such an approach will be more congenial to those readers who, like me, have discovered that knowledge is not merely perspectival, nor found wholly in a system of thought, but is found in a Person. I would hope, however, that any who value the human imagination might be convinced to go at least part of the way with me and allow themselves to be affected by these astounding texts. For to read is to be changed.

Feast of Saints Peter and Paul, 2006

INTRODUCTION

Vision-Report as Artifact and Polemic

Readers of the New Testament have frequently overlooked its vision-reports, thinking of these as mostly confined to that eccentric last book of the biblical collection, the Apocalypse. In fact, the vision-report, though not a dominant genre, shines forth at crucial moments, from the beginning of the Gospel narratives, through the Acts of the Apostles, to the Pauline and Catholic Epistles. The annunciation and visions surrounding the nativity, the Baptist's vision of the Spirit alighting on the young Messiah, the glory of the transfiguration, Jesus' declaration to the seventy of Satan's downfall, the resurrection, the ascension, Stephen's identification of Jesus as Son of Man, the inclusion of the Gentiles, the blinding call of Saul, the projected martyrdoms of Peter (John 21) and Paul (Acts 9:16; 21:11), the promised destruction of evil, and the glimpse of a New Jerusalem—all these dramatic moments come to the reader framed as reports of those who have seen the extraordinary. Besides all this, amidst the diversity of the New Testament writers, we find agreement with regard to the content of God's greatest "apocalypse"—that Jesus the Christ has shown forth, in a unique manner, the life and action of God.

So then, the New Testament writings, though not replete with vision-reports, are studded at key moments by them and are predicated on the paradigmatic apocalypse of the Holy One. It is not, of course, that the early Christian writings present the Jesus event as a mere revelation of hidden reality for the informed mind, as is the tendency in gnostic writings. One of the earliest criteria for authentic Christian witness was the insistence, after all, that the fleshly visitation of the Messiah was active and effective (and not simply a "sign" or an "appearance," 1 John 4:2); yet Jesus, by his coming, has also committed an interpreted "vision" of the mysterious Godhead to the believing community:

> In that same hour he rejoiced in the Holy Spirit and said, "I thank thee, Father, Lord of heaven and earth, that thou hast hidden these things from the wise and understanding and revealed them to babes; yea, Father, for such was thy gracious will. All things have been delivered to me by my Father; and no one knows who the Son is except the Father, or who the Father is except the Son and any one to whom the Son chooses to reveal him." Then turning to the disciples he said privately, "Blessed are the eyes which see what you see! For I tell you that many prophets and kings desired to see what you see, and did not see it, and to hear what you hear, and did not hear it." (Luke 10:21–24 RSV)

This passage (paralleled substantively in Matt. 11:25–27 and 13:16–17) indicates that the presence of the Son was understood as providing a kind of "vision" or "foresight" of those things that remain unseen, accompanied by an authoritative interpretation of them. These "mysteries" are described as having been vouchsafed to a first generation and communicated among the company of the faithful. Alongside this startling passage, the so-called "Johannine bolt from the blue,"[1] we may place the following verses from John, Paul, and the Catholic/General Writings:

---

1. The original phrase seems to be that of Karl von Hase, who spoke of "an aerolite fallen from the Johannine heaven" (*"ein Aerolith aus dem johanneischen Himmel gefallen"*) in *Geschichte Jesu, nach akademischen Vorlesungen*, 2te Aufl. (Leipzig: Breitkopf u. Haertel, 1891), 527.

No one has ever seen God; God the only Son, who is intimate with the Father, has exegeted him; "Show us the Father." . . . "The one who has seen me has seen the Father"; "I pray . . . also for those who believe in me through their word, that they may all be one"; "I made known to them your name, and I will make it known." (John 1:18; 14:8–9; 17:20–21, 26)

We preach Christ crucified, a scandal to Jews and foolishness to Gentiles, but to those who are called, both Jews and Greeks, Christ the power of God and the wisdom of God. . . . We impart a secret and hidden wisdom of God, which God decreed for our glorification before the ages. . . . This is how one should regard us—as slaves of Christ and custodians of the mysteries of God. (1 Cor. 1:23–24; 2:7; 4:1)

We were eyewitnesses of his majesty. For when he received honor and glory from God the Father . . . we heard this voice carried from heaven, for we were with him on the holy mountain. And we have the prophetic word made more sure. You will do well to pay attention to this as to a lamp shining in a dark place, until "the day" dawns and the morning star arises in your hearts. (2 Pet. 1:16–19)

In many and various ways God spoke of old to our fathers by the prophets; but in these last days he has spoken to us by his Son, whom he appointed the heir of all things, through whom also he created the world. He reflects the glory of God and bears the very imprint of his nature. (Heb. 1:1–3)

That which was from the beginning, which we have heard, which we have seen with our eyes, which we have looked upon and touched with our hands, concerning the word of life—even the life that was shown forth, and we behold it, and testify to it, and proclaim to you the eternal life which was with the Father and was shown forth to us. (1 John 1:1–2)

All the selections above present the revelation both as something that has been seen and heard in a first instance, and as something that can be transmitted as more than a recorded and remembered teaching—truly communicated to the Christian community as a shared and sacred mystery. The revelation thus involves both the sight of the glory of God in Jesus and the words that interpret what has been seen. This is in harmony with the broader Hebrew and Christian tradition, where God is depicted as communicating by both vision and audition; frequently the two are conjoined so that revealing mystery is placed in the context of interpretive word or interpretive word is made vivid or enhanced by vision. So it is that the vision-report, which likewise is composed of images and words, may become an apt representation, in miniature, of the gospel; for the "gospel" is not simply a deposit of "good news" but also the representation and interpretation of the epic story directed by God, in which God himself[2] has acted and continues to act.

In other religious traditions, visions frequently take on the connotation of privileged and esoteric illumination. While a sense of awe surrounding things visionary is retained in these New Testament texts, there remains, because of the centrality of the Christ event, an assumption that the interpreted vision is common property among the faithful: "But we *all* with unveiled faces behold the glory of the Lord" (2 Cor. 3:18). In this sense, New Testament visions are "demystified" and directed toward a common end: their significance is defined insofar as they indicate, in one way or another, the great *apokalypsis* that has already been made known. The visions, though frequently symbolic (so either bizarre or artful in representation) are not left, so to speak, to "stand alone," but serve a particular higher purpose (along with other contingent purposes as well). For this reason, a consideration of the various rhetorical functions of vision-reports in the New Testament is intriguing, for where we find vision-reports, we inevitably find argumentation, either explicit or implicit.

Readers of visions typically have pursued two separate aims— there are those who attend to the phenomenon of the vision itself, and there are those who attend to the art or aesthetics

2. Despite twenty-first century concerns regarding masculine language for God, I will retain the conventions of the canonical texts that we will be reading. This will render observations on the text more authentic, particularly in analysis of those sections where masculine-feminine imagery comes into full play.

of the report. Those who engage specifically with visions may be motivated either by fascination for or distrust of the visionary's claims; those who set themselves to analyze the narrative elements of the vision-report are perhaps less subjectively engaged at the outset, though they may well react to the skill (or otherwise) of the author as their analysis proceeds. Within the academy, biblical specialists have likewise tended to approach the visions of the Hebrew and Christian texts and traditions in either phenomenological or literary terms. In the first case, the vision-reports are considered as raw material, primary data for a study in various cultural responses to or beliefs about the numinous.[3] Others have fastened upon the literary techniques that surround the biblical narratives, tracing the typical contours of the apocalyptic genre[4] or visionary sub-text[5] within host genres, and either marveling at the deft use of the form by a particular author or cringing at what they have deemed to be a naïve passage embedded in the Scriptures. This bifurcation of study into "anthropology" and "literary studies" has meant that, until rather recently, vision-reports have seldom been examined for their palpable rhetorical power or in terms of the diverse rhetorical roles that they play in their various literary and social contexts.

3. See, for example, the anthropologically oriented studies on the prophetic literature of the Hebrew Bible in such volumes as *Interpretation* 32 (1978). Of particular interest here is Robert R. Wilson, "Early Israelite Prophecy" (pp. 3–16), in which prophets are described in terms of their "central" or "peripheral" position in society and their activity is seen in light of divinization and shamanistic activity.

4. See, for example, the findings produced by the Society of Biblical Literature Seminar devoted to apocalypses: John J. Collins, ed. *Semeia* 14 (1979); Adela Yarbro Collins, ed. *Semeia* 36 (1986).

5. On this, see John S. Hanson, "Dreams and Visions in the Greco-Roman World and Early Christianity," in *Aufstieg und Niedergang der römischen Welt*, 2.23.2, ed. Wolfgang Haase (Berlin: de Gruyter, 1980), 1395–1427. Hanson's analysis of the vision-report is very helpful, sketching the shape and conventions used in this literary form and illustrating by means of various kinds of literature. I am not convinced, however, by his studied conflation of "dream" and "vision" into one form, "the dream-vision"; see esp. p. 1408, where he speaks of the near "impossibility" of making this distinction. Though the forms are similar and do overlap, not all New Testament visions are reported as having occurred within the context of a dream; comparison of "waking" and "dreaming" visions may be an important avenue of inquiry.

Vision-Report as a Literary Form

The vision-report as a literary form is a complex subject that deserves and has received attention in its own right. The present study adopts a rather wide definition of "vision-report," understanding it as a literary form (whether or not it is based on a previous oral report) that is signaled by various conventions, that is placed in various literary contexts, and that is put to numerous uses by the author, who incorporates it into a larger work. John Hanson, in describing what he calls the "dream-vision report," indicates that this literary form includes:

- a setting with various details of the visionary's context and mindset
- characteristic terminology that identifies the sequence as a vision
- audio-visual, auditory[6] only, or visual only content of deep significance, related in the first or third person
- a description of the seer's reaction and response

Hanson concludes:

> The fully recounted dream-vision report is a relatively short narrative of a dream or vision which exhibits most or all of a characteristic set of components that include the dreamer, place, time, mental state, dream figure, message and/or scene, reaction and response, along with one or more technical terms. The subject matter has great variety, but it is almost always revelatory, containing some type of message or pertinent information related to the dreamer and his circumstances.[7]

He completes his outline of the literary form by speaking of the "function" of vision-reports, which occurs in various narrative

---

6. Properly, this "vision" is actually an "audition," but Hanson considers the audition to be "a designation . . . of dubious value" ("Dreams and Visions," 1411). This is debatable, particularly if one is concerned to show the interplay between what is seen and what is heard.

7. Hanson, "Dreams and Visions," 1413.

contexts, so that this may "direct or redirect the movement of the narrative, and not simply that of the dreamer."[8]

Hanson's detailed compilation of formal and constituent elements is most helpful, though his emphasis on content rather overshadows the discussion of function, as is often the case in literary analyses. Indeed, had he paid more attention to function, Hanson may have revised his opinion that the vision-report is "frequently understandable" in itself, "not requir[ing] the literary context for coherence."[9] That many visions frequently have "oracles" or "auditions" embedded in them would call this assertion into question. They are, indeed, used within the context of a larger narrative, and this makes it highly unlikely that they are stand-alone revelations, though certainly the symbolic and allusive impact of a visionary sequence can never be transposed wholly into words. Visions are, after all, visions, and to "decode" them into a proposition or method is to change not only the form but also the meaning. There are, however, rare "visions" that are woodenly allegorical and patently artificial, whose purpose is simply to teach, and where propositions have borrowed the garb of vision in order to sustain interest. One might, for example, cite the "Animal Apocalypse" of *1 Enoch* 89:41–50, where the symbolism is pedagogical, having a one-to-one correspondence with its meaning, and open to decoding. Each symbol in this allegorical history refers to one thing or one person, with the "rams" being King Saul and King David, the "beasts" the Gentiles, the "sheep" the people of Israel, and so on. Vision-reports sometimes have this kind of "steno"[10]

8. Ibid.
9. Ibid.
10. The term "steno," in contrast to "tensive," was originally used by Philip Wheelwright (*Metaphor and Reality* [Bloomington: Indiana University Press, 1962], 555) and has become current in biblical studies through the efforts of Norman Perrin in such articles as his "Eschatology and Hermeneutics: Reflections on Method in the Interpretation of the New Testament," *Journal of Biblical Literature* 93 (1974): 3–14. A strict polarization between these two types of symbolism is aptly questioned by John J. Collins in "The Symbolism of Transcendence in Jewish Apocalyptic," *Papers of the Chicago Society of Biblical Research* 19 (1974): 5–22. Collins cogently argues that even in symbolic pieces that would generally be considered "steno," there is "an evocative power" (p. 15) that cannot be fully rendered in decoding prose. Given this "remainder" of symbolic meaning, it is probably more accurate to speak of tendencies

(one-to-one) symbolism, and are "self-interpreting." More often, though, vision-reports are allusive, with the symbolism going off in various directions, ringing different bells all at once. Symbolism like this tantalizes; it is puzzling and mysterious. Typically in the Scriptures, such visions also include various verbal indicators—an interpreting angel, an oracle or "word" about the vision, a reflection by the seer—in order to guide the reader.

However, many aspects of the vision-report are indeed left to stand on their own: one of the aims of the vision-report seems to be to surround, to overwhelm, to surprise the reader. It is as though we are seeing the vision "by proxy," through the eyes of the seer, and must be taken away by the mystery and enter into it. Words are given to help us, but not to neutralize the mystery. Thus, if Hanson is concerned to allow the "givenness" and the mystery of a vision to stand (so that the vision-report is seen as coherent in itself), his words concerning their "self-interpreting" quality make sense. However, in the Jewish and Christian traditions, vision and words are typically conjoined, even while some aspects of the vision are left to make an imaginative rather than a cognitive impact. Indeed, with the exception of the long visionary sequences of the Apocalypse, virtually every example of vision-report in the New Testament is connected with a clear interpretative word or directed context, even while the imagination is engaged by the inherent mystery of the vision. It is, then, by the combination of vision and word, and by its place within the larger narrative, that the report makes its rhetorical impact. As for the Apocalypse, we shall see that the visions contained therein also are interpreted by narrative context and word, though apocalypse by its nature is a particularly "open" genre that speaks as much to the heart as to the mind. We are concerned, then, for function and effect, not

---

toward steno symbolism and to acknowledge that there is never a simple one-to-one correspondence between the symbols and their interpretation. However, the distinction made by Wheelwright and Perrin is still helpful in pointing out that some symbolic systems are more "flat," corresponding directly to denotations that may be otherwise and less picturesquely expressed, even if the prose cannot adequately capture the affective connotations that the original symbolic language awakens. Other symbolic passages are more characteristically centrifugal and polyvalent, in both denotation and connotation; it is with these that we are particularly concerned in this study.

simply for the structure and content of the vision-report—thus, rhetorical analysis is of great help. This study will consider a selection of New Testament vision-reports that fill the literary and formal criteria set out by Hanson and others, look to the function of these reports within their narrative framework, and consider how the reports make a rhetorical impact by their connection with the implicit or explicit argumentation of the author.

The Contribution of Rhetorical Analysis

The advent of rhetorical studies within the arena of biblical analysis has been nourishing for biblical studies, especially because rhetorical methods have the potential to bring together concerns that typically have been divided. Rhetoric, after all, is interconnected with the historical, the social, and the literary. Inquiry into the mode of argumentation found in a particular piece also leads the student to consider the various moments in the writing-reading process that have often vied for attention: the "intent" of the writer, the text "in itself," the "response" or even "creative collusion" of the reader. Rhetorical analysis is interested in the speech craft of the writer (sometimes as put into the mouth of a character in the text), in the persuasive power of the speech itself (as encoded in the text), and in the effect on the listener (i.e., characters listening within the text, the implied reader, the reader more-or-less contemporary with the writer, and other subsequent readers). By its nature, then, the study of rhetoric has an integrative aspect, for it is concerned with communication.

However, it is also the case that interest in rhetoric has emerged during a time when the discipline of biblical studies has become increasingly introspective. As Stamps remarks, "New Testament scholarship, especially since the flood of rhetorical studies which have emerged . . . is in a reflective and reflexive mode."[11] The proliferation of volumes and series such as *Semeia* and *Biblical Interpretation* dedicated to multidisciplinary methods dem-

11. D. L. Stamps, "Rhetorical Criticism and the Rhetoric of New Testament Criticism," *Literature and Theology* 6 (1992): 272.

onstrates that Stamps is right. The bewildering plurality in biblical studies (and, more broadly, in religious studies) has led some
to consider whether there remains a unified academic discipline,
or whether the fragmentation is terminal, so that Religious Studies departments ought to be collapsed and parcelled out into the
larger areas of philosophy, literary studies, and the like. Some
brave souls have tried to rearticulate a common core and have
used theological, sociological, or ideological terms to tame the
monster. Over ten years ago Vernon Robbins responded to the
challenge of the "significant divisions of the house in New Testament interpretation" by attempting to "organize a conversation"
on the stories told about one New Testament narrative.[12] This
approach is well summarized by the title of his article: "Using a
Socio-Rhetorical Poetics to Develop a Unified Method." He asks
the poignant questions, "Is it possible for the groups to talk to
one another? Is it possible for one group to use insights, strategies,
and results from another?"[13] Robbins intends by his project to go
beyond mere exegesis: he wants to "formulate issues in a manner
that can enable dialogue to begin."[14]

In light of these larger issues, we see that what has been valued
as a strength of the rhetorical method(s)—adaptability and an
ability to bring together historical, literary, and reader-response
concerns—is also a complicating feature. This is because those
who engage in a rhetorical approach frequently concentrate more
on their particular method, its potential, and its distinctiveness
in the context of multiple reading methods, than on the texts
that they hope the method will illuminate. The reader thus finds
himself or herself faced with at least two objects of concern: the
text itself and the lens used to see that text. From one perspective, this is a necessary encumbrance of critical study, for readers
who claim "simply to read the text" are blithely unaware of the

12. Vernon K. Robbins, "Using a Socio-Rhetorical Poetics to Develop a Unified
Method: The Woman Who Anointed Jesus as a Test Case," in *1992 Seminar Papers*,
ed. Eugene Lovering, Society of Biblical Literature Seminar Papers Series 31 (Atlanta:
Scholars Press, 1992), 303.
13. Ibid.
14. Ibid.

intricacies involved in reading and may well mistake their own assumptions for those of the author. It is important to know something about the glasses, or instruments, by which we see the world around us, in terms of both their benefits and their constraints; if I use my reading glasses while driving, I may end up with a nasty surprise.

However, introspection can also become so wholly consuming that little "seeing" goes on beyond the preliminaries of method. Indeed, the flourishing of the field of rhetorical studies has been marked by competing claims and debates regarding the benefits of one method over another so that there are many contenders for our attention. Besides Robbins's meta-methodical approach,[15] rhetoricians in biblical studies recognize the more classical approach[16] (which uses ancient Greco-Roman speechcraft as a source for the analysis of biblical texts), the eclectic and motivational approaches of Wilhelm Wuellner[17] and Walter Fischer,[18] and the "new rhetoric" of Chaim Perelman and L. Olbrechts-Tyteca.[19]

15. Robbins's overtures have been marked by an attention to text as well as an introspective analysis that many, including this writer, find immensely helpful. Rhetorical analysis inevitably leads the scholar to think about why one does what one does since the method is hybrid in nature, unless it is done as a sterile five-finger exercise. As we shall see in chap. 3, Robbins has articulated socio-rhetorical analysis as a kind of meta-criticism, a comprehensive method with at first four, and now five, levels of analysis. In seeking to demonstrate both the diversity of components of the text and the richness of "voices" found therein, Robbins has forged an authentic postmodern approach that commands attention.

16. See, for example, the several works of Burton L. Mack, Vernon K. Robbins, and George A. Kennedy.

17. Wilhelm Wuellner, "Where Is Rhetorical Criticism Taking Us?" *Catholic Biblical Quarterly* 49 (1987): 448–63.

18. Walter R. Fischer, "A Motive View of Communication," *Quarterly Journal of Speech* 56 (1970): 131–39.

19. Chaim Perelman and L. Olbrechts-Tyteca first published their treatise on informal reasoning under the title *La Nouvelle Rhétorique: Traité l'argumentation*, 2 vols. (Paris: J. Vrin, 1958). It was subsequently published in English as *The New Rhetoric: A Treatise on Argumentation*, trans. John Wilkinson and Percell Weaver (Notre Dame, IN: University of Notre Dame Press, 1969). In this volume Perelman and Olbrechts-Tyteca, with insights from the realms of philosophy, ethics, law, politics, and even contemporary journalism, work out a theory of argumentation with consideration for classical categories, probability theory, and the role of the reader.

A Literary-Rhetorical Strategy

The discussion of various approaches to rhetorical study is intriguing, and new insights have emerged through the interventions of those who concentrate on the rhetorical dimension of the text by the use of one strategy or another. However, I do not intend in this study to champion one particular method. Rather, I aim to attend to the literary and rhetorical dimensions of vision and vision-reports in the New Testament, suiting the various tools of these approaches to the particular text at hand. Though the social dimensions of these texts must surely come to the fore from time to time, the focus of this study will be literary-rhetorical rather than socio-rhetorical. When social and rhetorical concerns are married, texts can often be construed in terms of power plays and suasion in the sense of empowerment or disestablishment. Though these dynamics are significant, I seek a less cynical or violent reading of texts that befriends rather than interrogates: this stance emerges more naturally in an approach that focuses on the literary and rhetorical facets of what is being read and how these make their impact on a sympathetic community of readers. I want to celebrate the texts as important in their own right, and not simply as windows into the culture that produced them. We have to do with vision-reports within a classical corpus that deserves our admiration as readers of literature while it also continues today to exercise a quickening function that is analogous to the deep impact made on earlier generations. In other words, it is good to allow such vibrant voices to suggest the type of reading that best suits each of them rather than to approach them with a ready-made method to which they must be subjected.

For these reasons, the analyses of the chosen texts will be deliberately eclectic, paying heed to the insights of the various literary and rhetorical methods without attempting to form a meta-method that is all-consuming. The purpose of the study is not to be encyclopedic in terms of saying everything that can be said about the various texts. Instead, the goal is modest and the focus fine rather than broad. I aim to highlight and compare how it is that in vision-reports *word* and *image* work together, either as equals or with one of these elements dominant and the other supportive. These twin themes of word and image, manifestly dominant in both the Jewish and Christian traditions, thus serve as an entrée into the vision-reports of this corpus, specifically those of the New Testament. Such numinous passages frequently have been disclosed by literary criticism to be significant artifacts of the tradition, as also they have been seized on by phenomenologists in an attempt to describe the religious genius of Christianity: they possess considerable suasive power. Those for whom the texts serve more than a literary or sociological function may well ask how this persuasive dimension coheres with the theological purpose(s) of the text—how the vision-reports in their particularity show forth the One who has been called the Word and Image of God and how they elicit a response from those who read, hear, and see.

In this study, then, we will hearken to the rhetorical dimensions of the New Testament vision-report, engaging in a close analysis of several significant texts, while also comparing the particular way in which the vision-report is deployed in each passage to further the argument at hand. The rhetorical analysis of vision is in its infancy, so far as the study of the New Testament is concerned: beginnings have been made in the research on apocalyptic discourse conducted by the Society of Biblical Literature Rhetoric in the New Testament Seminar,[20] but there is still a good deal more to be learned about the rhetoric of vision-reports per se. Here we will give close attention to passages from the Pauline letters, the Gospels, Acts, and Revelation, with regard to both literary and rhetorical details, and then compare these texts to each other, so that they may be traced along a spectrum of hermeneutical polyvalence and univocity. It will be seen that each of the pieces emerges as a powerful example of early Christian rhetoric, a notable *poesis* to be admired, and a

20. Two comparative volumes have emerged from this group and those associated with it: Carey and Bloomquist, *Vision and Persuasion*; and Duane F. Watson, ed., *The Intertexture of Apocalyptic Discourse in the New Testament*, Society of Biblical Literature Symposium Series 14 (Atlanta: Society of Biblical Literature Press, 2002). The first of these attends to pieces that may be considered under the definition of the genre "apocalypse." The second is a broader study of apocalypticism as seen in New Testament discourse that adopts the socio-rhetorical method of Vernon K. Robbins for its structure.

testimony to the persuasive power of the earliest Christian authors. Moreover, the particular relationship of each vision-report to the overall process of argumentation will be seen: some visions bring speech to an apt and powerful conclusion; others direct the polemic of a narrative through recapitulation or strategic placement; still others, embryonic in form, subtly shape the message of the passage in which they are embedded; and extensive visions allow the readers' imaginations freer reign even while they are guided by propositions included within the vision sequence.

Clearly, vision-reports are used in both explicit and implicit ways, and at different points of a narrative or argument, to achieve different purposes and with differing effects. Inherent in the vision-report is a "liveliness" that allows the report to take on a life of its own, more or less unhampered by the overall argumentation. Sometimes this vitality enhances the explicit argument, and at other times it complicates or even clashes with it, producing an ambiguous or sophisticated rhetorical situation. Yet, because the Christian texts tend not to report visions for their own sake, the report is not permitted to break entirely free of its moorings. It will be seen that where propositional language ("word") dominates, the text tends to be more directly polemical, less "open" in possibilities of interpretation; over against such texts stand more allusive passages in which images dominate, though these are given some direction or interpretation by attached or embedded propositions.

These texts may be put on a spectrum, ranging from overt polemic to suggestive vision, the former appealing mostly to logic, the latter making an impact on the imagination:

$\longleftarrow$ ————————————————————————————— $\longrightarrow$

Verbal, Polemical, Closed   Visual, Symbolic, Open
(appealing to logic)   (appealing to the imagination)

At the outset of this study we might expect that the former texts (i.e., the "verbal" ones) exhibit the strongest persuasive power, whereas the latter (the "visual" texts) would have mostly an aesthetic appeal. Surprisingly, it will be seen that rhetorical or directive power persists throughout these texts, whether they are predominantly propositional or primarily imagistic in nature. "Closed" polemical texts that are clinched or directed by speech make a *sharp* impression on readers; "open" symbolic texts that work mainly through imagery and echoes make a *deep* impression. Even in the latter cases the polyvalent potential of the vision-report does not render this genre a literary Rorschach test, though some imaginative, heedless, or violent readers have occasionally co-opted the reports for purposes that run absolutely contrary to their literary and historical contexts.

The vision-report becomes, as it were, a "hard case" scenario for the ever-present and increasingly urgent questions attending the contemporary study of hermeneutics. We have, in this last generation, witnessed a sea change in the academic approach to interpretation. There has been a decisive shift from the "objective model," which stressed a scientific distinction between "what the text said" and "how it is to be applied," to more subjective and pluralist presuppositions, in which the importance of the text is no longer seen as meaning determined by the author, by the text itself, or even through various criteria accepted by a community of readers. The emphasis now, by and large, is on the "openness" of the text and the multivalent potential that it provides for the imaginative and/or cause-engaged reader. Creativity and ideology are indeed frequently mixed in amazing ways as readers of biblical texts adopt the stance of moralists and critics, but when questioned about the suitability of their presuppositions, they demur that they are simply "playing" with the text. The distance evident between the presuppositions of the ancient world and our own has led to the adoption of a hermeneutics of suspicion among many, now de rigeur among a readership that is disturbed by the way in which religious texts have shaped our imaginations. This study, though in the first place concerned with the diverse ways in which vision-reports are framed and directed in the New Testament, is also an overture toward the adoption of a different stance—a hermeneutics of welcome. For the texts (along with their authors and diverse readers prior to our own age) may be fruitfully approached as welcome guests, rather than as inscrutable strangers, hegemonic hierarchs, or violent enemies. It is to this quest that we turn in the conclusion.

1

MAKING A CASE

Word Clinched by Vision

(2 CORINTHIANS 12:1–10; ACTS 7:54–60)

Classical Rhetoric and Vision in New Testament Texts

In dealing with New Testament texts that are straightforwardly polemical, it has become common to consider them in terms of Greco-Roman rhetoric on the assumption that at least some if not all of the first-century authors had a foot in two worlds—that is, they had a general knowledge not only of the Hebrew traditions but of the classical traditions as well. This is most demonstrable in the case of Luke, who knows well the Septuagint, that Hebrew Bible of the Diaspora, even while he addresses his ideal reader, "excellent Theophilus," in a manner informed by classical *bios* and "history." It is also true of Paul, a Jewish Roman citizen, who, in the estimation of most scholars, appears to have manipulated the conventions of the ancient rhetoricians. Given that Paul's writings are designed to persuade and that Paul demonstrates an acquaintance with Greco-Roman strategies, it is not surprising that the

31

first major study of a New Testament book in terms of classical
rhetoric tackled his most polemical letter, Galatians.[1]

Following the first closely argued rhetorical analysis of a New
Testament book, offered by Hans Dieter Betz,[2] students waited
several years for a self-conscious methodological description of
such a method. This was provided by George A. Kennedy, who
outlined the immense potential of studying the New Testament
documents in the light of classical rhetoric.[3] Kennedy's pioneer-
ing book was followed by numerous studies, including the significant interventions of Burton Mack and Vernon Robbins,
who, in *Patterns of Persuasion in the Gospels*,[4] introduced New
Testament students to the classical "elaboration of the *chreia*,"
that is, the schoolboy's creative speech, constructed to elucidate
and demonstrate the saying, or *chreia,* of a noteworthy person.
Here New Testament students were reminded that rhetorical
training was commonplace in the ancient world, and so it is
plausible that the New Testament writers were acquainted with
the conventions.

1. Hans D. Betz, *Galatians: A Commentary on Paul's Letter to the Churches in Galatia,* Hermeneia (Philadelphia: Fortress, 1979). Betz's approach has become com-
monplace, but it has also been challenged; cf. Philip H. Kern, *Rhetoric and Galatians: Assessing an Approach to Paul's Epistle*, Society for New Testament Studies Monograph Series 101 (Cambridge: Cambridge University Press, 1998).

2. Betz's book on Galatians was paralleled by W. Wuellner's articles, which applied classical rhetorical conventions (coupled with modern rhetorical theory) to Romans and 1 Corinthians. The New Testament academic world had been prepared for this turn to the artistic and persuasive nature of their documents by J. Muilenburg's celebrated 1968 Society of Biblical Literature presidential address (subsequently published as "Form Criticism and Beyond," *Journal of Biblical Literature* 88 [1969]: 1–18), which had issued a plea for new ventures beyond those currently done under the aegis of form criticism. The work of scholars such as Amos Wilder and Robert Funk had also highlighted the persuasive and aesthetic qualities of New Testament passages prior to the advent of more focused rhetorical studies. On these developments, see Duane F. Watson and Alan J. Hauser's helpful brief introductions to the study of rhetoric in the New Testament and the Hebrew Bible, along with their thorough bibliographies to the early nineties (*Rhetorical Criticism of the Bible: A Comprehensive Bibliography with Notes on History and Method* [Leiden: Brill, 1994]).

3. George A. Kennedy, *New Testament Interpretation through Rhetorical Criticism* (Chapel Hill: University of North Carolina Press, 1984).

4. Burton L. Mack and Vernon K. Robbins, *Patterns of Persuasion in the Gospels* (Sonoma, CA: Polebridge, 1989).

Since that time, Burton Mack's little handbook *Rhetoric and the New Testament* has become the standard text by which religion and seminary students are introduced to this approach, for it elucidates the major themes, strategies, and modes of Greco-Roman rhetorical analysis and shows how these might be used in a study of various New Testament texts.[5] This handbook necessarily adapts and amplifies Kennedy's original approach so that narratives as well as more directly polemical pieces may be read in terms of the classical conventions. The neophyte in rhetorical analysis is taught to establish boundaries for a passage that may be fruitfully subjected to a rhetorical analysis; to consider the sort of rhetoric (judicial, deliberative, epideictic)[6] that is at work in a

5. Burton Mack, *Rhetoric and the New Testament* (Minneapolis: Fortress, 1990). Mack's book, however, is hardly a dispassionate description of classical rhetoric as it applies to New Testament texts. The last half of his little manual is given over to an application of classical models to various New Testament texts by which he shows the disappointing inferiority of New Testament argumentation (by the standards of Greco-Roman rhetorical conventions), namely, its preference for mixed modes and incoherent appeals to the supernatural. Mack opines that the New Testament's arguments must not have been very persuasive to non-Christians and that its main success was as an anti-pagan, anti-Jewish invective designed to create uniformity in the new movement. His treatment here is consonant with his judgment regarding the Gospel of Mark, which he declares "canonized a remarkably pitiful moment of early Christian condemnation of the world" (*A Myth of Innocence: Mark and Christian Origins* [Philadelphia: Fortress, 1988], 376). Mack's purpose seems designed to inoculate students against the power of New Testament rhetoric, for he engages in a thoroughgoing hermeneutics of suspicion and resistance. Though convenient for size and comprehensive concision, students may receive here more (or other) than they expected.

6. Judicial speeches are either apologetic or accusatory and seek to arbitrate the facts of the past: did the person do it or not? Deliberative speeches look to the future, asking which is the better or pragmatic thing to do, which is the better way to behave or the better attitude to adopt. Epideictic (literally, "appropriate for display") speeches concern "honor" and look to the present, either celebrating a noteworthy person (e.g., an encomium) or object or event, or inducing the audience to vilify an unsavory object or person or event in a formal manner. For a detailed discussion of the encomium, see chap. 2, where Acts 22 is discussed in light of this rhetorical mode. Examples of the vilifying invective are rare in the New Testament, possibly due to the dominical injunction "Judge not," an instruction found also in Paul (cf. 1 Cor. 4:5). A notable exception is Matt. 23:1–38, which in its final context may be seen to function epideictically, that is, to incite disapprobation of the scribes and Pharisees on the part of its readership. Certainly, the discourse begins with Jesus objectifying these parties, directing the "crowds and disciples" to consider them in third person plural references. However, the actual woes (Matt. 23:13–29) are addressed in the second

given passage; to investigate the purpose of the rhetorical ploys (i.e., the creation of *ethos*, *logos*, and *pathos*) at various moments of the speech-act; to decide, within the argument of the passage, which "proofs" are advanced and to what end; and to ask how the passage contributes to the argument of its larger text. Those who have been influenced by Mack will also contrast New Testament argumentation with the classical modes and note where they diverge from their most apposite templates.

Questions and Debates

It is natural enough, in the wake of a new movement, that creative ventures should be accompanied by questions and disagreement. Some scholars, particularly those who believe that some of the New Testament writers were insulated from the larger culture, have even questioned whether Paul can be assumed to have known the conventions he putatively exploits. I. H. Marshall, for example, in his introduction of the New Testament to senior students, comments that "Paul's letters . . . do not contain any significant evidence of a Greek education" and "his manner of argumentation is generally thought to reflect a rabbinic training."[7] This view of Paul's pedigree and especially of the scholarly consensus is a little unusual, and may reflect an overreaction against the current emphasis on a Hellenistic milieu for the New Testament. Few will follow Marshall's implication that Paul is unmarked by classical

---

person to the scribes and Pharisees; since these have formed part of the crowd at the level of the story, the words may also be heard as warnings to be heeded rather than as simple vituperation, despite the unfortunate history of interpretation that ensued in some quarters. Hovering on the verge of negative epideictic, this section seems to hold back from outright epideictic and instead conjoins its description of undesirable action with prophetic indictment and warning. A more clear-cut example of negative epideictic is seen in Rev. 18:21–24, where "Babylon" is ceremoniously judged and maligned. Even here, however, the rhetoric is unusual, since it is framed symbolically so that the object of vilification remains "a mystery" (Rev. 17:5) and therefore open to interpretation.

7. I. Howard Marshall, Stephen Travis, and Ian Paul, *Exploring the New Testament*, vol. 2, *A Guide to the Letters and Revelation* (Downers Grove, IL: InterVarsity, 2002), 37.

rhetorical conventions, a claim that would put a significant brake on the rhetorical analysis of at least half the New Testament. Other questions have been frequently addressed to those who endorse the rhetorical approach, however. Are strategies designed to understand oral speeches applicable in the context of written epistles? What about the difficulty in determining a "rhetorical unit?" Is it not the case that we can easily confuse authorial intent with the readers' perceptions? What are we to make of the lack of consensus regarding "species" of speech? Is it fair to hedge one's bets by characterizing awkward passages as "mixed" in rhetorical genre? At what point does the heuristic value of these pursuits give way to a multitude of qualifications and debates?

Notwithstanding these concerns, it has seemed right to many New Testament scholars to continue this mode of inquiry so that rhetorical analysis is now thoroughly established in the arsenal of the exegete. Indeed, the movement is mature enough to have become self-reflective, for good or for ill.

If the fruit of rhetorical analysis has seemed abundant enough so that not a few are committed to the project, the connection of rhetoric with the vision-report is not so well demonstrated. To some it may seem bizarre to analyze the vision-report in terms of classical models since a vision-report would be an unusual component for formal argumentation in any of the three milieus, whether courtroom, assembly, or public gathering. However, to debate a point by reference to a reported vision is not so far a cry from, say, Plato's compelling cave allegory or Lucian's ironic visit to the Island of the Blessed in the *Vera historia*. A creative speaker might well use the vision-report as a building block in an argument if its significance were manifest to his designed audience. Consider the folk wisdom of the consummate "rhetorician" Tevye (*Fiddler on the Roof*), who convinces his wife Golde against the impending marriage of their oldest daughter to the village butcher. Faced with the task of changing his wife's mind, Tevye relates a concocted "visitation" of his mother-in-law, who putatively has come back from the dead to disapprove the match and to suggest an alternative suitor. Tevye thus employs the vision-report as the major "proof" in his demonstrative speech, and so directs his wife to discover the most "pragmatic" course of action. This is, of course, a domestic and ironic example of the form that such rhetoric might take, but the New Testament documents are also, in some respects, *Kleinliteratur*. In the first-century world the genre of vision-report was a commonplace, ready-to-hand for the daring rhetorician, who might use it sincerely and not necessarily with a Tevyan "wink" to the audience.

Quintilian,[8] in outlining the strategies available to the aspiring rhetorician, describes the move known as *demonstratio* as the expression of the matter at hand with words so that it appears to be borne up "before the eyes" (*res ante oculos*) of the audience. *Demonstratio*[9] was part of the arsenal of the rhetorician and might be used to set forth in a vivid manner the statement of the case (*narratio*) or dramatically to confirm an argument. Given the wide-spread awareness of rhetoric in the ancient world and the commissive aspect of the gospel, we should not be surprised to discover that *demonstratio* plays an important role in the rhetoric of at least some New Testament writers. In Galatians 3:1 Paul speaks about his practice of "portraying" (προεγράφη)[10] Jesus Christ as crucified "before the eyes" (κατ᾽ ὀφθαλμοὺς) of his listeners. It would seem, then, that in the rhetoric of those for whom divine revelation was an important and authoritative factor, *demonstratio* sometimes assumed a peculiar shape—that of the reported vision.

At first glance, the student of classical rhetoric might assume that vision-report falls neatly into the category of "nontechnical or uninvented proofs." However, Mack declares that such mi-

8. *Ad Herennium* 4.55.68.

9. The technique is also described by other rhetoricians under other labels. See Quintilian's discussion of *visio* (*Ad Her.* 9.2.40) and Cicero's treatment of the figure in which the matter is placed *sub oculos* (*De orat.* 3.202).

10. See Betz, *Galatians*, 131n33. From the perspective of rhetorical practice, Betz argues for this reading and against the translation "*proclaim* publicly." While he assumes that Paul is exaggerating his practice by ironic reference to the rhetorical *topos*, it is worth considering what Paul's rhetorical strategies might have been in such homiletical portrayals of Christ crucified. Could first-century piety and devotional rhetoric have been enriched by precursors to later meditations on the details of the cross (cf. the medieval poem, *The Dream of the Rood*)? I am indebted to my colleague Ian Henderson for this suggestion.

raculous proofs "actually must have been invented," so that their marshalling "must have been a challenging undertaking for early Christian authors."[11] In a less skeptical vein, we may consider the framing of the vision-report as an integral part of argumentation that had to be artfully performed in order to have the desired effect. At this point invention and nontechnical proof come together, since within a worldview that is hospitable to the numinous, the *vision* could make its impact as a non-technical proof—a fact of the case—whereas the *report* requires invention. So then, we may consider the use of visionary narrative as a figure within an argument even where the vision-report is also appealed to as an authoritative "trump card."

Two obvious passages from the New Testament corpus employ the vision-report as a means of completing an argument or bringing it to a full culmination: Paul's "I know a person in Christ" passage, and Stephen's "I see heaven opened." In 2 Corinthians 12:1–10, Paul uses the "report" in an overt manner in order to bring a complex case to a striking conclusion; in Acts 7:55–56, the vision provides a narrative cap to Stephen's interrupted speech, as well as a stunning climax to Luke's martyrological and doxological narrative. In both cases, the openness of the vision-report is well suited to complexity, allowing Paul to bring home a two-pronged attack and permitting Luke to attend to both the drama of the immediate narrative and the greater purposes of his corpus. We begin with the most direct and explicit use of vision, 2 Corinthians 12.

Vision-Report as Climactic Argument: 2 Corinthians 12:1–10

In turning to this passage, we find ourselves in the midst of a closely debated section set within a letter that also is marked by academic controversy. Paul himself writes no full-blown apoca-

---

11. Mack, *Rhetoric*, 40. Mack does not mention visions explicitly, but it is certain that he would classify these along with miracles, oaths, prophetic predictions, "and the like."

lypses or vision-reports—despite the well-meaning efforts of a second- or third-century forger, by whose hand we have the so-called *Apocalypse of Paul*. Yet many of Paul's letters, most notably 2 Corinthians, bear the imprint of the visionary traditions, using themes, forms, and ideas typically found in vision literature in ways that both engage and surprise the reader. Paul's rhetoric in using such means is of necessity subtle, since it is governed as much by his reserve toward things normally construed as visionary as it is by his acceptance and experience of them. After all, his purpose in the letters is practical rather than speculative. So he mines his repository of resources, pulled from various sources—Hebrew Bible, second temple literature, Greco-Roman literature, and the cultural realities associated with these. In mustering these resources, he directs even visionary elements toward a careful and enticing presentation of how the body of Christ should live together in the light of the apocalypse par excellence that he declared to have been already revealed but has yet to be grasped fully.

Second Corinthians is not patently a literary unit to all scholars. The ongoing debate concerning its integrity and the sequence of its various parts as they relate to Paul's ministry with the Corinthian church is well known. Whether or not an intelligent defense can be made for the book's unity, it is not surprising that these thirteen chapters have been collected in a spot together within the Pauline corpus. Whatever their literary relationship, they are marked by a similar perspective—by the sense that the drama of the church in this world is interconnected with a reality that is not normally seen but opened (indeed, rendered present) to those who are in Christ, through the ministration of the Holy Spirit. As a complication, Paul finds himself in debate with those "super-apostles" who set great stock by personal visions and revelatory experiences. Thus he aims to pull his Corinthian flock back to a less elitist vision more centered on the One who has revealed God. As a result of competing contingencies, Paul's depiction of things visionary is (to say the least) ambivalent, and the letter proceeds by both direct and polemically inverse references to visions of the unseen but ever-present heavenly world.

A quick flight over the letter shows that, despite all its textual complications, every part is informed by Christian visionary themes or by apocalyptic forms.[12] Paul begins by treating affliction and consolation (1:3–11) in terms of the consoling God "who raises the dead" (1:9) and in terms of a future hope (1:13–14). He goes on to tackle problems in Corinth by providing for them a dual stance: actions done "before the face of Christ" and in full knowledge of Satan's "machinations" (2:10–11). Similarly, the apostolic ministry is depicted in dualistic terms (2:14–17) from the perspective of life and death, and perhaps with an echo of *merkabah* mysticism,[13] a practice not unrelated to that of the apocalyptic visionary. Chapters 3 and 4, drawing as they do on key revelatory moments in Israel's history, are fully framed in apocalyptic terms (but see especially 3:7–18; 4:3–14), as will soon become apparent. In chapter 5 the future hope typically is disclosed in terms of both positive hope and judgment (5:1–10), and then the apostolic ministry is viewed from the perspective of Paul's reformulated apocalyptic world-view (5:14–17). The thematically connected sections of 6:1–13 and 7:2–4 deal with the "Day" (now present) and the open heart and are punctuated by the textually controversial and decidedly apocalyptic discourse of 6:14–7:1. Paul's subsequent discourse on repentance (7:5–16) is perhaps atypical for him, but its contrast of "godly" and "worldly" grief, and their diverse fruits of "salvation" and "death" (7:10–11), is clearly informed by an apocalyptic perspective. Chapters 8 and 9 discuss the collection, apostolic ministry ("the glory of Christ!" 8:23), and human giving in the light of the revealed gift of Jesus Christ (8:9), which is at the

12. "Apocalypse is a genre of revelatory literature *with a narrative framework*, in which a revelation is *mediated by an otherworldly being* to a human recipient, disclosing a transcendent reality" (John J. Collins, "Introduction: Towards the Morphology of a Genre," *Semeia* 14 [1979]: 9). My added italics indicate attention to formal features.

13. *Merkabah* (literally, "chariot") mysticism was practiced by some rabbis following in the tradition of Ezekiel, who saw the heavenly "chariot of God" during a vision at the Chebar River. Allusions or echoes, rather than outright citations of text, are notoriously difficult to nail down but are well-established features in sophisticated literature. See J. M. Scott, "The Triumph of God in 2 Cor 2:14," *New Testament Studies* 42 (1996): 270, for a possible allusion to *merkabah* mysticism in Paul's writings.

same time God's "indescribable" gift (9:15). Chapter 10 describes Paul's own apostolic rhetoric in terms of cosmic battle (10:3–6), and 11:2–3 employs the protological and eschatological imagery of virginity and the serpent (cf. Rev. 12). In contrast, Paul's opponents are described as using an inverse apocalyptic discourse that obscures rather than reveals, and as having undergone a twisted transfiguration (μετασχηματίζεται, 2 Cor. 11:14) that corresponds diabolically to the transformation of the saints. While the "chaste virgin" has her high calling, these pseudo-ministers will reap their own end (τέλος, 11:15). As a climax to Paul's argument, 12:1–10 employs the form of a vision-report with rhetorical flair and to surprising effect. Finally, the letter closes by relativizing notions of power and weakness through Paul's underlying revelatory story of Christ (13:4).

It is clear, then, that the climactic vision-report of chapter 12 sits comfortably within the themes and concerns of the letter as a whole and within the logical flow of chapters 10 through 13. Whatever one's view of the unity of the letter, the closure at the end of chapter 9 and the new invocation at 10:1 render 2 Corinthians 10:1–13:10 a major rhetorical unit, in which Paul's authority as an apostle is at stake. However, this unit also exhibits Paul's concern for the well-being of the Corinthians: Πάλαι δοκεῖτε ὅτι ὑμῖν ἀπολογούμεθα. κατέναντι θεοῦ ἐν Χριστῷ λαλοῦμεν· τὰ δὲ πάντα, ἀγαπητοί, ὑπὲρ τῆς ὑμῶν οἰκοδομῆς ("All along, have you considered us to be offering an 'apology' of ourselves to you? Instead, we have been speaking before the face of God, in Christ. And all of this, dear ones, that you might be edified!" 2 Cor. 12:19). Paul's own reference to the various modes of rhetoric—in this case, apology versus deliberation[14]—confirms our decision to consider this vision-report mainly in terms of classical rhetoric, with its various categories, templates, and tropes.

The same debate that has raged over Galatians—that is, whether it is apologetic or deliberative—could be duplicated regarding this

---

14. Paul enjoys, at the end of his "fool's speech," pulling the rug out from under his listeners' feet and directing them to rehear his words in terms not of self-defense (an apology in the judicial mode of rhetoric) but in terms of exhortation (the deliberative mode).

passage. It may be helpful to distinguish between the form and the actual direction of argument in a speech. From the aspect of form there is little doubt that 2 Corinthians 10–13 is apologetic.[15] Moreover, the apology is offered in the form of a "foolish speech," as has been accounted for in the readings of Betz and others, and therefore cannot be taken at face value. Paul is engaged in a subtle argument, which has both judicial (apologetic) and deliberative aspects—perhaps, as we shall see, even epideictic. The commingling is not naïve but a mixture that evidently plays with the Hellenistic rhetorical conventions. The proliferation of irony and sarcasm throughout the section mean that the apology is not made for its own sake but is subordinated to a greater cause, as Paul himself declares at the conclusion (12:19). In this manner Paul frames his argument by means of what has been called "preterition"— that is, showing reticence about his argument and the means by which he must work it through.[16] By placing his apology within the larger context of edification, Paul indicates that his major concern is to direct his hearer toward attitudes and actions for the future—clearly a deliberative stance.[17] Readers aware of the various cultural conventions from which Paul draws have had a complex and engaging task. It is as though, through the completion of difficult homework, Paul leads his hearers to make his worldview their own.

Paul's vision-report and its *sequelae* (12:1–10) might be understood as occurring at the climax of the *argumentatio* section,[18]

15. See Hans D. Betz, who compares this to the "Socratic apology" in *Der Apostel Paulus und die sokratische Tradition: Eine exegetische Untersuchung zu seiner "Apologie" 2 Korinther 10–13* (Tübingen: Mohr Siebeck, 1972); and Jerry W. McCant, who prefers the "philosopher's apology" as a model in "Paul's Thorn of Rejected Apostleship," *New Testament Studies* 34 (1988): 555.

16. Perelman and Olbrechts-Tyteca, *New Rhetoric*, 487.

17. Note also that Wilhelm Wuellner considers Paul's argument beginning at 1 Cor. 1:9 to be a "mixed" speech, an "epideictic apology" ("Where Is Rhetorical Criticism Taking Us?" 460). See also the composition analysis of Max-Alain Chevallier, which demonstrates the pastoral nature of the unit, in "L'argumentation de Paul dans II Corinthiens 10 à 13," *Revue d'Histoire et de Philosophie Religieuses* 70 (1990): 3–15.

18. The interesting treatment by David F. Ford and Frances Young sees the vision-report as part of the emotional peroration of the entire letter (*Meaning and Truth in 2 Corinthians* [Grand Rapids: Eerdmans, 1987], 39). While a case can certainly be made for looking at

after an *exordium* at 10:1–6 and the statement of the case (*narratio*) in 10:7–18. This works well within the scheme followed by classical rhetoricians who developed "the complete argument": in following the conventional structure, Paul is able to set himself up as one engaged in a "fool's speech," adopting an anticipated form while speaking nonsense:

Exordium (Introduction)	10:1–6
Narratio (Proposition and Reason)	10:7–18
Argumentatio[19] (Argument, combining various strategies, ending with vision-report)	11:1–12:10
Peroratio (Conclusion)	12:11–13:10

As he states the case, Paul initiates a two-pronged argument: self-evaluation and self-commendation are not seemly; rather, the Lord's commendation is valuable, and boasting in the Lord is fruitful. The proofs begin at 11:1, where Paul introduces his own self-evaluation and commendation as "foolishness," going on to his past experience with the Corinthians, his pedigree, his experiences of humility, and probably a parody of the *corona muralis*.[20] Paul, the first down the wall of the earthly city, then goes on in 12:1–10 to describe one who surpassed others in ascending to the heavenly realm—only to learn that there is no human glory in such experiences. In his own defense, Paul in fact appeals to topics often found in epideictic discourse, that is, the character strengths and notable achievements usually recounted in an encomium. His impassioned argument, based on his human pedigree and exploits, is capped by a reference to his otherworldly experiences and his resultant identity as one who is "weak, and therefore strong." This clinching argument is followed by the conclusion at 12:11–13:10,

---

the letter as it stands, the obvious signals at the end of chap. 9 and the beginning of 10 make unavoidable the consideration of chaps. 10–13 as a unit. Moreover, it seems more natural to view the peroration as beginning at the point where Paul distances himself from the foolish discourse, that is, at 12:11, and appeals directly to the Corinthians.

19. This moment in the speech is also sometimes called *confirmatio*.

20. This "walled crown," made of gold in the form of turrets, was one of the most prized military awards, given to the man who first breached the wall of a city during an attack (cf. Suetonius, *Divus Augustus* 25).

in which Paul comments on the methods that he has used during his "apology" and goes on directly to address his audience. Within the structure of the argument, the vision-report thus plays its role as a nontechnical (i.e., uncontrived) authoritative proof. Even while Paul appeals to his vision, however, the basis of that proof is undermined by his ironic stance, for the vision is placed within the mouth of a "boastful fool."

The direction in which the irony moves bears consideration. Is Paul's irony directed against ecstatic experiences per se? Against this view must be set the persuasive arguments of James Tabor.[21] He insists that Paul refrains from divulging the essence of his vision because of its sacredness rather than because he considered such visions insignificant. Rather, Paul is reporting "a privilege of the highest order" and thus "nothing in the context of 2 Corinthians 12 should lead one to conclude that Paul disparaged such experiences."[22] But if Tabor is correct and Paul is not contesting claims to visions per se, why does he speak ironically? The answer lies in the specific use to which Paul puts his report: such experiences should not, he implies, be baldly mustered as "nontechnical proofs" in an apology. Indeed, he considers himself a fool to engage in this kind of discourse, though his audience is accustomed to such claims from other leaders. Paul, however, has been "compelled" by the suspicion of his audience and by their expectation that he will offer them a visionary credential; yet he indulges them only in an ironic mode. From Paul's cruciform perspective, the signs of true apostleship are displayed by one who considers his achievements as though they were "nothing"; the apostle's task is to point beyond himself to the One who has been seen.

The adroitness of Paul's discourse is highlighted when we consider the way in which he plays with the conventions of the genre of apocalypse—both its typical elements and its structural contours. Second Corinthians 12:1–10 has, as its "intertext," the entire genre of apocalypse rather than any one specific example and may be

21. James D. Tabor, *Things Unutterable: Paul's Ascent to Paradise in its Greco-Roman, Judaic, and Early Christian Contexts* (Lanham, MD: University Press of America, 1986).
22. Ibid., 21.

aptly compared both to apocalypses with a historical dimension and to those with a heavenly dimension. So there is an immediate connection with several apocalypses that include the rapture of the visionary into the heavenly realms, such as *1 Enoch* (extant, at least in part, in Paul's day) or the later *Ascension of Isaiah*.[23] Such writings stress the spatial axis over against historical apocalypses, which are more oriented to the temporal. Frequently Paul's "apocalypticism" has been understood only in terms of features that are to be plotted along the temporal axis. This is not entirely misguided, since Paul's greatest *apokalypsis* is of course the historical revealing of the Son of God in a surprising resurrection. However, Paul also has a sense of standing "in the presence of God" (cf. 2 Cor. 4:2) and sees an ongoing connection between the unseen world and the life of the church. This final section of the letter, though it is framed ironically, demonstrates that Paul was personally knowledgeable about those visionary experiences that informed the "apocalypses with otherworldly journey." Moreover, his use (and playful "abuse") of various formal features of these writings indicate he was aware not only of the experience but also of the apocalyptic writings associated with visionary illumination. In terms of Vernon Robbins's categories, 2 Corinthians 12 is "thick" with both scribal and cultural intertextures.

Here the rhetorical prowess of an apostle who "wrote weighty letters" comes to the fore. Paul's method here is not mere citation, nor simple recontextualization, but a total reconfiguration of the genre so that it becomes at the same time a supreme apocalypse and an anti-apocalypse—and here we must amplify our discussion of rhetoric by an appeal to literary genre. The mold is broken. After all, scribes recorded their visions in order to give their readers a proxy experience of their exploits and, through the visions, to lend them knowledge of the divine drama, a reason for patience, and a desire for holy living. The apocalypticist typically offered his visions pseudonymously; Paul declines to name a notable namesake but simply speaks anonymously of "a person/human being

23. These apocalypses were called type II, "Apocalypse with Otherworldly Journey," and subdivided into three categories by the Society of Biblical Literature group. See the chart in Collins, "Morphology," 14–15.

(ἄνθρωπον) in Christ" whom he "knows" (12:2). The name by which he wants to be known,[24] the only boast (12:5) he can make, is that this person is "in Christ." Further, unlike the apocalyptic visionary, Paul never actually passes on to his hearers a single detail of the vision(s) or audition. Certainly, in some apocalypses particulars are kept from the reading through the technique of "sealing" the vision; Paul's reticence is more thoroughgoing than this convention, however. The tone leads us to infer that had Paul related such details, the narration would not have achieved the desired goal of illuminating the readers. Besides presenting to his reader a narrative framework, a third person account, and an (undisclosed) audition and vision, Paul also refers to an *angelus interpres,* or interpreting "angel" (ἄγγελος, 12:7)—of the Satanic variety.

While appealing to his own exploits, Paul has refused to give content to the vision. Nor do we get a description of the "paradise" or an explanation of the numbered heavens or a description of the visionary conquest of each gate at each heaven, such as we might have expected in reference to Paul's excellence as a seer. In fact, he makes much of spurning the fine distinctions of the mode of ascent ("whether in or out of the body, I don't know, God knows"), perhaps himself acknowledging that this is in fact a matter of much speculation among some (the pseudo-apostles?). But mirror-reading, always a risky enterprise, is frequently frustrated in this letter. The reader is hampered by Paul's seemingly deliberate lack of disclosure at this point—a reticence that he does not exhibit in regard to more practical matters, such as his support by the churches in Macedonia.

So then, the formal features plus the esoteric language ("paradise," "third heaven," "angel") evoke a whole corpus of visionary and mystical literature that serve to further his ironic purpose. Paul sets up the expectations of the reader but then leads the argument

24. A sole voice argues that the visionary is not Paul on the basis that Paul himself eschewed mysticism as grounds for ecclesial authority (see Michael Goulder, "Vision and Knowledge," *Journal for the Study of the New Testament* 17 [1995]: 53–71). Goulder, though well meaning, flattens out the complexities of Paul's position and has not swayed the consensus position that Paul refers to himself.

in a different direction. Those conversant with the formal features
of the apocalypse anticipate an interpretation of the vision and
perhaps even some *paraenesis* ("exhortatory instruction"). The
surprising interpretation given through Paul's inverse "angel" is
that insight into God's mysteries should not elate the one illumined;
rather, weakness is the true source of strength. Whatever the nature
of Paul's "thorn," it serves as a memorial to the visions, a kind of
inverse stigmata, over against the resultant "glory" of seers like
Moses. It is permanent rather than fading, a seeming shame, but
a sign that points to true glory.

Interestingly, the double-edged sword of irony and the speculative atmosphere of the vision account may assume their own
unruly life. Contrary to Paul's stated intent, the hearer may be
tantalized by the brevity of his vision account. We are led to muse
about whether or not Paul hints at the contents of the vision: could
ἀποκαλύψεις κυρίου (12:1) possibly be a subjective genitive, to be
translated "apocalypses *about* the Lord"; does Paul envision a
two-stage journey from third heaven to paradise; what did Paul
hear; and what exactly is the difference between an in-the-body
and an out-of-the-body experience? Within the context of Paul's
argument, such speculative details are quickly abandoned, but
they are nonetheless raised during the reading of this "report"
that refuses to report. Paul's reader is at liberty to pause at the
forbidden points and so enter a provisional part of the world
evoked by the text rather than going on immediately to hear the
apostle's rhetorical point. Indeed, that creative anonymous writer
of the *Apocalypse of Paul* resisted the overall argument of the section entirely and disobediently remained in the realm of speculation that Paul was at pains to prevent. In doing so, he seized on
an "opening" in Paul's own text but did not follow the cues of
the passage in placing the apocalypse within a "fool's speech," a
boasting to be rejected.

Yet despite the danger latent in irony, Paul's proof does establish a kind of authority. The argument works on several levels: if
the listeners require "supernatural" proof, he could give it, but
he won't; Paul's very reticence should be an indication to them
of his real motives and trustworthiness. That is, his obedience in

the matter of not divulging that which is not to be uttered and his turning back to the theme of weakness for the sake of glorifying the Lord serve as an example to his listeners of what they should value. Paul has his cake and eats it too in that he has claimed the fact of his heavenly journey without inviting his listeners to enter into its intricacies, all the while insisting that such talk is futile. Further, their very accusation of weakness is turned around to have a positive value: the only enduring lesson to be learned is that of human weakness and divine grace.[25] In handling this contest of spirituality, silence becomes a preferred weapon in Paul's hands as he directs his hearers away from ordinary means of judging shame and glory, and away even from the debate in which he is embroiled, toward a larger canvas, a larger drama, within which he urges them to see his, and their, place. "Have you been thinking all along that we have been offering an apology defending ourselves before you? We are speaking in Christ before God . . . for the sake of building you up" (12:19).

In adopting this mixture of direct and indirect polemic, Paul shows himself prepared to take a notable risk: he extends liberty to his readers. Indeed, though he styles himself as an instructor, he also offers the Corinthians, and later readers, the courtesy of an invitation to see, think, and enter the story with him. "Spaces" for action by the reader are amply provided in the argument and in the embedded narrative. The liminality inherent to a discourse that is both ironic and visionary provides a mixed blessing—enlivening Paul's argument, but also threatening to break its moorings. As Karl A. Plank points out, "Writing and reading are fraught with risk. . . . The risk: both writers and readers may be surprised by what occurs through the collaboration of the other."[26] The first-century reader may have been tempted to ignore Paul's plea against

25. For a similar reading of another "boasting" passage, see Karl A. Plank, *Paul and the Irony of Affliction* (Atlanta: Scholars Press, 1987), 92. There Plank concludes that Paul's argument works by "compelling his audience to reinterpret the very categories through which they have challenged his authority." Hence, "[i]n the world which Paul's text discloses, weakness no longer signifies simply powerlessness or the absence of God, but the presence of divine power."

26. Ibid., 91.

an undue adulation of spiritual and visionary exploits. For the twenty-first century reader the challenge will come at a different point. Rather than being seduced by the unseen world, we are more apt to refuse to place Paul's rhetoric, apocalyptic or otherwise, within his proffered meta-narrative. Without the central lifted veil, that is, the "unthinkable gift" of God in Messiah Jesus, Paul's talk of weakness and strength becomes a mere power play, and his reserve toward personal visionary experience is rendered insincere. The complexity of his rhetoric is flattened, and Paul's "authority to build up," as well as his motivation, is subjected to cynical questioning. The only answer to such questioning is to change vantage points, as Paul himself pleads, so that the readers themselves adopt a new identity within a larger readership, seeing reality from a new vantage point, from a new "where" and "when."

Vision-Report as Peroration: Acts 7:54–60

Our second example of a speech completed by vision-report is found in Acts 7. Here Stephen's last rhetorical stand is completed by a dramatic opening of the heavens for Stephen's benefit, his report of this vision, and his ensuing martyrdom. Stephen's speech itself (7:2–53) is far longer than most of the speeches placed in the mouths of Lukan characters and provides a carefully worked out judicial argument that transforms apology into accusation. Various critics have brought rhetorical tools to bear on the speech, finding clear structural divisions of *exordium*, *narratio*, *argumentatio*, and *peroratio*.[27] Stephen's speech not only follows the usual logical flow of an extended argument but also conforms to the emotive moments with which the beginning, middle, and end of a speech are connected: Stephen's character, or *ethos*, is carefully established at the beginning; the *logos* or rationale offered matches the expectations of the audience in this scene, paying special attention to their concern for temple and Torah; and as we come toward the end,

---

27. For one such scheme, see Jacques Dupont, "La structure oratoire du discours d'Etienne (Actes 7)," *Biblica* 66 (1985): 153–67.

Stephen makes an ill-advised appeal to *pathos,* or the emotional
sensibilities of his hearers. Perhaps the appeal is more designed to
make its impact on the readers of Luke's narrative.

On all accounts, by Acts 7:51 Stephen has come to his impassioned peroration, signaled by his direct invocation of his audience and his modification of the phrase "our fathers" to "your
fathers." He has succeeded in turning the charges of blasphemy
against temple and Torah back onto his accusers. It is remarkable that few of those who deal with this passage go on to talk
about the effect of Stephen's vision, even though we are told by
one writer (if only in a footnote), "This vision caps the speech, as
the resurrection/ascension/sitting at God's right hand . . . capped
the crucifixion."[28] However, one of the tricks in marking out rhetorical units for inscribed speeches, rather than actually delivered
speeches, is that their logical boundaries do not necessarily correspond to the embedded speech proper within the larger text.

The vision is not simply a dramatic cap; it is an integral part
of the rhetorical situation. It is the dramatic conclusion and final
proof both of Stephen's innocence and of the apt condemnation
of his accusers. Dramatically, it extends the peroration, or conclusion, when the listeners would rather abort it—their already
aroused emotions are worked into a frenzy. Logically, it confirms
the judgment that Stephen has already delivered. Stephen, as a
masterful orator, uses both action and words in the finale to his
peroration. His calm gaze into heaven is in striking contrast with
the fury of the listeners; his vision-report is a pointed continua-
tion of the earlier interrupted reference to "the righteous one."
Just as Stephen's speech was introduced as inspired (6:15), so too
is his vision-report (7:55) annotated by the remark that he was
"filled with the Holy Spirit": thus, the *ethos* established at the
beginning of the speech is sustained until the climactic moment.
Israel received the law from the angel of the Lord; Stephen, filled
with God's grace and power (6:8), with a face like an angel (6:15),
has interpreted the holy history of Israel; now, while rejected by

28. John J. Kilgallen, "The Function of Stephen's Speech (Acts 7:2–53)," *Biblica* 70 (1989): 186.

his listeners, he passes on to them the mysteries more normally seen by angels.

The rhetorical unit for the entire speech, then, is not 7:1–53 but extends at least to verse 57. As Max Turner observes, Stephen's vision is "a charisma specifically related to the content of the preaching" and "heightens the effect of that preaching."[29] Moreover, it is not only a question of heightening but of extending the preaching at its critical and emotive point, that is, at the peroration in which "the appropriate mode of persuasion was *pathos*."[30] It is only after the vision-report that the hearers stop their ears and pursue their own agenda; Stephen's final two words are directed toward Jesus rather than his audience, although of course they have a rhetorical effect on the reader. The setting is re-established in 7:58–60 and the finale of the story is given. The narrator's argument, of course, continues in that Stephen's hearers re-enact the verdict of 7:51, adding a new martyrdom to those already mentioned. Depending on the perspective, then, the rhetorical unit could be marked off fruitfully as either 7:1–57 or 7:1–60.

What is particularly interesting is the way Stephen's argument in the concluding vision is preempted, or at least contained, by the narrator's interpretation of it. Contrary to the usual order of apocalypses and vision-reports, the reader comes to the interpretation of Stephen's vision prior to the vision itself. That is, before we hear Stephen's own words, the narrator interprets to us what Stephen will report: "Stephen, in a state of fullness by the Holy Spirit . . . saw the glory of God . . . and Jesus" (7:55). This displacement of the interpretation may be explained by reference to Luke's theological concern to safeguard the vision from error: it is the *glory* of God (δόξαν θεοῦ, 7:55) that is seen by Stephen, since no one can see God; it is *Jesus*, and none other, who is the Son of Man. However, such observations only explain the content of the narratival interpretation, not the phenomenon of reversal of interpretation and vision. Doctrinal points could easily have been

29. Max Turner, "The Spirit of Prophecy and the Power of Authoritative Preaching in Luke-Acts: A Question of Origins," *New Testament Studies* 38 (1992): 69.

30. Burton L. Mack, "Elaboration of the Chreia in the Hellenistic School," in Mack and Robbins, *Patterns of Persuasion*, 55.

made had Luke followed the usual order for an apocalyptic vision, where story frame is followed by vision, then by interpretation:

> "But he . . . gazed into heaven and said,
> 'Behold, I see . . .'
> That is to say, he saw the glory of God and Jesus."

The reversal of vision and interpretation has a dramatic effect in that it gives an immediate identity to "the Righteous One" while allowing for a natural repetition of the phrase "standing at the right hand of God." Again, the reader comes to the actual vision-report with an interpretation at hand—there is no need to puzzle over the mystery, since this has already been dispelled. Stephen's words are therefore encountered not so much as an intriguing mystery but as a satisfying conclusion to a lengthy judicial speech. Moreover, the reversal prevents a double interruption of the narrative. Luke may now proceed directly from Stephen's vision to the murderous reaction of the crowd, rather than inserting an interpretation of the vision-report. The pace from lengthy speech, to aroused pathos and contrasting vision, to martyrdom is thus smoothly accelerated. Finally, Stephen's vision is placed in a privileged position in terms of its dramatic impact. It is Stephen, rather than a narrator, who has the last coherent word; his clarity is juxtaposed with the inchoate rage of the "witnesses" (οἱ μάρτυρες, 7:58). Stephen, the true witness, confirms his word by his martyrdom; the judicial "witnesses" at this trial scene are reduced to the status of a lynch mob even while the narrator ironically gives them their technical title. By their actions they confirm Stephen's words: "You always resist the Holy Spirit! Was there ever a prophet your ancestors did not murder?" (7:51b–52a). In all these ways, by disposition of the details and by deft dramatic touches, the vision is contained and directed while its main themes are highlighted, bringing the polemic of Stephen to a rhetorically satisfactory ending.

The effect of the whole is that Luke has, so to speak, out-perorated Stephen. First, there is in verse 54 the "intentional interruption," which David Aune tells us is a literary device "common to historians and novelists" that "heighten[s] the drama of particular episodes."[31] Stephen has already aroused the *pathos* of his hearers within the narrative—and readers outside of it. The narrator increases this arousal of emotion by providing an interruption that focuses on the emotional states of those enacting the drama. When the speaker is reintroduced in verse 56, his words assume the form of a vision-report, so that not simply the *ethos* of the speaker with the angel's face lends the words authority but also the very form in which they are given. Finally, the actions that follow serve as dramatic confirmation of the truth of Stephen's words: it is not he who is on trial but the very ones who fancy themselves as witnesses to his blasphemy. In contrast, Stephen's manner of death recalls the death of Jesus himself, and so reinforces the acquittal in a near-subliminal way.

The unusual stance of the Son of Man, who is seen "standing" rather than enthroned, is emphasized through repetition and has received numerous explanations.[32] The "standing" contrasts curiously with the scenes portrayed both in Daniel 7:13–14 and Luke's first volume (Luke 22:69), and is surely not a gratuitous description. This detail could well evoke the picture of a parallel trial scene in heaven where the Son of Man adopts the standing position of the witness, both to acquit Stephen and to condemn his detractors. The competent reader, stimulated by reference to the Son of Man, may be led to recall the whole Daniel scenario, in which the heavenly court sits in judgment (Dan. 7:26). Just as Luke has extended the conclusion of Stephen's speech by the action, so the trial then would be extended spatially, beyond the earthly actions into the visionary sphere seen by Stephen. Such techniques are excellent examples of the distinction that John Kilgallen makes between "an actual, intended-to-be delivered speech and a purely literary never-to-be-delivered speech," a distinction that is "revealed by the degree of unity between the latter type of

31. David E. Aune, *The New Testament in Its Literary Environment* (Philadelphia: Westminster, 1987), 127.

32. For an example, see the appeal to form—that the verb ἵστημι is typically used to evoke a supernatural vision—in S. Léglasse, "Encore ἑστῶτα en Actes 7,55–56," *Filologia Neotestamentaria* 3 (1990): 63–66.

speech and its context."[33] The speech of Stephen, artfully designed to hoist the accusers by their own petard, has been given an extended and incisively dramatic conclusion, complete with the most authoritative utterance imaginable for its designed audience. The skillful dovetailing of speech with narrative frame shows Luke to be a master of narrative as well as of rhetorical techniques.

A final word regarding the interplay of the rhetoric of narrative and speech is perhaps in order. Stephen's vision-report is introduced by the typical ἰδοὺ θεωρῶ ("Behold, I see . . . ," 7:56) of the seer. However, this demonstrative word ἰδού may also serve to indicate a change of direction in the overall argumentation of the narrative, which has been forensic. With this word and the remarkable example of the first Christian martyr, the reader is perhaps directed toward an action that goes beyond simply assessing accusation and defense. The return to the narrative frame indicates a return to an implicit deliberative mode. Christian readers are directed toward the open heaven, the Son of Man standing for them, their inevitable conflict with those who refuse to hear, and the example of the faithful who have gone before. Luke ensures by the shape of his narrative that in the witness of Stephen they hear an echo of the Messiah—a boldness coupled with unusual humility and gentleness. The same rhetor who indicted those "stiff-necked people" pleads in his death, "Lord, do not hold this sin against them" (7:60).

Thus a frankly judicial situation is afforded the hint of the deliberative, as might be expected in a sacred writing. As Mack points out, "In general, early Christian rhetoric was deliberative in the sense that every aspect of the new persuasion (including the imagination of founder figures and founding events, beliefs, behavior, and the adjudications of social issues) had to be approached as a matter of policy that would determine the future of (membership in) the community."[34] Here, as in Luke 10:18, the question of authority comes firmly to the fore: the wonder of the vision at hand is not allowed to predominate, since it is the "apocalypse" of the Jesus-event that must remain authoritative.

---

33. Kilgallen, "Function of Stephen's Speech," 184.
34. Mack, *Rhetoric*, 35.

The identity of ὁ δίκαιος (Acts 7:52), the righteous Son of Man, and the paradigmatic importance of his words and death overshadow the innocence and rhetorical flair of Stephen. For Luke, the open character of the vision-report provides a pliable and evocative ingredient in a complex narrative, one that is concerned to justify Stephen, identify the Son of Man, and suggest a stance for the faithful—all while serving as a pointer to the larger salvation history that directs his narrative.

Assessing the Cost of Authority

Reflection and comparison of 2 Corinthians 12 and Acts 7 elucidate several ways in which the vision-report may be pressed into the service of formal and narratival argument. The first vision was brought forward in the full heat of the argument but ironically so as to transmute its apologetic effect into the deliberative mode; the second found its place at the critical point of the peroration, and by it the author was enabled to extend the arguments of an apologetic speech beyond the bounds of the oration proper and into the narrative. The suggestiveness of vision is a helpful vehicle for the complexity of each piece. Both of the discourses, through their recourse to vision, are directly concerned with the issue of authority: Stephen's words issue from one with "the face of an angel" and are confirmed by an extraordinary vision of the Son of Man; Paul's arguments for his own authority are offered shame-facedly and point ultimately to the Lord's authority (2 Cor. 11:17). The way in which each of the visions works within its overall argument demonstrates the insufficiency of Kennedy's suggestion that Christian "radical rhetoric"[35] (that is, prophetic or absolute assertions) ought to be classed separately from argument that uses *enthymeme* (that is, more carefully contrived logic).[36] In these vision-reports we have seen the fusion of the non-technical (the vision) and the invented (the report).

---

35. Kennedy, *New Testament Interpretation*, 22.
36. For a more detailed explanation of *enthymeme* and an example of its use in the New Testament, see p. 126, n.31.

Those analyzing the New Testament no doubt have been comfortable to bracket radical rhetoric because of its strangeness and the fear that it might wholly subsume more conventional argumentation. However, the use of rhetoric in these passages does not demonstrate a strong-arming rhetor or a hopelessly naïve ideal reader. In the Stephen episode, the vision might have assumed a more triumphalistic conclusion had Luke not evoked wistful allusions to Jesus' own death. The reader is directed away from Stephen's vindication to another, more significant figure. In the Corinthian correspondence, where we might most have expected this rhetoric to steal the stage as nontechnical proof, Paul's irony disassociates vision from authority. Perhaps Graham Shaw is too hasty in asserting that in his rhetorical manipulation "the Christian Paul [becomes] not perhaps so different from the persecuting Saul."[37] It is not that visions are deployed as the final authoritative argument to stop the mouth of Paul's detractors, as might have been possible in a full-blown apocalypse. Paul's aim really may be a gentler one. Such an assessment depends largely on whether there is evidence of playfulness in the text, evidence that Paul expects his hearers to enter freely into the irony and laugh at themselves as he laughs at himself.

Finally, even though the visions function within the logic of these two arguments in a remarkable and directed manner, we have seen that each of the vision-reports still retains the potential to take on a life of its own. Here are two unusual cases of the collision of polyvalent and deductive speech, of symbolism and argumentation. Both of these speeches carefully circumscribe the polyvalent potential of the vision, using it as a building block within a discernible polemic. In the Stephen episode, this direction comes through sequence, since the vision is carefully introduced and then made clear by a prevenient interpretation: the actors in the passage and the reader are under no illusion as to the meaning of Stephen's words—that Jesus is the Son of Man and the fulfillment of sacred history. Though prepared to play with convention, Paul is

37. Graham Shaw, *The Cost of Authority: Manipulation and Freedom in the New Testament* (Philadelphia: Fortress, 1983), 125.

also determined to leash the power of his reference to visions and does this by an almost heavy-handed use of rhetoric. Despite his best efforts, however, the suggestiveness of his journey to paradise may continue to tantalize the reader who refuses to follow the direction of the text toward grace and weakness.

Though these two cases, framed in argumentative and narrative form, have demonstrated how two different New Testament writers can use the conventions of *ethos*, *logos*, and *pathos*, combined with the ploys of classical rhetoric, in order to mount a case, it is clear that neither passage fits perfectly into the usual templates. This lack of commensurability between the text and the pattern may be explained in two ways: first, the texts were not originally designed as sheer speeches; second, a descriptive approach that attends mostly to form and technical detail may be unequal to the potency of the speech-acts. Wilhelm Wuellner has argued that classical categories are insufficient to capture polemical power, and he has indicated the potential of a broader rhetorical criticism to disclose the rational, cognitive, emotive, and imaginative dimensions of the text.[38] Further investigation of the rhetorical use of visions in the New Testament is needed to uncover the intriguing ways in which these dimensions may reinforce each other, or even conflict.

---

38. Wuellner, "Where Is Rhetorical Criticism Taking Us?" 461.

2

DIRECTING THE ARGUMENT

The Power of Repetition within Narrative

(ACTS 10:1–11:18; 9:1–25; 22:1–22; 26:1–24)

Containing the Explosive

Our consideration of two of the best-known vision-reports in the New Testament (2 Cor. 12:1–10; Acts 7:54–60) disclosed the potential for variation that this form possesses, its latent subtlety, and the unusual ways that it can be taken into service in the explicit or implicit argument of a case. Both Paul's sustained argument in the fool's speech and Luke's suggestive argument in the Stephen narrative come to a conclusion in their vision-reports; yet each argument moves toward a different end, making its particular impact on the reader. Paul works through irony, Luke through drama, in order to coax the ideal reader to a desired conclusion. In all this, however, the polyvalent potential of vision is not thoroughly tamed. Indeed, the latent strength of the form may, when encountered by a resistant or whimsical reader, burst the bounds of its argumentational wineskins. Readers who are allergic to being strong-armed might well refuse the directive word of Stephen, the human *angelus interpres* (interpreting angel), and so dismiss the preceding tendentious historical survey as well; imaginative readers might decide to ignore Paul's irony and thus find themselves in a cul-de-sac of speculation—the very opposite of the apostle's intent in his impassioned peroration. Even where the vision-report is used in a tightly controlled manner it cannot be totally leashed, for the collusion of the reader is required and the signals of the text are not univocal.

A different way of directing the power of the vision-report is seen when it is employed within a narrative through repeated tellings rather than at a key point in the action. Rather than allowing the shock wave of the vision to make its grand but unpredictable mark on the reader, as when the report is used at the culmination of an argument, the author may harness the potential polyvalence of the vision and actually play this out in an extended and complex narrative. This is a less forceful technique since it does not use the vision-report in order to "pull out the big guns" and coerce the reader. However, there is something to be said for the use of controlled and smaller explosions over against a dramatic blast. By working with the potential of the form through repeated and varied narration of its strange details, the narrator may well carry more readers safely along. The value of repetition for the purpose of emphasis and mnemonics is, of course, well documented as a heuristic device in theories of education. In art forms it is used less pragmatically but with equal calculation: consider the reappearance of a musical motif in a single movement of a piano sonata—its various soundings at the beginning, through the complications of the middle section, and in reprise. Sometimes a composer will exploit the possibilities of a motif throughout the different movements of the sonata, to the delight of the audience—we are astonished to hear a largo motif reframed in the presto finale. Meaning changes according to context, according to placement, and according to the voice that is used. A generation that has grown up with the existentialist doctrine of the "naiveté seconde" should know intuitively that to hear something twice is to hear it differently. Again, the contemporary world has been marked by the anthropological theories of Lévi-Strauss and others concerning the power of repeated myth-making in dealing with contradiction and mystery.[1]

We will engage in a close analysis of two examples where the phenomenon of repeated vision discloses the masterful rhetorical art of Luke: the sequence of Peter's encounter with Cornelius (Acts 10:1–11:18), and the underlying extended narrative of Acts, which features three modulations (Acts 9:1–25; 22:1–22; 26:1–24) of Saul/Paul's call vision. As in the first section, we take our cue regarding method from the text, which may be fruitfully analyzed in terms of literary and narrative criticism as well as in terms of classical rhetoric. Then, since we have discovered that these methods, though helpful, are insufficient to disclose the entire potential of New Testament rhetoric, recourse will also be made to more contemporary approaches to rhetoric. The analysis of inner "texture" (especially "narrational" and "argumentative texture") performed by an application of Vernon Robbins's socio-rhetorical method will also be helpful in confirming our observations of the Saul/Paul stories.

The analysis will, in the first place, underscore what we have already seen—that the vision-report has the potential to take on a life of its own and threatens to break loose from its narrative context even while it is gently but significantly guided through repetition. We are also concerned in our two examples of repeated narrative to see the vision-report as a component of the writer's speech craft (sometimes as put into the mouth of a character in the text), as part of the persuasive power of the speech itself (encoded in the text), and as making its impact on the listener (i.e., characters listening within the text, the implied reader, the reader more-or-less contemporary with the writer, and other subsequent readers). In the case of the Cornelius-Peter complex, the emphasis will be on reader-response theory, as we seek to demonstrate

---

1. Adela Yarbro Collins makes use of such insights in her consideration of cyclical sequences in the book of Revelation in "What the Spirit Says to the Churches: Preaching the Apocalypse," *Quarterly Review* 4, no. 3 (1984): 73.

one possible view of the relationship of the "scribal" rhetor, the rhetorical text, and the hearer/reader. In the case of the narratives of Paul's call, literary concerns will come to the fore as we see the use of repetition skillfully employed in the creation of a "narrative hologram" that functions as a prism for the light that is directed through the rich text of the Acts of the Apostles.

Repeated Vision-Reports within a Directed Narrative: Acts 10:1–11:18

As a final coup in his treatment of Acts 10:1–11:18, the Cornelius-Peter episode, Ernst Haenchen makes his famous pronouncement:

> Here stands revealed a peculiarity of Lucan theology which can scarcely be claimed as a point in its favour: in endeavouring to make the hand of God visible in the history of the Church, Luke virtually excludes all human decision. Instead of the realization of the divine will *in* human decisions, *through* human decisions, he shows us a series of supernatural interventions in the dealings of men: the appearance of the angel, the vision of the animals, the promptings of the Spirit, the pouring out of the ecstatic πνεῦμα [Spirit/spirit]. As Luke presents them, these divine incursions have such compelling force that all doubt in the face of them *must* be stilled. They compellingly prove that God, not man, is at work.[2]

Haenchen's problem with this narrative, in fact with Lukan narrative in general, is that "Luke has forsaken the dimension of reality in which genuine decisions of faith are taken" and "substituted a string of miracles."[3] His assumptions regarding the foreclosing power of the supernatural on human debate or endeavor recall the comments of George Kennedy, who, as noted above, categorized the "radical rhetoric of authority" separately from the rhetoric of propositional argumentation.[4] Similarly, Burton L. Mack points

---

2. Ernst Haenchen, *The Acts of the Apostles: A Commentary*, trans. Bernard Noble and Gerald Shinn (Philadelphia: Westminster, 1971), 362.

3. Ibid., 363.

4. Kennedy, *New Testament Interpretation*, 22, 93.

out that nontechnical or uninvented proofs (including tales of the miraculous or prophetic reports) were "highly prized" in early Christian circles even though they "were not thought [by the classical rhetoricians] to challenge the ingenuity of the rhetor."[5] Although Mack allows for ingenuity on the part of early Christian authors to invent these nontechnical proofs of the miraculous sort, it is clear that he considers the function[6] of these to differ from that of more carefully (and successfully) contrived rhetoric.

What happens, however, in the case of Acts 10:1–11:18, where we encounter a narrative in which are set a series of vision-reports? Here, to do justice to the rhetoric, we must attend not just to the deployment of vision-report as a type of *demonstratio* but also to its careful framing and repeated use within a larger narrative. This complex of story framework and embedded visionary narratives enact a new chapter in Luke's presentation of the experience of the early church. That we are dealing with a pivotal episode is clear from the bare fact of the missionary speech included within the narrative at 10:34–43. As Dibelius reminds us, one of the major purposes of such speeches in Acts is to give special emphasis, to "heighten" the moment.[7] Further indications of the importance of this episode may be seen in the subsequent reference to it in chapter 15, its extended nature (the repetition of the visions from scene to scene), and its status as the final missionary proclamation of Peter—or indeed of the apostles, if Paul is to be differently conceived in Luke's scheme. So then, the episode is crucial. But what is the direction of the rhetoric in this overall narrative, and how is it furthered by the vision-reports? Again, are there any moments of polyvalence within the visions that might complicate or run counter to what seems to be the overall rhetorical thrust?

To answer this we need to consider the crafting of the narrative in these two chapters and Luke's method in presenting the visions

5. Mack, *Rhetoric*, 40.

6. Mack suggests that appeal was made to the miraculous and supernatural in the "quest for firm foundations" having a privileged position over human argumentation (ibid., 39).

7. Martin Dibelius, *Studies in the Acts of the Apostles*, ed. H. Greeven, trans. Mary Ling and Paul Schubert (London: SCM, 1956), 119, 166.

as they move toward the deliberative stance of the apostles at 11:18: "*So then* [the Attic ἄρα replaces the more usual οὖν] God has granted even the Gentiles repentance unto life." Programmatic for our analysis is the peculiar function of a vision-report that has been embedded within a narrative, over against a vision-report used within argumentative speech (as in 1 Cor. 12). Due to the complex nature of the passage, we must engage in at least a dual task, paying heed to both rhetorical and narratival strategies. We will first observe the intricate structure of the narrative, then the differences in the recapitulations of the vision-reports, and finally proceed to an assessment of the way in which the repeated visions function within the argument of the narrative as a whole.

The Structure of the Narrative

Given the complexity of the narrative structure, a chart may be helpful. Figure 1 is designed to demonstrate the relationship between the two visions (I and II)—their configuration, interaction, and reconfiguration as they are either reported or interpreted throughout the narrative. These visions of Cornelius and Peter may be seen to surround the missionary discourse and lead toward the conclusion of 11:18.

A quick glance at the shape of this narrative goes part way to explain its dramatic power—if not to evoke it, as would a reading from beginning to end. We find here an artful adaptation of the conventional twin-vision motif, found in a more ornate fashion in the previous episode of Saul and Ananias (Acts 9:1–19). Double visions are usually narrated in such a way as to confirm an impression or course of action for both involved parties: see, for example, Judges 13 (the visions of Manoah and his wife regarding Sampson's birth), Luke 1:5–45 (the interconnected visions of Zechariah and Mary), and *Aseneth* 19:7–8 (the ratification of Aseneth's affirming vision by Joseph). It is interesting to note that the double vision, which is found frequently in romance literature, is not a common feature of biblical rhetoric, perhaps because visions are usually vouchsafed to the elect and need no confirmation by a second party. Eli, for example, does not receive a complementary vision

Figure 1: Entwined and Recapitulated Visions in Acts 10:1–11:18

Vision Ia Cornelius and angel (10:1–8)
  Third person, narrator
  Setting and preparation, 1–3a
  Vision and address, 3b
  Human reaction, 4a   link 9a
  Angelic message, 4b–7a
  Visionary frame closed, 7b
  Retelling (implied), response, 8

Vision IIa Peter and animals (10:9b–20)
  Third person, narrator
  Setting and preparation, 9–10
  Vision and address, 11–13
  Human reaction, 14
  Audition, 15
  Threefold repetition, frame closed, 16
  Meditation, response, 17–20

link 21

Vision Ib Cornelius and angel (10:22–23)
  Introduction, 22a
  Angelic message, 22b   link 23b–26

***Vision IIb** Peter and animals (10:27–29)
  Setting, 27
  Visionary interpretation, 28

Cornelius & Peter meet

  Addition: "so that he could hear
    what you have to say."
  Response, 23a

  Interpretation: "no person unclean
    whom God has called clean."
  Response, 29a

link 29b

      Vision Ic Cornelius and angel (10:30–33)
        First person
        Setting, preparation (addition: "praying"), 30a
        Vision (alternate: "in shining clothes"), 30b
        Angelic address and message [reaction missing], 31–32
        Response, 33
        Addition: "Now we are all here in the presence
          of God to listen to everything . . ."

          Peter's Missionary Speech (10:34–43)
            Exordium = link and interpretation of Ic, 34–35
            Narratio: proposition "Lord of all," 36
                Reason, 37–38
            Confirmatio, 39–43a
            Conclusion, "everyone who believes in him
                receives forgiveness . . . ," 43b

          Narrative frame, dramatic *sequelae*, 44–48

      Peter's "Defense" = Vision IIc and Id (11:1–18)
        Setting and accusation, 1–2
        Introduction, 3

Vision IIc = *Exordium*, 4–10
  Vivid first person   link, 11–12a
  Additions: "It came to me . . ."
  ". . . entered my mouth."

Vision Id = *Narratio*, 12–14
  Addition: "an angel in his house."
  "a message through which . . . your
  household will be saved."

  Confirmatio, 15–17
    Comparison, 15; citation, 16; pathetic appeal, 17
  Conclusion enacted by opponents, 18

* Here the vision is intimated ("God has shown me") rather than clearly reported.

for the benefit of Samuel: God's word is for the latter alone. In the Cornelius-Peter episode, the complementary visions go beyond this simple confirmatory function and are key to the furthering of the story. Indeed, Luke's care in showing divine confirmation may indicate the debate that consumed the early church, and possibly Luke's readership, concerning the status of Gentile believers. The twin visions are recapitulated as the two primary actors come together—a total of five vision-reports. They are then given a climax two-thirds of the way through the narrative by Peter's missionary speech. Finally, they are each rehearsed once again in Peter's "defense" to bring the action and thought to a satisfying conclusion.

The visions and narratives appear in this order: Ia (10:1–8), IIa (10:9b-20), Ib (10:22–23), IIb (10:27–29), Ic (10:30–33), Peter's missionary speech (10:34–43), and Peter's defense (11:1–18), in which we find IIc and Id as part of the argumentation. The conclusion, which we might have expected from Peter's own mouth, is actually spoken by his erstwhile "opponents," making for a very effective closure: "So then, God has granted even to the Gentiles repentance unto life" (11:18). While a string of visions might have had an episodic appearance, the visions are in fact carefully united and given dramatic contours through the way that they are joined, and through their connection with the two speeches. We have no difficulty in determining the beginning and end of the passage and its subordinate parts, since as readers we are given very pointed temporal, spatial, and conceptual indicators. All of the following features work toward a well-conceived whole: a strategic use of links, the parallel manner of presenting the visions and subtle manner of offering interpretation, and the symmetrical characterization of the two principal characters.

The first link, verse 9a, joins together the two scenes of Caesarea and Joppa by reference to the time of day and a "meanwhile" technique. The link between visions IIa and Ib (v. 21) is dramatic, using Peter's statement to underscore the quest of the God-fearers and the coming together of the two parties; his question for clarification invites the retelling of Cornelius's vision by his emissaries. At 23b–26, the narrative itself links together visions Ib and IIb through attention to the change in time and place, the momentous meeting of Cornelius and his expectant clan with the apostle, and the deliberate equalizing of the two major actors: Cornelius's humility is rewarded by Peter's demurring and affirming word, ἀνάστηθι, "Arise!" Again, at 29b, a link is given through a leading question that provides a natural shift from Peter's experience to the second retelling of Cornelius's vision (Ic). Cornelius's own invocation of the presence of God (33b) and Peter's recognition of God's impartiality (34–35) link together vision Ic and Peter's missionary speech in a very complex manner.

The unfolding of the story leads the reader initially to consider Cornelius's vision as prerequisite to the Gentile reception of the gospel from Peter's lips. However, the self-declared stance of Cornelius in the presence of God and Peter's unusual *exordium* suggest that the rehearsal of Cornelius's vision is equally a prerequisite, freeing Peter to speak as he does. By introducing his speech with a commentary or interpretation of the words of Cornelius, Peter presents himself as one who is as much a convert to the new situation as Cornelius will be a convert to Christianity. Peter's own preparation has come about not only through his own complementary vision, or through the word of the Spirit, but through the experience and understanding of the seeker Cornelius. At the conclusion of the speech, we leave Peter in community with the new converts. This situation is "heard about" in Jerusalem (Ἤκουσαν, "they heard" is the initial word of chapter 11) and commented on specifically by Peter's detractors (11:2–3), thus linking the two scenes. Finally, within Peter's defense, visions IIc and Id are linked through the way Peter, in his narration, ranges three emissaries from Cornelius who stop at his house alongside the six with Peter who enter the house of the Gentile. That is, Peter refers to the three from Caesarea (11:11), explains that the Spirit told him to "make no distinction" (12a) between them and his own party, and then speaks of the "six brothers" who accompanied him to Cornelius's house (12b). The text itself is unclear as to whether "the six" include the "three" or are separate—the narrator seems to have heeded the command not to differentiate!

A second unifying feature is the parallelism of visions and the deft manner in which Luke works interpretation into the narrative. While there are some differences between the structures of the visions, they follow a general form of setting and preparation, vision and address, human reaction and closing of the frame, often with a response. Such a pattern is similar to many vision-reports, for example, *4 Ezra* (10:59–12:49; 13:1–58) or *Shepherd of Hermas* (*Vis* 1.1.1–1.4.3; *Vis* 2.1.1–2.4.3; *Vis* 3.1.1–3.1.5). What is significant in the Cornelius-Peter sequence of visions, however, is the lack of an explicit interpretation following the vision itself: this is a feature that is a highly conventional part of visionary literature, particularly when the visions are being used to make doctrinal points. Luke, however, allows the interpretations to slip in at key points of the drama. For example, vision Ic (10:30–33) and Peter's missionary speech are linked together by means of Peter's *exordium*, which also doubles as interpretation of vision Ic, which Cornelius has just reported (10:31–32). In this way, the introduction to Peter's speech completes Cornelius's vision, adding the "divine" interpretation of it. Elsewhere interpretive details are fitted into subsequent tellings of the vision rather than given their natural place, as we will note below. Or, as in 10:27–29, interpretation is offered casually, as if a mere comment on the unusual direction of the action, as when Peter remarks on the meaning of his previous vision as he enters Cornelius's house. Robert Tannehill points out that "the close connection between the speeches and their narrative settings is . . . shown by the fact that some of the repeated elements may occur in one case in the speech, in another case in the setting";[8] the same may be said for the connection between the vision-reports and their narrative settings.

The effect of this ad hoc insertion of interpretation into the action, rather than its formalized inclusion at the close of each vision, is such as to characterize interpretation as part of the natural unfolding of events—an emergence of understanding, one accessible to anyone of reason and insight. In esoteric literature, such

---

8. Robert C. Tannehill, "The Functions of Peter's Mission Speeches in the Narrative of Acts," *New Testament Studies* 37 (1991): 414.

as the genre of apocalypse, the more common rhythm is that of a vision followed by the words of the *angelus interpres*. Luke's organic inclusion of interpretation within the narrative has the rhetorical power to draw the reader into the discussion, for we get no sense of a mystery being "decoded" by an expert. Here is a significant case in which Haenchen's dictum concerning compulsion "by divine incursion"[9] is not subtle enough. There is an undeniable rhetorical force to the narrative, but its character is the type that wins by finesse rather than by playing an oracular or visionary trump card.

A final unifying factor may be seen in the introduction and presentation of the major actors, a feature made possible by the parallel vision format but also enhanced by allusion and symbolism. Both Cornelius and Peter are at prayer and are addressed by God. Further, the *ethos* of both is established through the use of sacrificial language. At 10:4 the angel refers to the God-fearer's prayers and alms as a memorial before God, recalling other angelic references to prayer:

> While I was speaking and praying, confessing my sin and the sin of my people Israel, and presenting my supplication before the LORD my God for the holy hill of my God; while I was speaking in prayer, the man Gabriel, whom I had seen in the vision at the first, came to me in swift flight at the time of the evening sacrifice. He came and he said to me, "O Daniel, I have now come out to give you wisdom and understanding. At the beginning of your supplications a word went forth, and I have come to tell it to you, for you are greatly beloved; therefore consider the word and understand the vision." (Dan. 9:20–23 RSV)

> And so, when you and your daughter-in-law Sarah prayed, I brought a reminder of your prayer before the Holy One; and when you buried the dead, I was likewise present with you. When you did not hesitate to rise and leave your dinner in order to go and lay out the dead, your good deed was not hidden from me, but I was with you. So now God sent me to heal you and your daughter-in-law Sarah. I am Raphael, one of the seven holy angels who present the

9. Haenchen, *Acts*, 362.

prayers of the saints and enter into the presence of the glory of the
Holy One. (Tob. 12:12–15 RSV)

In light of the similarity between Cornelius and heroes from Jewish
literature, the reader is predisposed to view this Gentile sympatheti-
cally. Pointed reference to Cornelius's household and to the ascension
of prayers at the traditional hour also cast Cornelius as a kind of
priest for his family and close associates: this role is continued in the
story at 10:24, where Cornelius has called together his household
to hear God's word. In the case of Peter the imagery is even more
pointed, since he refuses the unclean at 11:8 in words that echo
those of the priestly Ezekiel: "Nothing unclean has ever entered my
mouth" (cf. Ezek. 4:14). What ensues from the command differs,
however: Yahweh compromises in the case of Ezekiel, whereas Peter
is given the same command to eat three times.

In all this, both Peter and Cornelius, Jew and Gentile, are commended to the reader with equal intensity and with similar intertextual echoes of erstwhile famous figures. Perhaps there is even a
little more sympathy directed toward Cornelius, whose status may
be less obvious, so that their visions, and the combination of their
visions in the retelling, will be given equal weight by readers in the
unfolding revelation. In this story, a cultically clean Peter and the
penultimately pure Gentile Cornelius are brought together to herald
and, in fact, to enact the mission to the Gentiles. As in the story of
another centurion (cf. Luke 7:1–9), emphasis is placed not simply
on God's prerogative to act but also on the deserving status of this
God-fearer. The picture evoked by Luke in the telling, retelling,
and final union of the twin visions within Peter's defense seems to
be that of two "houses" coming together, as we shall see.

It's All in the Telling: The Recapitulation of the Visions

We move on now to analyze differences and variations in the
subsequent retellings of each vision. It should not come as a surprise to us that Luke does not repeat the visions verbatim, for the
differences between retold visions in Acts have often been noted,
as in the case of Paul's three conversion reports, which we will

consider below. The differences between the retold visions of Acts 10–11 are particularly noticeable due to their proximity one to the other. If we were dealing with an author whose approach to vision and audition were oracular we would expect the fullest treatment of the visions to come first, in the narrator's own account, and the subsequent retellings to be derivative. Such would be the kind of narration expected of Luke by the reader who has been convinced by Jervell (or Haenchen, for that matter) that Luke is "the fundamentalist—*sit venia verbo* [pardon the expression]—in the New Testament."[10] In such a situation, determinacy rather than an open "text" (or vision-report) would be the name of the game. In fact, very significant details are added to the subsequent retellings; interpretations or applications are placed within the second and third tellings as part of the vision and not as mere interpretation or gloss.

Compare, for example, visions IIa, IIb, and IIc, with their emerging force. IIa (10:9b–20) begins as a typical vision with Peter in the usual preparatory stance of prayer and hunger (cf. 4 Ezra 5:19; 6:30–31; 10:23–25)—although he is about to break his fast, both physically and cultically. The visionary language is typical too: "heaven is opened" (cf. Rev. 4:1) and "something like" (τι ὡς; cf. *dĕmût* in Ezek. 1:26, etc.) a sheet is let down. The divine audition is followed by human refusal, then a repeated command. God has the last word, but Peter is not given an explicit interpretation yet. However, by IIb (10:27–29), presumably through the prompting of the Spirit to go with Cornelius's emissaries, Peter has drawn the analogy of unclean food to "unclean" Gentiles. He declares to his Gentile audience, "God has shown me not to call any human being [ἄνθρωπον] common or unclean." At this point we do not get a complete retelling of the vision (hence the asterisk in the chart)—Peter has another type of speech to make. The new interpretation, however, recalls Peter's entire vision and places its memory within the context of the new scene. We as readers, though not Peter's in-text audience, know that it is through

10. Jacob Jervell, "The Center of Scripture in Luke," in *The Unknown Paul: Essays on Luke-Acts and Early Christian History* (Minneapolis: Augsburg, 1984), 122.

the sheet vision that God has given Peter this new insight. There
is to be a very thorough rehearsal of Peter's vision, however, in
chapter 11: sequence IIc (11:4–10) provides a first-person account,
appropriately vivid, with a fourth group of animals added (wild
beasts) and the sheet being let down specifically "from heaven"
to "where Peter was" (11:5). It is not enough for Peter simply
to state that he has never eaten unclean food, but he must state,
with prophetic flourish, that it has never "entered his mouth."
Unclean food may never have entered Peter's mouth, but Gentiles
are on the verge of entering his house, and he is about to go into
their domain as well.

If there are interesting variations on Peter's vision, then the four
rehearsals of Cornelius's vision are even more telling of Luke's
art. Vision Ia (10:1–8) has an extended introduction and preparation section in which Cornelius's devout character is carefully
established for the rhetorical reasons of *ethos* as outlined above.
Again, emphasis is placed on Cornelius's perspicacity or "clear
sight" of the vision, although no detailed description of the angel
is offered. In 10:22 the rehearsal of vision Ib is much briefer, and
yet an apt detail is added, considering the position of the suppliants
before Peter: the angel has instructed Cornelius to send for Peter
"so that he might hear what Peter had to say," a reason not given
in the first telling of the vision. The third vision of Cornelius, Ic
(10:30–33), is more vivid (as with Peter's first-person vision-report,
IIc) describing the Godfearer's action of prayer as preparatory for
the vision (10:30), emphasizing the glory of the epiphany, disclosing God's active stance of hearing and remembering, and adding
Cornelius's own expectation that God has commanded Peter to
give him a word (10:33). By the fourth telling of the vision (Id,
11:12–14), the gathering together of the details and their elaboration are decidedly pointed. Vision Ia has briefly mentioned the
"entering" (εἰσελθόντα, 10:3) angel, although we have not been
given an exact setting for Cornelius's prayer so it is not clear where
the angel has entered; vision Ib gives the purpose for calling Peter
to Cornelius's house; vision Ic gives the setting of Cornelius praying in his house and the angel standing before him. It is vision
Id, however, that brings the details together, making unavoidable

the picture that the angel did not simply appear before Cornelius but entered and stood "in his house" (ἐν τῷ οἴκῳ, 11:13) to give a momentous message. It is in vision Id as well that we hear the angel *tell* Cornelius that Peter "will bring a message through which you and all your house [πᾶς ὁ οἶκός σου] will be saved" (11:14). Here what appears to be a theological reflection on the vision is placed within the vision itself as the angel speaks.

Rhetoric and Household: The Tendency of the Argument

It is this picture of the angel entering the house of Cornelius for the ultimate purpose of the salvation of that household that deals the masterstroke of the argument. The reader is alerted to the importance of the house/household theme by the repetition of the Greek words οἶκος and οἰκία (words that mean, variably, "house" and "household") throughout chapters 10 and 11. At the beginning of the episode, Cornelius and his household (οἶκος) are described as devout God-fearers; emphasis is placed on Peter's sojourn in the tanner's house (οἰκία) by the sea; Peter is on the roof of this house; Cornelius's messengers stop outside the gate of the house (οἰκία) of Simon; they say that Peter is to come, at the word of the angel, to Cornelius's house (οἶκος); Cornelius tells Peter that he had been in his house (οἶκος) praying; Cornelius tells Peter that he had been instructed in a vision to send for him at Simon's house (οἰκία); Peter tells the circumcised believers that he and his companions entered Cornelius's house (οἶκος); he tells them that the angel stood in Cornelius's house (οἶκος); and salvation was to come to the house (οἶκος) of Cornelius. We can add to these the repetition of different forms of εἰσέρχομαι ("to enter") at 10:3, 25, 27; 11:3, 8 and be fairly certain that we are to take heed of such actions as going into houses or refraining from going into houses. Out of delicacy for Peter, Cornelius's messengers stop short of entering until invited; Cornelius falls at Peter's feet when Peter crosses his threshold;[11] Peter comments on

---

11. The rendering of the NRSV (Peter's "arrival" vs. "entry," 10:25) obscures the importance of this motif, which is better preserved by the RSV, despite the difficulty of Peter's entering twice (10:25, 27). The repetition of the verb in the context of, first,

his unusual entry as he goes in with Cornelius. The first crosser
of the line, however, has been God's angel—first in chronology,
but last and decisive in the rhetorical arsenal. Of real interest is
the effortless way in which this detail finds itself worked into the
final vision-report. With it the speaker says, but with understated
finesse, "In case you didn't get it, the angel entered first, so who
are you to criticize?" It is in Peter's final speech that all the events
of the last chapter are summarized, connected with the Lord's own
words, and pressed home; as a cap for the reader, the detractors
themselves acknowledge the rightness of what has happened and
leave us with a conclusion.

So then, Peter's explanation before the circumcised believers
in Jerusalem takes on the shape of an eccentric defense: vision IIc
(11:4–10) functions as an *exordium*, establishing Peter's character
through his priestlike unwillingness to become impure; vision Id
(11:12–14) functions as the *narratio*, demonstrating how the entry
into a Gentile home finds a divine precedent; the references to Jesus
and the prophet's words at verses 15–17 function as *confirmatio/
argumentatio*; and the deliberation of the group itself (v. 18) acts
as a conclusion. Despite the use of the adverb καθεξῆς ("orderly")
at Luke 1:3 and Acts 11:4, we have neither here nor in Luke's
writing as a whole a simple chronological account of what has
taken place; rather, there is a studied "sequencing" and shaping
of the narrative in order to enhance its rhetorical power. What
has begun as Peter's apology is transformed into a deliberative
situation in which a precedent has been set for a future Gentile
mission. That is, the focus on the question, "Did Peter break the
law?" is replaced by an argument for the mission to the Gentiles:
"So then, to the Gentiles, God has also granted repentance unto
life." The issue of entry into Cornelius's house is replaced by the
issue of Gentile homes being united to the household of God.

It should be pointed out here that, technically, Cornelius is not
the first Gentile to receive salvation in the Acts narrative. Pride
of place belongs to the Ethiopian eunuch, who is converted on

---

Cornelius's obeisance and, second, Peter's interpretive explanation, is logical rhetorically,
even if it is problematic in terms of narrative.

the desert road. But as Dibelius points out, "apparently it means much more for Peter to enter the Gentile house."[12] The question is not simply whether a Gentile can be converted; it is about the inclusion of Gentiles as a whole within the household of God. Indeed, this entire episode, with its wordplay on "house/hold" is reminiscent of the interchange between David and the LORD in 2 Samuel 7, with regard to the temple and the seed of David.

If it seems that the angel's entry into and stance within Cornelius's house may be a fortuitous phrase without polemic purpose, note that I have only been able to find one other instance in similar epiphanic passages. Elsewhere in the New Testament, angels appear *to* people, but in *Joseph and Aseneth*, which has several other parallels to the Acts,[13] we hear that the angel of the Lord, the one who is "chief of the house of the Lord," "enters the chamber" (εἰσῆλθεν, *Aseneth* 14:5–8) of Aseneth and that Aseneth marvels that he has "entered our house" (εἰσῆλθεν εἰς τὴν οἰκίαν, 6:2). It should not be surprising, given this emphasis on boundary-crossing, to learn that the major theme in the Aseneth story is her conversion to Judaism, that purity—cultic as well as moral purity—is a major motif, and that the central problem addressed by this novel is how Joseph, the patriarch, could possibly have married a Gentile.[14] *Joseph and Aseneth*, like Acts, is concerned with how Gentiles can be joined to the household of God, although it gives a different answer.

How, then, do the visions function within Luke's major argument? It can be seen from the narrative chart that the visions

---

12. Dibelius, *Studies*, 118.

13. Similar motifs and images occur in the conversions of Aseneth and Saul/Paul—the twin-vision technique, the concept of an eternal vocation from God, and a preponderance of light symbolism, for example. The dating of *Joseph and Aseneth*, however, remains uncertain (see Edith Humphrey, *Joseph and Aseneth*, Guide to Apocrypha and Pseudepigrapha 8 [Sheffield: Sheffield Academic Press, 2000]), and thus no case of "borrowing" may be here adduced with confidence. It may be that both books, as religious "action" narratives, simply draw from a similar linguistic and cultural thesaurus.

14. Indeed, the same dramatic and winsome type of language used in *Joseph and Aseneth* is used in Acts to describe purity: Peter has never so much as allowed unkosher food to "enter his mouth"; Aseneth, though Gentile, is virginally pure and has never "so much as had a male child" enter her chamber or sit on her bed.

prepare dramatically for the argumentative section of the narrative in 11:15–18: twin visions are related, the recipients are gradually brought together as more interpretive details are added, and a penultimate climax is created in Peter's missionary speech and the resultant conversion of the Gentile house. Moreover, the council's query about Peter's behavior is answered by reference back to the visions so that the recapitulation of the visions actually forms the major portion of this final speech—a speech in which apology is transmuted into deliberation. In Peter's reply, the vision-report is used to establish *ethos* (Peter was unwilling to transgress) and to set forth the real matter at hand, that God has justified entry into the Gentile domain. Perhaps it seemed at the first telling of Cornelius's experience (10:1–8) that the "vision" (what Cornelius *saw*) was far less important than the content of the angel's *message* that Cornelius is pleasing to God and that he should send for Peter. In this sense, Ia appears to be more of an "audition," a word from God that prepares the reader to accept Cornelius and that moves the action along to the meeting of Cornelius and Peter. However, the narrator has indeed called Ia a "vision" in which Cornelius saw "clearly," and in Ic further emphasis is placed on the brightness of Cornelius's vision. What Cornelius clearly saw was an *entering* (εἰσελθόντα) angel, although the startling content of this vision is not made clear until the final retelling at Id. Peter's speech discloses the implications of the vision: Cornelius saw the holy angel (entering and) standing *in his (Gentile) house.* Luke holds back the vital detail until the best dramatic moment, underscoring his point that entry into the Gentile domain has been enacted by God and is therefore to be pursued. The visions and speeches are internally connected in order to press home Luke's argument.

Does This Piece Fit?

Some commentators have criticized the missionary sermon of 10:34–43 as being out of line with the situation at hand. It seems to me that attention to the tendency of the visions and certain details of the missionary speech show that this criticism is unwarranted.

The major question to ask in analyzing such a narratival sermon is what should be placed or understood to stand in the foreground. If verses 36 and 42–43 are seen to be central, as I have indicated in the charted presentation of the proposition of the speech (see figure 1), then the emphasis of the missionary speech is on the universality of the gospel, that Jesus is Lord of all:

> Proposition (v. 36):[15] "As to the word which God sent to the children of Israel bringing the good news of peace through Jesus Christ: This (Jesus Christ) is Lord of all."
>
> Final confirmation (v. 42): "And he commanded us to preach to the people, and to testify that he is the one ordained by God to be judge of the living and the dead."
>
> Citation (v. 43a): "To him all the prophets bear witness . . ."
>
> Conclusion (v. 43b): "that every one who believes in him receives forgiveness of sins through his name."

As Burchard argues, "[Peter's] main purpose is not to preach the gospel to Cornelius; it is rather to assure him that the coming of Christ is the culmination of God's dealings with Israel, the people to which the worthy soldier wanted to belong all along."[16] Seen this way the speech is not simply a tool to heighten the episode with contents that have little connection with the burden of the narrative. Rather, the speech makes explicit what the twin visions have already suggested and what will be pressed home in Peter's concluding speech in Jerusalem. Kennedy may be right in arguing that there is no "serious rhetorical problem"[17] to be overcome by Peter in his address to Cornelius's household, so far as their receptivity is concerned; there is, however, a serious rhetorical obstacle

---

15. Here we adopt the reading of Christoph Burchard, "A Note on 'RHMA in *JosAs* 17:1f.; Luke 2:15, 17; Acts 10:37," *Novum Testamentum* 27 (1985): 293.

16. Burchard argues that the best translation of 10:36 views τὸν λόγον as an accusative of respect, emphasizing "This is Lord of all" as the word of God ("A Note on 'RHMA," 294). In his view, the core of Peter's speech is vv. 34–36 inclusive. I would prefer to see vv. 34–35 as an introductory statement in which Peter addresses the situation and prepares for the statement of universality in v. 36.

17. Kennedy, *New Testament Interpretation*, 122.

in the narrative as a whole, acknowledged even in Cornelius's action of prostration as Peter "comes in"—that is, the problem of whether the event should be taking place at all. It is this problem that the speech of Peter addresses, while of course it also sounds the recurring note of the proclamation found throughout Acts. For Kennedy, Peter's missionary speech is epideictic, focusing on and celebrating the mighty acts of Jesus; however, I agree with Burchard that this speech has rather a deliberative flavor, pointing the reader to the issue of the universal gospel.

Open and *Closed Case*

Another issue that has been debated in this episode is the strange silence whereby Peter's vision is not applied explicitly to food laws (its most obvious connection, since Peter is told to eat) but to Gentiles themselves. It would seem that Luke is at great pains to avoid the obvious implication of the vision. In support of this it should be noted that Luke likewise does not follow Mark 7 in applying Jesus' words regarding the washing of hands to food (Luke 11:38–40, versus Mark 7:18b); similarly, he avoids emphasizing Jesus' table fellowship with a leper (Simon) and simply describes him as a Pharisee (Luke 7:36–50 versus the tradition cited in Mark and Matthew). Again, in Acts 15, the issue of table fellowship among Jewish believers is not actually broached. Rather, the council discusses appropriate behavior of only the Gentile believers. It may be that Luke, with his concern for historical development of the church, does not anticipate in his narrative actions that will be taken later: Jesus did *not* declare all foods clean but left that for the Spirit to make clear. Alternatively, it may be that Luke was comfortable with two standards and expected Jewish believers to maintain dietary purity but Gentiles to follow a modified code.[18]

Be this as it may, it is not at all clear that Luke's own lack of application regarding food laws forbids readers from adducing the vision's "obvious" meaning. Indeed, it is by no means clear that vi-

18. Michael Pettem, "Luke's Great Omission and His View of the Law," *New Testament Studies* 42 (1996): 35–54.

sions by and large have one obvious meaning, although they may be directed along one line to the exclusion of others within a range of possibilities. In fact, it is at this point that the polyvalent character of symbolism works to Luke's advantage. Had Luke primarily been concerned with table fellowship of Jew and Gentile believer, then this line might have been followed in the retelling and interpretation of Peter's vision. Luke's real focus here is, however, on the Gentile mission, and so the message derived from Peter's vision is that "no one whom God has declared clean should be considered unclean." The symbolism of the sheet of animals is very rich, conjuring up notions of completeness—all animals, cultically pure and impure, come down together from heaven—as well as addressing Peter's pressing practical problem of whether he should heed Cornelius's emissaries. Critics who have halted with confusion at Peter's refusal to kill, suggesting that he could have devoured the clean animals, are insensitive to the way in which vision functions. The sheet evokes the completeness of God's household *as well as* presenting an opportunity to challenge the assumptions of the circumcised.

Moreover, although the lesson drawn from the sheet vision underscores persons rather than food, food is not uninvolved in the Acts account since Peter is accused of (and does not deny) eating with Gentiles. The vision, then, offers several connected but different directions of thought—the breadth of God's household, the importance of direct action in the Gentile domain, the implication that purity laws may not apply any more, and so on. It is the second of these paths that Luke specifically treads in the telling and retelling of these visions: he is concerned with a direct mission to the Gentiles. The polyvalent potential of vision is demonstrated, however, by the fact that at least some later ecclesiastical traditions have appealed to the sheet vision as primarily indicating the abrogation of kosher laws.[19] Depending on how one sees Luke's

19. Most ancient commentators—an exception would be Cyril of Alexandria (*Contra Julian* 9.318–19)—use the vision of the animals in the sheet as an occasion to talk about "the nations." Calvin, by contrast, fastens on the abrogated Law and the papal regulations against bacon on fast days (*Calvin's Commentaries: The Acts of the Apostles 1–13*, trans. J. W. Fraser and W. J. G. McDonald [Grand Rapids: Eerdmans, 1965], 296).

view of food purity and Jewish Christians, some of the reverbera-
tions of the polyvalent vision may have a complicating effect on
the overall argumentation. It may be difficult for those who are
entrenched within the ongoing tradition of the western church to
sort out the constraints of interpretation that would have directed
a first readership: we tend, despite all efforts, to read Acts from
the side of Galatians and later Reformation church history.

In the light of the postmodern situation, however, the polyvalent potential of vision may well appear to offer permission
for twenty-first-century interpreters to read this vision sequence
against the grain of Lukan ethics and theology. Already we have
noted the potential conflict of symbolism with argumentation in
such passages as 2 Corinthians 12, and we will see this even more
clearly in our treatment of the Apocalypse as we move to more
open uses of the vision-report. There is a particular penchant of
our age for inclusivism, indeed a veritable crescendo of voices that
are, from various standpoints,[20] now identifying inclusivism with
the gospel. Eugene Rogers,[21] for example, has argued in connection with Pauline theology that Paul's gospel of the "inclusion of
the Gentiles" as branches grafted in "against their nature" (Rom.
11) might offer an opening for the "inclusion" of those whose
sexuality is considered to be "against nature" (Rom. 1) so that
Paul spoke "truer than he knew." A similar reading of this vision
sequence might well lead the inclusivist theologian to co-opt it
along with, for example, certain readings of the parable of the
good Samaritan as a plank in the proclamation of a new gospel.
Such moves, which are being made even in passages that do not

20. One might cite the well-known work of Elisabeth Schüssler Fiorenza, who
makes this move most decisively in her *Rhetoric and Ethic: The Politics of Biblical
Studies* (Minneapolis: Augsburg, 1999), and Eugene F. Rogers, who adopts this view
of gospel as foundational for his more focused polemic in *Sexuality and the Christian
Body: Their Way into the Triune God* (Oxford: Blackwell, 1999). The perspective
has percolated from the academic sphere into popular discourse in the writings of
John Shelby Spong, for example, *Why Christianity Must Change or Die: A Bishop
Speaks to Believers in Exile* (New York: HarperCollins, 1998), and Michael Ingham's
Mansions of the Spirit: The Bible in a Multi-Faith World (Toronto: Anglican Book
Centre, 1997).
21. See esp. Rogers, *Sexuality and the Christian Body.*

offer the polyvalent complications of the visional, must be addressed seriously from those who continue to read the visions in harmony with historic Christianity. What are the limits, or the controls, that the text itself offers amid the imaginative scope that it offers? In the book of Acts, it is obvious that chapters 10 and 11 are to be read as a preface to the unfolding proclamation of the gospel concerning Jesus and that the orderly decisions of, say, the council of Acts 15 are as significant as the visionary shock of Acts 11. Decisions as to the implications of Peter's vision are made by reference to the believing community (11:17–18), a theme sustained in the larger and more complex decision of the council concerning directives for Gentile believers (15:23–29). There the gathered church weighed together the issues and paid attention to the cues latent in the revelatory words and symbols.

This strategy of the earliest faith community is instructive for the reader who desires today to heed the cues of the biblical text. As in other literature, some cues in Scripture are more "open" while others are more directive; nevertheless, the text itself provides the "lures"[22] for the interpreters who are interested in hearing another voice, another story, rather than engaging in their own free creation or storytelling. In reader-response theories of this sort an accent is placed on the part of the interpreter, who is understood as reconfiguring, even "re-creating," the text. However, a hermeneutics of reception is, as complementary to a critical mind, fruitful for any reader of any text—receptivity is important if readers want to hear anything other than their own thoughts echoing back at them. To call a text "open" is to suggest that it has a range of meanings, but not that it should be treated like a wax nose. Reading a text is less like the subjective tracing of patterns in the clouds than it is like the inductive/deductive work necessary in performing (i.e., interpreting) a musical score. There is room

22. Russell Pregeant, *Christology beyond Dogma: Matthew's Christ in Process Hermeneutic*, Semeia Supplements 7 (Missoula, MT: Scholars Press; Philadelphia: Fortress, 1978), 45. I adopt this terminology from process hermeneutics because it seems an apt description of the interaction between text and reader, without intending to import all the other methodological and philosophical foundations of this school of interpretation.

for argument between one school and another concerning the performance of Bach and even more scope for variation between one performance of Debussy and another, but some renderings just will not work. From this perspective, one of the roles of the sympathetic reader is to respond to the indications of the text's language, be it relatively open or closed. Listening from within the context of a faithful community requires this same kind of active listening and engaged spectatorship, but it goes beyond this to demand a corporate rather than merely individualistic herme-neutic. It can never be a matter of action solely on the part of one "re-creating" interpreter, since those whose perspective has been shaped by the incarnation and the communion of saints will be optimistic that true communication can take place between the canonical voices and today's community. For a reader within the Christian community this also will mean giving priority to how other Christians have heard and seen, and continue to hear and see, the passage in question. This would include a certain reserve regarding a reading that is utterly novel or wholly eccentric.

Synergy and Interpretation

We began this consideration of repeated vision-reports by citing Haenchen's dictum that human decision is often, in Luke's work, left behind for a sequence of visions and divine actions. What we have instead observed in Acts 10–11 is the merging of speech and vision-reports within Luke's narrative so that the rhetorical purposes are accomplished in a compelling yet refined manner. While it is certainly the case that God is presented as the main actor in this episode, human decisions and interpretations of di-vine visions are evident throughout. Unlike the usual strategy of the genre apocalypse, the visions are not given an authoritative interpretation by an *angelus interpres*; rather, they are understood through the meditation, speeches, and unfolding events enacted by the human players in the drama. Moreover, Luke seems happy to import interpretation into the visions as the action develops, demonstrating how human understanding enriches the significance of the visions. The Cornelius-Peter episode is obviously about coming to understand God's purposes for the Gentile community, but at every step of the way human thinking and action are involved. Thus the visions do not present a fait accompli but are artfully presented and combined to lead the hearers within the story, and the readers of the story, to certain conclusions. The way in which Luke carefully intertwines narrative, argumentation, and vision-report may stand as a picture of his view of the relationship between the human and the divine—here we see cooperation rather than coercion, disclosure rather than determination.

This literary-rhetorical consideration of Acts 10:1–11:18 has shown some of the ways in which a text has "a say" concerning its own signification: structure, directed argument, key motifs or words, the arrangement of details to work toward conclusion, intertextual echoes, and the like. The perception of such details will no doubt be weighted differently from reader to reader, according to their various approaches and understandings of Acts, the Bible as a whole, and other related texts. What an interpreter will see in this complicated narrative will no doubt be affected more than a little by the working hypothesis concerning what the book of Acts is all about. Again, one's view of the appropriate literature to be placed alongside the passage for comparison, as well as one's view of Luke and his milieu—for example his rhetorical competence or the likelihood of his knowing the double-vision tradition—will also make its mark on the reading offered.

Helpful in schematizing and clarifying these different contextual foci is the four-part typology of Elizabeth Struthers Malbon,[23] in which she suggests an abstraction (never found in a pure form) of "literary" and "historical" contexts and shows the intersection of these with "internal" and "external" contexts. The text can function as mirror and/or window, and different interpreters will locate their engagement with the text at different quadrants of the typology. The diverse concerns of rhetorical criticism, especially the rhetorical criticism of a narrative, underscore Malbon's insistence that it is necessary to envisage the inter-relationship of

23. Elizabeth Struthers Malbon, "Texts and Contexts: Interpreting the Disciples in Mark," *Semeia* 62 (1993): 83.

these contexts. In the case of rhetorical criticism, both literary and historical contexts are germane since we are discussing the purposeful creation of a persuasive technique and form. Here "internal" "literary" and "external" "literary" contexts are constantly informed by, especially, "external" "historical" context. Other readings will shift the concern. Despite various possible construals of a text and that text's unusual relationship with the interpreter(s), the literary work is not wholly dependent on these construals (nor is it "autonomous"). Rather, it is "heteronomous"[24] and calls in this otherness to be so engaged. Interpretation cannot proceed in a vacuum, but interpretation is about understanding a text. When we hear an ancient text, then, is it a matter of our being moved by a determining argument, or of our determining argument(s) within the text, either as single readers or as readers in a community? Never a completely patent process, this quest is delightfully complicated in the reading of Acts 10:1–11:18 by the role of an inherently open genre (the vision-report) within what is not entirely an open and shut case.

Directing an Extended Narrative through Repeated Vision-Reports: Acts 9:1–25; 22:1–22; and 26:1–24

In the Cornelius-Peter-Jerusalem council sequence the interrelationship between word and vision has been seen to be enmeshed and mutually interpreting. Our analysis confirms the trenchant observation of Luke Timothy Johnson: "the apparent redundancy of this passage is the most important clue to its interpretation."[25] As we go on to consider the thrice-told report of Saul's vision, we encounter a similar blending of what is seen with what is heard—indeed, perhaps a conflation of these categories. The Saul/Paul narratives recall to my mind a humorous scene from the days when I was becoming acquainted with the liturgical church. Imagine with me an informal ("low") Anglican church in Montréal. The situation: all are listening to what may be euphemistically characterized as a "strongly prophetic" reading from the Bible. The reader: a friend and colleague, new to the church, and definitely not of Anglican formation. My friend arrives at the end of the colorful passage, redolent of gloom and doom, and pauses a little in confusion. He is unsure of the appropriate ecclesial etiquette, but looking behind to the rector, puts on the appropriate tag with a questioning voice: "This is the word of the Lord?" As you can imagine, the congregation's response, "Thanks be to God," was mingled with laughter: the difficult content of the biblical passage and the reader's insecurity in the ecclesial context had conspired to add an unanticipated polyvalence to a conventional phrase.

The narratives of Saul's Christophany present us with a similar, if not as refreshingly comic, dilemma. These are passages that have presented exegetes with numerous challenges, ranging from disputes about whether Paul is here "called" or "converted," through efforts to harmonize the discrepancies in the passages, to complex discussions of sources or the art of Luke. However, in the context of our study—the analysis of the rhetorical role of vision-reports within narrative and discourse—there is a more obvious question. Ananias declares that Jesus "appeared" to Paul (9:17), and Barnabas introduces Paul to the apostles as one "who had seen the Lord" (9:27). But where is the *vision* on the Damascus road? A sympathetic reader might agree: "This is the *word* of the Lord?" But is it a vision? We see no throne room, no figure at the right hand of God (as in Stephen's story), no description of face or loins or white hair: none of the visionary details found in apocalypses or prophetic epiphanies. The account seems to focus on what Saul *hears*, either directly or through others, rather than on what is *seen*.

What exactly does the author intend by characterizing the revelation as a vision while scarcely reporting any visionary content at all? If audition or oracle is the key revelatory medium in these sequences, why are the experiences persistently designated as visionary?[26] It seems inadvisable to reduce this dilemma to

26. See Acts 9:10 and 26:19.

semantic quarrelling, or to plead that academics make a nice distinction between "audition" and "vision" that would have been incomprehensible in the ancient world. The narratives, in fact, not only use the word "vision" but increasingly highlight the themes of blindness/opening of eyes and light/dark *alongside* references to hearing and witnessing. A recent socio-rhetorical analyst of this passage comments, "The language of divine revelation, through visual as well as verbal media, dominates the discourse."[27] What does it mean, then, for Luke to clothe "the word" with the garb of vision? How does this understanding of envisioned word direct the rhetoric at the various levels of narration in these three parallel but unique passages and in the development of Acts across their recurrent narration?

As we approach this repeated vision-report, then, we have several questions on the agenda. First, what difference does it make to see chapters 9, 22, and 26 as concerned with vision and not simply declarative proposition? Next, granted that there are vision-reports included here, where exactly do these occur, and how do they function within the narratives of chapter 9 and the two speeches of chapters 22 and 26? Finally, faced with the recapitulative but transformative nature of these accounts, how do these vision-reports contribute to the overall rhetorical flow of Acts? We will take each passage in turn, looking for indications about the nature of the revelation, observing the place of the vision within the passage, and suggesting a rhetorical lens whereby each passage can be fruitfully understood. By way of conclusion, we will consider the variations and the development of the three accounts taken together. Though rhetorical tools will be helpful, especially in the analysis of the second and third renditions (for these occur in the immediate context of a constructed "speech"), the question of literary strategy will be more dominant here because, as with Acts 10:1–11:18, we are dealing with an extended narrative.

27. István Czachesz, "Socio-Rhetorical Exegesis of Acts 9:11–30," *Communio Viatorum* 37, no. 1 (1995): 8. Czachesz constructs an instructive table on page 6 of this article, in which he demonstrates the repetitive and progressive patterns that emerge when we attend to words associated with seeing and speaking. Of interest, too, is the centrality of the word ὄνομα, *name*.

Seeing and Not Seeing; or, Vision within Visions: Acts 9:1–25

The complexity of Acts 9:1–25 is manifest by reference to the various ways in which it has been understood and the multiplicity of source and form critical studies from which it has suffered. It has been understood in terms of a "healing" story adulterated by the Lukan theme of Paul's commission,[28] as a call narrative modeled on the narratives of Old Testament prophets and other noteworthy parabiblical characters,[29] and as a conversion story in which the blinding has a corrective function.[30] The blinding motif itself has been assessed variously as traditional or as an artifice of Luke.[31] We are not concerned here with source-critical analysis, with which analysts of these passages have had a "field day,"[32] nor in discovering underlying forms, but rather with the narrative per se. The ambiguous presentation of Paul's experience has itself produced various verdicts: "[Luke] wishes to insist that Paul did see Jesus . . . [in a revelation] to be accepted on a par with the other appearances of the Risen Lord";[33] it "must be called an audition rather than a vision";[34] the categories of vision and audition are "sometimes . . . interchangeable" as can be seen in the curious phraseology of Acts 22:17, "I *saw* him *saying* to me."[35]

28. Charles W. Hedrick, "Paul's Conversion/Call: A Comparative Analysis of the Three Reports in Acts," *Journal of Biblical Literature* 100 (1981): 415–32.

29. K. Stendahl, *Paul among Jews and Gentiles* (Philadelphia: Fortress, 1976).

30. D. Hamm, "Paul's Blindness and Its Healing: Clues to Symbolic Intent (Acts 9, 22, and 26)," *Biblica* 71 (1990): 70; and Beverly Roberts Gaventa, *From Darkness to Light: Aspects of Conversion in the New Testament* (Philadelphia: Fortress, 1986).

31. See, for example, the call of Samuel, of Isaiah, and of Aseneth in the romance *Joseph and Aseneth*. On the commission call in particular, see John T. Townsend, "Acts 9:1–29 and Early Church Tradition," in *1988 Seminar Papers*, ed. David J. Lull, Society of Biblical Literature Seminar Papers Series 27 (Atlanta: Scholars Press, 1988), 119–31.

32. Richard Longenecker, *The Acts of the Apostles*, Expositor's Bible Commentary 9 (Grand Rapids: Zondervan, 1981), 317.

33. David M. Stanley, "Paul's Conversion in Acts: Why the 3 Accounts?" *Catholic Biblical Quarterly* 15 (1953): 329–30.

34. Hamm, "Paul's Blindness," 64.

35. Benjamin J. Hubbard, "The Role of the Commissioning Accounts in Acts," in *Perspectives in Luke-Acts*, ed. Charles H. Talbert (Edinburgh: T&T Clark, 1978), 192.

One commentator, Marion Soards, refrains from a decision and simply places inverted commas around the word "vision."[36]

Despite the paucity of visionary details, we are, I think, constrained by the narrative to consider the narrative in terms of vision because of the way in which it is subsequently interpreted for us in Acts (9:17, 27), because of the implicit contrast of Paul's experience with that of his companions (who hear the voice but behold no one, v. 7), and because of the strong apocalyptic or epiphanic themes of the chapter. The light, the prostration, the audition and dialogue, the command to rise, the devastating effect on the recipient, the recipient's prayerfulness and fasting, and the subsequent role of a (human) *angelus interpres,* Ananias, are all evocative of the Danielic visions (especially Dan. 10). Taken together, the speechlessness of his companions, the helplessness of Saul, and his privileged reception also recall Daniel, where the visionary is himself "speechless" (Dan. 10:15), helpless (10:8, 17), and the "only one" to see the vision (10:7) among those present.

In contrast to the intricate description of the epiphanies seen in the later prophets and apocalypses, we are told in this vision-report only that a "light" shines around Saul, a "light" that is subsequently identified or associated in the audition with "Jesus" and interpreted later by Ananias and Barnabas as an appearance of "the Lord." As a sequel to this initial nonvision, however, there is an elaborate disclosure of another vision vouchsafed to Saul: within a vision seen by Ananias (9:10), the Lord tells Ananias (and so, the reader) about a vision that Saul is currently having (9:12). From one perspective this can be understood as a variation on the "double dream" common to Hellenistic writings, seen also in our previous passage (Acts 10–11). However, in this chapter the interconnected visions are not exploited in the usual manner as interauthenticating; rather, they function to let us know what is going on "in the meantime" to Saul. Moreover, the layered construction, in which the Lord himself relates Saul's vision, highlights

---

36. Marion L. Soards, *The Speeches in Acts: Their Content, Context, and Concerns* (Louisville: Westminster John Knox, 1994), 178, 180. Soards refers specifically to the narratives of chaps. 22 and 26, but the issue is identical. See also Isa. 2:1; Amos 1:1; Mic. 1:1; and Hab. 1:1, where the prophets "see" God's word.

what it is that Saul is seeing and foreshadows the healing to come. From the perspective of a reader in sympathy with Luke's aims, a vision reported by the Lord takes on an authority and importance far beyond that of one related by an omniscient narrator or even by the recipient himself.[37] Saul has "seen a man called Ananias coming in and laying on his hands, so that he may see *again*" (9:12), or perhaps, as one writer suggests, "so that he might look *up*"[38]—that is, for divine help.

The two visions, the blinding light identified with Jesus and the restoration of sight by the touch of a follower, are complementary: they are quite deliberately linked by the oracle "I am Jesus, whom you are persecuting" and by Ananias's address to Saul as "brother" (9:17). The combined effect of the extended narrative is to illuminate three questions of identity for Saul: the light signifies Jesus, the Lord; Jesus is intimately associated with his followers; Saul is re-envisioned as a "brother," rather than as persecutor, through integration with Jesus and his followers. Ironically, it is in being blinded that Saul really begins to see. It is in his state of blindness that he is brought to pray and sees in a vision his cure. Nor is the "seeing" finished at the point when Saul "looks up" or "sees again," for through Ananias we know that "the Lord" has much to "show" Saul "concerning what must be suffered because of [the Lord's] name" (9:16). This emphasis on the "name" of the Lord and the prominence of the community of faith in the newfound

37. Czachesz suggests that the discourse between the Lord and Ananias should be understood in terms of a deliberative speech, with the speech's "thesis" identified as the Lord's command that Ananias go to visit Saul and the "rationale" given that Saul is having a vision that this will happen. It is unfortunate that this sensitive interpreter does not notice that he has had to add the "because" in order to force the double vision into the role of a rationale for the thesis. Certainly one of the functions of the double vision is deliberative, but it seems that Czachesz is more on the mark when he notes that the "main rhetorical task of the text" is "to convince the reader about the radically new calling of Saul" ("Socio-Rhetorical Exegesis," 12). The double vision serves to convince the reader; on the level of the narrative, however, it is the dominical word to Ananias that Saul is "God's chosen instrument" that effects a change in the balking Ananias. To cut a dialogue into the template of a speech-format, deliberative or otherwise, is to miss the various ways and intersecting levels through which this passage works.
38. Hamm, "Paul's Blindness," 65.

identity of Saul militates against any reading of this episode that might overstress the "individualistic character" of Saul's vision as presented in Acts.[39] The emphasis is on who Saul is in connection with the Lord and the church; indeed, the predominance of future tenses in this chapter indicates its place as a preparation for Paul's identity and ministry in the later chapters of the Acts.

D. Hamm has characterized the dynamic between blindness and sight, audition and vision: "Though the experience was *physically* an audition rather than a vision, he realized, in the end, that he had indeed (*spiritually*) seen the Lord, that his eyes had been opened."[40] It seems to me that this critic is right in what he affirms but wrong in what he denies. The second revelation of Paul is manifestly, within the narrative, a vision, complete with details, even though Paul's eyes are blind; Ananias and Barnabas, and later in the overall Acts narrative, Paul himself, characterize the first revelation of Paul as a vision even though the only detail given the reader is that of the light and its association with Jesus. It is probably beside the point to wonder about the phenomenology of the vision as physical or spiritual, given the fact that visions occur in dreams as well. Rather, we might say that the puzzle encountered by the reader—a vision without much that is seen—mirrors the ambiguous state of Saul, the blinded one who is beginning to see (Luke's reticence about the vision here matches that of Paul himself in 2 Cor. 12). Saul's epiphany is not that he has encountered a mystical being with intriguing symbolic features, but to fall helpless before the light, to hear Jesus identified with the followers of the Way, and to receive healing by the hands of one of these. It is a vision concerned with bonds of affection, or *koinōnia*, in the first place. It is interesting to note with Luke Timothy Johnson that again Acts may here be read,

39. For example, Czachesz extrapolates from the esoteric character of the vision (seen only by Saul, Acts 9:7; cf. Dan. 10) that Saul's vision bolsters prophetic individualism ("Socio-Rhetorical Exegesis," 24), confirming Paul's independent status and thwarting any institutionalization of power in "the board of apostles" (ibid., 29). He surely overplays his hand in making such clear ideological distinctions in the reading of an ancient text that does not share our contemporary allergy to authority and hierarchy.

40. Hamm, "Paul's Blindness," 64.

as in Acts 10–11, in conjunction with the apocalyptic romance *Joseph and Aseneth*, especially in terms of the protagonist's role in the exemplification of piety.[41] Piety is detailed, of course, in the context of communion—a theme dear both to the novel *Joseph and Aseneth* and, it appears, to Luke.

We move on from a discussion of thematics to a discussion of actors and action. An observation of the place of the visions within the narrative of chapter 9 shows that they occur in all three of the subsections: 9:1–9 includes the first nonvision-report of light and audition (vv. 3–5) at dead center and also leads inevitably to the second section through the revealed instructions, "you will be told what you are to do." Then, 9:10–16 is signaled by the change in scene and actors, with Ananias's vision coming close on the heels of the story frame. Most of the words in this section are attributed to "the Lord," with a few demurrals from Ananias, and there is in the center of the audition the vision-report by the Lord himself of what Saul has been seeing (v. 12). The section closes with intimations of more visions to come ("I will show him . . ."). The final section, 9:17–19, has a healing in the central place, but since the healing issues in Saul's ἀνάβλεψις ("looking up/seeing again") the miracle has at the very least a semantic connection to "vision." In looking up to Ananias and accepting the appellation of "brother," it may be said that Saul's initial vision is complete. The sight is sealed by Saul's baptism, resumption of eating, and *koinōnia* (communion) with the disciples. We see, then, that the visions interrupt the action and set in motion a new plot; they prefigure new action, direct it, and seal it. In this narrative the Lord is the director and major actor; Saul's helplessness is in view. An actantial analysis of the narrative,[42] calling attention to the dynamics between the "actors" or "actants," makes this clear:

---

41. Johnson, *Acts*, 167.

42. Actantial analysis is a procedure for analyzing and portraying narratives developed by the French-Lithuanian structuralist A. J. Greimas and first applied to biblical studies by Roland Barthes in his discussion of Gen. 32:22–32. Like other schools, it is based in a particular view of reality and power relations but can be used beneficially even by analysts who do not share Greimas's philosophy. For a simple account of how

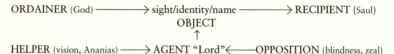

ORDAINER (God) ————————> sight/identity/name ————————> RECIPIENT (Saul)
                                              OBJECT
                                                ↑
HELPER (vision, Ananias) ————> AGENT "Lord"<————OPPOSITION (blindness, zeal)

When we freeze the action, as above, at the point when the Lord speaks to Saul, we see that Saul is passive, with God as ordainer, the Lord (Jesus) as the agent, and the vision and the human interpreter Ananias as the powers that will transform Saul.

We may then go beyond "surface structure" to give attention to the levels of narration. These also disclose a special emphasis on Saul's divinely reported vision—specifically, the second report of this—which is enveloped in the center of the central section:

> Scene I   9:1–9   Paul meets/hears the Lord, is blinded
> Scene II   9:10–16   A. Ananias receives/hears a vision
>   B. The Lord reports the vision **that Paul has seen,** 9:12
>   C. Ananias argues and the Lord prevails
> Scene III 9:17–19   Ananias fulfills the visions and restores Paul's sight.

It is interesting to recall the linguistic analysis done by Hellholm and Aune on apocalypses, where embedded oracular utterances— structural digressions—show themselves to be sheltered mysteries with special authority and purpose in determining key themes.[43] Here in Acts 9, the embedded vision/oracle occurs at 9:12: the narrator *tells* us that Ananias *heard* the Lord *"say in a vision"* that Saul *saw* a man called Ananias heal him. Though the extravagant epiphany of scene I grasps the readers' imagination most vitally, the deepest vision here is the domestic but dominical report of Ananias laying on hands and bestowing sight. Indeed, Luke does not actually recount, on the level of the narrative, that Ananias laid hands on Saul—it is enough for us to have heard the Lord's own report of Saul's vision and for the narrator to

to use this method, see Etienne Charpentier, *How to Read the Old Testament*, trans. John Bowden (London: SCM Press, 1985).

43. See D. Hellholm, "The Problem of Apocalyptic Genre and the Apocalypse of John," in *1982 Seminar Papers*, ed. Kent Harold Richards, Society of Biblical Literature Seminar Papers Series 21 (Chico, CA: Scholars Press, 1982), 157–98; and David Aune, "The Apocalypse of John and the Problem of Genre," *Semeia* 36 (1986): 39–50.

report that "immediately" Saul's sight was restored. Ananias, however, needed a little more prodding, and so in verse 16, to clinch his argument with Ananias, the Lord speaks about additional visions that will be vouchsafed to Saul. It is a curious thing that the content of this embedded (thus accented) vision-report by the Lord is that of *human* action in the midst of a divinely conceived script; similarly, the intimated future vision that Saul will receive is about *his* destined action of suffering for the Name. The identity of the follower is bound up with the identity of the Lord.

Defense or Encomium? Acts 22:1–22

The second full-blown account of Saul's encounter (discounting the brief reportage by Barnabas in chapter 9) is found in Acts 22 as part of Saul's informal defense before the crowd in Jerusalem. We move, then, from straight narrative (chapter 9) to narrative within discourse. But this discourse itself forms a part of the mega-narrative of the entire book of Acts. We also move from third person to first person. Much ink has been spilled regarding the narrative discrepancies between the two accounts, concerning who heard but did not see, or who saw but did not hear. Despite the arguments of Haenchen[44] and Dibelius[45] that Luke seems untroubled by the surface contradictions, ingenious solutions continue to be suggested. These solutions detail the use of the accusative or genitive case[46] for φωνή ("voice, sound," 9:7; 22:9) or offer suggestions that the voice indicated in chapter 9 is Saul's while in chapter 22 the voice not heard is that of the Lord.[47] Of more interest in this study is the *effect* of the declaration in chapter 22 that Saul's companions did not hear—voice, sound, whatever—and its displacement in relation to the ordered events of chapter 9. This detail, taken with other

44. Haenchen insists that there is no distinction in meaning when the case of the word φωνή (voice) is changed (Haenchen, *Acts*, 322n2).

45. Dibelius argues that the discrepancies are the product of the independent nature of the speeches (*Studies*, 177).

46. G. Steuernagel, "AKOYONTES MEN TES PHONES (Apg. 9.7): Ein Genitiv in der Apostelgeschichte," *New Testament Studies* 35 (1989): 691–24.

47. F. F. Bruce, *The Acts of the Apostles* (London: Tyndale, 1951), 199.

narrative curiosities, is helpful in exposing the chapter's rhetorical impact, as we shall see.

As in chapter 9, the embedded account of Saul's conversion recalls epiphanic passages from the prophets, especially Daniel, and the other parabiblical or deutero-canonical writings. Seen in these, as in Acts, are the following features: intense light, prostration, privileging vision, double vocative, audition, command to rise and move to another place (cf. *4 Ezra* 9:24; Ezek. 3:22), and the effect of δόξα ("glory") on the seer. In fact, certain details of this report in chapter 22 are even more consonant with the "apocalyptic" atmosphere than chapter 9: first-person accounts are more typical, the description of the light as "strong" even at noonday and "from heaven" intensifies the epiphany, and the comment about his companions' confusion is reminiscent of Daniel 12:8, where the prophet says that he "heard but did not understand" what he had been told. Moreover, the discourse continues with an abbreviated version of the ensuing visitation by Ananias (22:12–16), in which Saul's healing is now downplayed while the significance of the epiphany is underscored. In chapter 9, Saul's commission was intimated in the vision to Ananias, but here it is transposed into Ananias's words to Saul. Like a human *angelus interpres*, Ananias "comes to Saul and stands by" him, explaining Saul's experience as one in which he has been chosen "to know [God's] will" and "to see the righteous One" and "to hear the voice out of his mouth" (22:14). There is also a striking transposition from future tenses in chapter 9 to past tenses in this narration. Paul then goes on in his discourse in 22:17–21 to relate the "temple vision," a trance in which he sees Jesus and receives explicit directions. As in the speech and apocalypse of Stephen, Paul is interrupted by the provoked crowd who is listening to his vision-report.

But we must back up slightly and consider the place of these revelations within the discourse. In his address, Paul labels his speech an *apologia* (22:1), and most commentators have been content to consider it in these terms while commenting that the speech serves better the overall purposes of Acts than the dilemma faced by the prisoner. In terms of form, the speeches before

Agrippa (26:1–23) and especially before Felix (24:10–21) are far more typical of the classical *apologia* ("defense"), using terms of address, acknowledging the charges, using careful argumentation, and appealing to justice. Some have suggested that the idiosyncrasies of the speech in chapter 22 are to be explained by its "Aramaic" flavor in comparison with chapter 26, where Luke "treats" the reader to an Attic variation on the same theme.[48] However, Dibelius points out that Acts 22 "shows no trace of Aramaic colour."[49] A better way of understanding the speech's unusual form might be by reference to its ad hoc nature. Before magistrates, Paul is prepared to offer a more traditional defense, whereas at this point Luke may well be presenting the harried apostle "in character" before a hostile audience at a dramatic juncture—he has just been rescued from a lynching. One would hardly expect the same evangelist who emphasizes Jesus' words forbidding careful preparation for trial (Luke 21:12–14) to depict Paul as perfectly "prepped" for testimony. Thus, as in the parallel case with Stephen, the speech takes a curious turn, not hearkening to specific charges or apologetic patterns of rhetoric, but appearing as "*mischform*" ("mixed in form").[50]

It may be that analysts have been so swayed by the dramatic situation and by the term "apology" that they have not noticed the curious first-person encomiastic[51] topics in Paul's address, that is, topics designed to bring the (reading?) audience to a point of praise. Rather than establishing a proposition and reason, as would be the case in a defense, the *narratio* (i.e., the major part of the argument) pursues details of Saul's past not yet related in Acts. Certainly, the autobiographical details have an ethical dimension within the dramatic situation, forging links between Saul and his Jerusalem hearers. However, for readers the speech functions more

48. Richard Pervo, *Profit with Delight: The Literary Genre of the Acts of the Apostles* (Philadelphia: Fortress, 1987), 76.

49. Dibelius, *Studies*, 179.

50. R. F. Collins, "Paul's Damascus Experience: Reflections on the Lukan Account," *Louvain Studies* 11 (1986): 114.

51. See p. 31, n.6 for a definition of the encomium alongside other modes of speech.

subtly to fill in the profile of Paul, reconfiguring their ideas of what is "honorable" and "necessary" and "right" by this new retelling of Paul's story. Though a first person encomium might be deemed unseemly on the level of the narrative, Luke has the perspective of his readership to consider and imports into Paul's speech frank self-referential details that most likely do not reflect the mode of the speech Paul would have directed to his audience. Instructive here may be the dynamic found in Paul's own autobiographical Philippians 3 or the "epideictic apology"[52] seen in 1 Corinthians 9 by Wilhelm Wuellner. Like the encomium, Paul's speech in Acts 22 traces origin, genealogy, and birth in verse 3a and then moves on to his "achievements" in verses 3b–21. Under these achievements, verse 3b treats his education and virtuous zeal for the law while verses 4–5 give examples of his deeds, calling forth the highest authorities as witnesses to these. From the perspective of the reader, the list of accomplishments has an ironic tinge, for we are aware of where the story is leading. The encomiastic narration of achievements usually ended by speaking of the virtuous man's blessings or endowments, and these we encounter as three revelations from God, in verses 6–11, 12–16, and 17–21. It is at this turn in the road, too, that the rhetoric is redirected, showing an unusual disjuncture between the autobiographical preparation for excellence and the endowments with which Paul has in fact been blessed.

Paul's *persona* in this chapter is less passive than the light-crazed and helpless one-time zealot of chapter 9, for he initiates a question to God: "What am I to do, Lord?" After he hears with his own ears the news of his election and commission, he has a subsequent vision directing him to the Gentiles. Following the pattern of other Lukan speeches, Paul reaches the climax of his message in this narrative, which is then underscored by a pattern of interruption (22:22). Luke also, in a deft stroke, comes quietly alongside the puzzled reader who may be wondering why Paul's ministry to his countrymen is not to be successful. The explanation comes to us in the words of the Lord, as Paul dialogues concerning his

52. Wuellner, "Where Is Rhetorical Criticism Taking Us?" 460.

calling. In this temple vision Paul argues with the Lord over his Gentile mission, suggesting that he is the perfect witness in the Jewish and Jerusalem milieu since they know his prior zeal and will marvel at the transformation. The Lord's words prefigure what is to happen in this situation—"they will not receive your testimony about me"—thus justifying the Gentile mission. Despite the interruption, Paul's speech is well framed in terms of a ring structure: in the closing verse there is a reference to Stephen (v. 20), which matches the opening reference to Saul's persecution (v. 4). Moreover, the final note to Stephen transmutes a typical concluding item of the encomium, that is, a word of memorial, which is here not applied to Paul but to the first martyr, whose ranks Paul seems bound to join.

There is no real conclusion to the speech, however. At the level of the narration, it fails as an apology, and it is not quite an encomium. After all, the reader has already heard of Paul's impending judgment in the prophecy of 20:25, 38, and the time is not yet right to celebrate Paul's honor—he still must witness before kings. Yet the speech has been skillful in transforming Paul from a converted zealot, who must be blinded before he can see, to a confidant of the Lord and a martyr-in-the-making. The speech takes, it seems, a detour with its first embedded vision (22:7–10) and builds to the climax of its third revelation (22:18), where Paul is sent from Jerusalem by the dominical voice in the temple. The narrative irony of the moment brings the reader on side to the same degree that it alienates the hearers within the story. Within the narrative, Jerusalem devotees are estranged by the direction of the speech—the rejection of Saul, who was nurtured in Jerusalem, who was redirected on a journey away from that city, and who has been blessed by the revelations that he has seen and has heard but which they have not understood. For the ideal reader, these are the very characteristics of a faithful follower of the Way. The encomiastic shape of the defense and the closing parallel to Stephen fill in and recall certain details that at this juncture in the Acts narrative accomplish the construction of Paul's character, a key element in these closing chapters of Acts.

From Apology to Mission, from Witness to Paradigm: Acts 26:1–24

The third and final rehearsal of Saul's conversion/call also occurs within the context of a forensic speech with a difference. Dubbed "the most atticistic"[53] of Luke's speeches (although I would grant this to the speech before Felix in chapter 24), it uses typical judicial techniques, apostrophizing the king, setting up the argument, employing ploys such as *litotes*,[54] and even using a rhetorical question (26:8). Moreover, the central audition is expanded for this setting by the addition of a Greek proverb intended as much for the "educated reader" as for Agrippa[55]—a situation made all the more curious since the audition is declared to have been in Aramaic. Despite these details, and the conventional orator's pose with which Paul begins, the speech does not conform purely to the apologetic mode: Luke's purpose is complex. What begins as a defense ends, as is whimsically pointed out by Agrippa, as a missionary speech. So we move with Paul from the judicial to the deliberative. Within this movement, the narrative of the Damascus light plays a crucial and focused role, for it is the only revelation employed as argument here. Moreover, elements that were dispersed across episodes in the earlier narrations will now be concentrated within this one narration.

Paul, given permission to speak, assumes the orator's position (26:1). His *exordium* (vv. 2–3) includes the customary *captatio benevolentiae*[56] before Paul goes on to establish *ethos* (vv. 4–5) in the narration proper, signaled by the typical Lukan phrase μὲν οὖν ("so then, indeed, accordingly," 26:4). Depending on whether the speech is understood as forensic or deliberative, the proposition and reason may be variously formed:

53. Pervo, *Profit with Delight*, 46.
54. *Litotes* refers to a double negative used to make a strong positive effect: "I was *not disobedient*," 26:19.
55. Dibelius, *Studies*, 173.
56. *Captatio benevolentiae*, a term derived from medieval rhetoric, is an ancient ploy by which the speaker "captures the audience's goodwill," often by praising them.

> Proposition: "I am not guilty:
>   Reason: *because* I am only on trial for the belief in resurrection
>   common to all the pious;" or
> Proposition: "God has raised Jesus from the dead:
>   Reason: [you can know this] *because* I am a witness to what I have
>   seen and heard."

The second set is more like an *enthymeme*, requiring that listeners import the proposition implied in 26:8 to complete the logic: "For God can raise the dead." Indeed, we begin the scene by assuming that the first apologetic argument is in view, while the second proclamatory argument comes increasingly to the fore as Paul mounts his evidence.

Paul's *confirmatio* begins with verse 9 (signaled again by the μὲν οὖν) as with breathtaking impudence Paul sets himself up as his own opposite (vv. 9–11). In this argument, the Damascus event takes the position of the analogy and example (vv. 12–18), non-invented episodes, yet carefully framed as proof. Within the mode of defense the Damascus event transfers responsibility for Paul's actions to God; within the mode of deliberation the event provides evidence for the resurrection of Jesus. Alongside such deft touches also appears an apt allusion to Euripides (*Bacchanals* 794) in the phrase "kick against the pricks"—a touch suitable for both the narrative level (considering Saul's educated audience) and no doubt appreciated by the Hellenistic reader of the Acts.[57]

Those revelations that were scattered across the narrative in chapters 9 and 22 are here collected into one dominical word, a word implicit in the appearance of the light (vv. 15–18). As Luke Timothy Johnson puts it, "The experience of the risen Lord bore implicitly within itself all the mandate and significance for Paul's

57. Some have likewise heard in 9:5 and 26:14 an echo of *Iliad* 22.8 in the question, "Why are you pursuing me?" This remains a possibility latent in the chap. 9 narrative and probably more noticeable in the Acts 26 version of Paul's story, where it comes in tandem with Euripides and is more naturally within the purview of the actors in the narrative. It would be a very subtle inference indeed for even a Hellenistic reader to "pick up" this echo in chap. 9, where the question is addressed to a Pharisee in a locale far removed from any Greco-Roman context.

life."[58] This distillation of themes does far more than simply re-
vamp what might have been a repetitive and "boring narrative."[59]
The audition in 26:15–18 functions as a collect, bringing together
all that we have learned through the repeated narratives and sum-
marizing the role of Paul and the progress of the gospel. Paul
continues his argument by offering himself, now "metamorpho-
sized," as an example (vv. 19–21) of one who is obedient, and
then cites the prophets and Moses as general authorities on the
resurrection of the Messiah, proclaiming light to his own people
and to the Gentiles (v. 23). Again, the key point is highlighted by
interruption, but there is a conclusion of sorts made possible by
the interrogations by Festus and Agrippa: Paul presses his missionary intent, concluding by setting himself up as a paradigm
for not only Agrippa but also for "all those who are listening"
(vv. 25–29).

Within the speech, key moments of the argument are highlighted by the repeated term of address, βασιλεῦ, "[O] King," in
verse 2 (the *exordium*), in verse 7 (the proposition), in verse 13
(the analogy/example), in verse 19 (the example), and in verse 27
(the conclusion). The central occurrence of the term, at verse 13,
signals the major proof of the speech, which is in fact the Damascus episode. Here the theme of brightness is greatly emphasized:
"a light from heaven, brighter than the sun, shining around me
and my companions." Moreover, everyone implicated in the story
is affected. The light shines around them all and everyone falls
to the earth, implying what will be made explicit in the audition:
what Paul has seen and heard is intended as direction and light

58. Johnson, *Acts*, 441. Johnson presents this third episode's conflation of themes
and events into the voice of the risen Lord in a psychological fashion, suggesting that
Luke intends us to understand that this is how Saul/Paul "remembered" the events
during his defense before Agrippa—not as coming via the mediation of Ananias nor
through a second temple vision but implicit in the first spectacular call. Though his
presentation is perhaps too "experientially" oriented for my comfort, it seems clear
that Luke does intend Paul's defense to serve as "a retrospective interpretation of the
narrative" (ibid., 442)—not simply the narrative of Saul's conversion and transformation but the narrative of Luke-Acts in general, in which light comes to Israel and
into the world.

59. Hedrick, "Paul's Conversion/Call," 427.

for all. Gone is the reference to Paul's blindness, the hand-leading of the companions, and the role of Ananias, for the emphasis has shifted from Paul's helplessness to his integrity, as well as to the light that is available to all through Paul's witness. One scholar uses the metaphor of a "literary *rheostat*"[60] that functions to brighten the light in the narrative and so to build up Paul's character. Curiously, however, as Paul's status grows, Luke is able to move beyond mere *Paulusbild* so that Paul becomes a paradigm for others who will transfer their allegiance from dark to light, from Satan to God (v. 17).[61] This imagery of light and darkness brings to fulfillment, indeed, a theme common to Luke's double-volume work, which began with the words of Simeon in Luke 2:32 regarding Jesus as "a light for revelation to the Gentiles, and glory to . . . Israel." At issue in this chapter is not so much the special status of Paul as one privy to a revelation but the portrayal of one through whom the revelation is being announced freely, to Gentile as well as to Jew. So the audition itself is heard in Aramaic but speaks with intertextual echoes so as to capture the attention of the Gentile as well. By the time we reach the end of the chapter, the verdict of Agrippa ("this man is doing nothing to deserve death or imprisonment") seems an afterthought—Paul's defense has been overtaken by Luke's greater purpose. Here, as Witherup suggests, "the figure of Paul crystallizes more clearly as a light to the Gentiles."[62]

Conclusion: A Narrative Hologram?

We have seen how a seeming nonvision, coupled with an embedded vision of healing and seeing (9:1–25), is transformed into a series of three revelations within a quirky encomiastic apology (22:1–22) and finally into the carefully distilled vision/audition that forms the substance of Paul's apology-cum-missionary speech

60. R. D. Witherup, "Functional Redundancy in the Acts of the Apostles: A Case Study," *Journal for the Study of the New Testament* 48 (1992): 70.
61. The theme of light and darkness in connection with conversion is traditional, of course, as articulated in Isa. 42:6–7, and is used in other Christian and Jewish pieces, such as 1 Pet. 2:9 and *Joseph and Aseneth* 8:10 and 15:13.
62. Witherup, "Functional Redundancy," 84.

before Agrippa (26:1–24). It is clear that these three passages provide a fruitful locus for the observation of what has been called
"functional redundancy" in Luke. Exegetes differ as to whether the
readers are expected to "adjust their understanding of the event
in the light of its subsequent narration,"[63] or whether they are
intended to import the material from earlier accounts into chapter
26, which has been abbreviated in order to avoid tedium. Even in
a linear reading of Acts, the reader will surely both supply details
and adjust his or her understanding during a retelling of the story.
In fact, the interrelationship between the accounts proves to be
far more subtle than mere correction or abbreviation, especially
with the possibility of reading and rereading that is offered by
the encoded text. Rosenblatt seems closest to the mark when she
characterizes the repeated visions as "a narrative pondering . . . an
exercise in reflection . . . a narrative hologram . . . [where] these
retold events are stilled."[64]

It has often been suggested that the elaborate and disorienting
images of the genre of apocalypse function to provide a mechanism
for the reader's vicarious ecstasy. In contrast, the very embryonic
nature of this light-vision (like that related by Paul himself in
2 Cor. 12) tantalizes the reader, beckoning more strongly with
each retelling: "What did Saul see?" As for what he heard, this
we are told in various forms, and to various effect, until by chapter 26 we find ourselves encoded within the text. Here the Lord
talks past Saul to those who will be "set apart by their faithfulness toward me," and Paul talks past Agrippa to "all who are
listening to me." We have seen how the three call narratives not
only use the word "vision" but increasingly highlight the themes
of blindness/opening of eyes and dark/light *alongside* references
to hearing and witnessing. The gospel, or word, is clothed with
the garb of vision. But the question to which Luke ultimately
directs us is not *what* Paul sees but *whom* he sees: Jesus and
the followers of the Way. In the first rendition of this story Saul

---

63. Hedrick, "Paul's Conversion/Call," 431.
64. Marie Eloise Rosenblatt, *Recurrent Narrative as a Lukan Literary Convention in Acts: Paul's Jerusalem Speech in Acts 22:1–21* (Collegeville, MN: Glazier,
1990), 104.

is, by implication, the only one of the travelers who has seen; moreover, his true "sight" begins in blindness. The artful retelling of the visions leads the reader to the place where, in chapter 26, Saul's healing virtually drops out of view, leaving vacant a broader arena where light is to be proclaimed and eyes are to be opened. Before our eyes appears an image of the whole story and of the main Actor, by which and by whom the reader is invited (indeed, urged) to enter.

The Shape of the Divine Comedy

In speaking of the anthropological notions disclosed in Luke-Acts, one commentator[65] aptly evokes the observations of literary critic Northrop Frye, who spoke poignantly of the "U-shaped story"[66] of Scripture. Such an appeal may certainly bear fruit; however, in our reading of the narrative we have discerned a rather different shape. Rather than a simple U-shaped drama, whereby humankind "gets . . . back"[67] what has been lost, it would seem that the narrative more nearly resembles a check mark, with the ending level of the narrative mounting far higher than the beginning point. This characteristic shape discerned in Luke-Acts is shared, it would seem, with the Pauline and Johannine constructions of salvation history, so that the reclamation of the Gentiles (Acts 10–11) or Saul's call (Acts 9:1–25; 22:1–22; 26:1–24) take their place as microcosms within the larger canonical story. Not only is the denouement higher than a mere restoration to the first state, but it would seem that the main actor disclosed in the drama is, after all, not humankind but an unmanageable God who eludes any human attempt at theurgy. This same astonishing and subversive power is seen in the repeated visions that we have read. It would seem, after all, that any attempt to contain the explosive force of such vi-

65. Czachesz, "Socio-Rhetorical Exegesis," 31.
66. See, for example, Frye's magnum opus, *The Great Code: The Bible and Literature* (Toronto: Academic Press Canada, 1981), 169–98.
67. Ibid, 168.

sions may be futile, for vision's emergent liveliness, the visionary polyvalence that threatens to complicate the author's purposes, seemingly finds its source in an original Light that can both blind and illumine. So we turn to strategic vision-reports of that Light as presented by the evangelists.

3

SHAPING THE NARRATIVE

Embryonic and Strategic Visions

(LUKE 10:17–24; 1:5–2:40; MATTHEW 17:1–8;
MARK 9:2–8; LUKE 9:28–36)

We have moved from the far pole of our continuum, that is, from the "closed case," toward "open potential" in vision-reports and find ourselves in the very center of the spectrum. Analysis began with two highly "intentional" or "specific" uses of the form, that is, Paul's "un-apocalypse" of 2 Corinthians 12 and Luke's "capping" vision for Stephen's speech: both these argumentative cases are brought to conclusion through the vision-report. This means that what has been heard is decisively completed—"clinched"—by a report of what has been seen. Next we considered Luke's deft use of the repeated vision-report within a larger narrative, first in the Cornelius-Peter sequence and then in the stories of Saul's call. These passages emerged as less overt in the exercise of power even while they are directed toward discernible ends. Now, at the center of our continuum, we aptly find visions that illumine the figure of Jesus, training a spotlight on him. Here we will find brief, even embryonic, visions that appear in strategic positions, calling attention to the main character of the biblical narrative. Yet it will be seen that as they retain this focus on the Christ, they also serve to direct the reader's gaze on matters not strictly "christological" but historical, ecclesial, missional, and pneumatological.

Let us go on to investigate how strategic and "unassuming" vision-reports shape the narrative—dare we say, how they shape its "message"? In Jesus' vision of the downfall of Satan, in the visions surrounding the birth narratives, and in the transfiguration stories, we may see how the evangelists, and particularly Luke, provide a balance of "open" and "closed" rhetorical argument in order to give the narrative a suggestive but coherent direction. To appreciate this dynamic is to recognize the space wherein the narrator's artistry, textual cues, and readerly imagination may fruitfully and faithfully cooperate. As with the preceding studies, the most useful rhetorical or literary approach will be suggested by the implicit argument of the passage and the relationship between each vision-report and its surrounding narrative.

Embryonic Vision Completed by Speech: Luke 10:17–24

The Elaboration of a Strange Chreia

We begin with Luke 10:17–24, which is thoroughly integrated into Luke's Gospel but is also a well-marked rhetorical unit. As such, it is a good candidate for comparison to "classical" rhetorical speech-craft, even though the speech act is also governed by its larger narrative framework. The setting is provided by the return of the disciples from their successful mission (v. 17); Jesus' response (vv. 18–20) is firmly linked to the public "prayer" (vv. 21–22) and the private word (vv. 23–24) by time markers ('Εν αὐτῇ τῇ ὥρᾳ, "in that same hour," v. 21, and the aorist participle στραφεί, "and when he had turned [himself]," v. 23). The change of setting in verse 25 delineates the end of the unit. Jesus' words do not constitute a full-blown speech but may be read (without forcing the classical template) in terms of what classical rhetoricians called the "elaborated *chreia*"[1]—that is, one of the prescribed compositional exercises of the *progymnasmata*[2] assigned to schoolboys in classical times. The goal of this particular exercise was to expand and illuminate a memorable saying (*chreia*) uttered by an authoritative figure, according to various preset patterns. When we compare this section in Luke against the usual parts of the "complete argument" or elaborated *chreia*, both the parallels and slight deviations are instructive:

Introduction ("Lord . . .")	10:17
Chreia ("I saw Satan fall . . .")	10:18
Rationale ("I have given you authority")	10:19
Opposite ("Nevertheless, do not rejoice")	10:20
Example ("He rejoiced in the Holy Spirit . . .")	10:21
[Analogy displaced]	
Authority ("Father, thus it was pleasing in Your sight . . .")	10:21b
("All things have been given . . .")	10:22
Conclusion ("Blessed are the eyes . . .")	10:23–24
[Contrast analogy included here]	

It will be noted that all of the anticipated parts of the elaborated *chreia* are present, with only the analogy missing from its usual position.[3] However, example, analogy, and authority all work toward the same end in an elaboration and make up what is called "the argument" in a full-blown speech. Since the example and the authority are well developed, analogy may be bypassed without weakening the argument.

1. As mentioned in chap. 1, Burton Mack and Vernon Robbins were key in elucidating this convention for a contemporary audience in *Patterns of Persuasion*. See also Mack's handbook *Rhetoric and the New Testament* for a brief discussion of *chreiai*.

2. The *progymnasmata* were a set of fourteen rudimentary exercises assigned as preparation for both the writing and declamation of speeches. The exercises concentrated on various parts of the persuasive enterprise. E.g., the exercise of composing a "narration" was preparatory for the *narratio* section of the complete argument.

3. It was not unusual, at any rate, for an elaboration to miss or reorganize certain steps.

The introduction conforms to the tone that was appropriately adopted in a speech that elaborated a famous saying, that of encomium or "praise" for the one from whose lips the *chreia* had originally come. In the classical speech, the schoolboy would introduce the *chreia* by referring to its originator in an approving manner; here Luke knits the passage into the larger narrative, and so it is the disciples who defer to Jesus as "Lord," beginning a sequence that will elaborate on his saying. Moreover, in the context of this story Jesus both utters his own *chreia* and performs the elaboration. That some of this elaboration is found in a different setting in Matthew's Gospel is testimony to the creative activity of Luke, who puts together various dominical traditions, and likely amplifies these himself, in order to complete the argument that takes its point of departure from Jesus' visionary *chreia*. So then, the evangelist uses the disciples and Jesus, all actors in his narrative, in order to present a speech that has been marked, to a greater or lesser extent, by his own invention.

In the conclusion of this section (vv. 23–24), the disciples are favorably compared to great figures of the past and contrasted with them in a surprising manner. Thus the polemical moment of "analogy" is imported into the conclusion rather than falling in its usual place in the center of the argument: the prophets themselves longed to look into the sight of Satan's conquest that these disciples are privileged to behold. This displacement of the analogy makes for an emotive and striking ending. We might also note that it aptly presents Jesus' words in character with Hebrew rhetoric, which frequently ends with a "two-way" word of wisdom rather than adhering rigidly to the classical model (cf. Ps. 1:6; Matt. 7:24–27//Luke 6:48–49). This observation has two possible explanations: either Luke is passing on a binary statement remembered by the earliest community as spoken by Jesus, or he is claiming the prerogative of the ancient historiographer, who ensured that the speeches spoken by his characters possessed verisimilitude.[4]

4. Jona Lendering, in his Internet article on Livy (http://www.livius.org/li-ln/livy/livy.htm#Life [accessed July 18, 2006]), explains as follows: "Although the presence of invented speeches strikes us as odd—they are not historical facts and do, therefore,

Let us consider the logic of the unit and how the vision works within it. In the last century, analyses of this Lukan passage tended to be atomistic, separating off "Semitic" and "Hellenistic" thought forms and appealing to the appearance of parallel portions in Matthew.[5] Our interest, however, is in the logic of the passage as it stands and how this fits into the overall aim of Luke's narrative. The reader has been made aware of the importance of the mission through an earlier extended monologue, complete with dramatic contrasts:

> "Woe to you, Chorazin! woe to you, Bethsaida! for if the mighty works done in you had been done in Tyre and Sidon, they would have repented long ago, sitting in sackcloth and ashes. But it shall be more tolerable in the judgment for Tyre and Sidon than for you. And you, Capernaum, will you be exalted to heaven? You shall be brought down to Hades. He who hears you hears me, and he who rejects you rejects me, and he who rejects me rejects him who sent me." (10:13–16 RSV)

With such dramatic dichotomies and the rejection of God's word as a backdrop, the reader continues in the narrative and is delighted by the unlikely success of the disciples: he or she is thus induced to enter into their astonished joy in verse 17. We have already noted how the brief vision-report of verse 18 may be taken as an unusual form of *chreia*, or memorable saying.[6] Again, we would expect the

---

not belong in a work of history—this way to embellish the plain facts was a normal practice in ancient historiography. (In fact, the custom is even older than historiography, because the first historian, Herodotus, introduced speeches in his *Histories* to emulate Homer.)" George Kennedy comments on the possible link between New Testament dominical discourse and the exercise from the *progymnasmata* known as *prosōpopoeia* (that is, the composition of a speech for either a mythological or historical personage in order to display character): "One of the most difficult questions in rhetorical criticism of the New Testament is whether the discourses of Jesus . . . should . . . be viewed in this light" (*New Testament Interpretation*, 23). To Kennedy's comment, I would add that the difficulty in making a sharp distinction between what is "invented" and what is "given" is a major factor in this complexity.

5. See, as exemplary, Rudolph Bultmann's treatment in *Die Geschichte der synoptischen Tradition* (Göttingen: Vandenhoeck und Ruprecht, 1957), 170–72.

6. Heinz O. Guenther describes a *chreia* as "a brief, succinct, rational saying, disinclined toward the world of the miraculous" ("Early Christianity, Q, and Jesus,"

elaboration of the *chreia* to commence with praise for the sage who authored the succinct word to be elaborated. Here, in the context of a gospel that centers around Jesus, an explicit encomium for Jesus is superfluous. Nonetheless, the disciples' introductory address sets up their master as an authority (κύριε, "Lord") whose very name has power (ἐν τῷ ὀνόματί σου, "in your name"). Jesus' response is arresting: "I saw Satan fall as lightning from heaven."[7]

Much has been written concerning this phrase, which Bultmann calls a "dark word" and which Samuel Vollenweider dubs "this remote word of Jesus."[8] The interventions of these two scholars (and others) go on to debate the nature of Jesus' saying: do Jesus' words (or Luke's facsimile of "a word of the Lord") imply an actual vision of Satan's downfall, or are they to be taken as merely an apocalyptic and metaphorical phrase designating the successful work of the seventy(-two)? Although we are not given other visions of Jesus in this gospel, the concept of Jesus seeing ecstatically is not dissonant with the general picture that Luke paints: a Jesus who is personally addressed at the baptism; a Jesus who prays prior to the transfiguration and enters into conversation with the supernaturally present Moses and Elijah; a Jesus who knows that his lieutenant has been demanded by the Archenemy; and (according to the traditional but not [say most] the original reading of 22:43–44[9]) a Jesus who is ministered to by an angel in Gethsemane. The Jesus of Luke's Gospel is no stranger to the spirit world, since he is shown in concourse with its denizens and

---

Semeia 55 [1991]: 64). As a *chreia*, then, this saying in Luke is remarkable, for as a report of the unseen world it partakes of the "miraculous."

7. In "Luke 10:18—Who Saw Satan Fall?" *Journal for the Study of the New Testament* 46 (1992): 25–40, Julian V. Hills mounts an intriguing but, in the end, unconvincing argument that the verb ἐθεώρουν (I saw/they saw) should be read as third person plural, in reference to the demons, not Jesus.

8. Samuel Vollenweider, "'Ich sah den Satan wie einen Blitz vom Himmel fallen' (Lk 10:18)," *Zeitschrift für die neutestamentliche Wissenschaft und die Kunde der älteren Kirche* 79 (1988): 187–203.

9. These two verses, though not in our earliest manuscripts (omitted in P[69], P[75], ℵ, A, B, N, T, W, and so on), appear very early in the tradition (ℵ*, D, L, D*, Q, Y, and so on). François Bovon seems to be reopening the issue in his Hermeneia commentary, *Luke 1: A Commentary on the Gospel of Luke 1:1–9:50*, trans. Christine M. Thomas (Minneapolis: Fortress, 2002), 1. We await the volume that will treat these verses.

as fully aware of its power, both for good and for ill. In the light of this characterization of the Lord, the most natural reading of this terse phrase would take it at face value, as a vision-report given by Jesus so as to interpret or to contextualize the success that the disciples have enjoyed.

The Impact of the Elaborated Vision

It seems, then, unnecessarily subtle to classify the vision-report as an artifice intended simply to make a theological comment. But even if the vision be taken as artificial,[10] this strange statement made by Jesus effectively strengthens his *ethos*, a quality already established by the disciples in their opening words. We may be reminded of the appeal to vision of a Martin Luther King Jr. or of the Canadian Prime Minister Diefenbaker: "I have a vision." The very style of Jesus, who solemnly declares "I saw," establishes his spiritual insight and unusual form of encouragement as matters that must be carefully heeded. He is the prophet, not simply the teacher. And yet he is also the teacher, responding to his disciples. Like the speech of the Cynic,[11] Jesus' address to his followers is friendly, though corrective—this in contrast to his debates with the Pharisees and other opponents, which are designed to undermine and uproot theological foundations, or even to condemn. In place of classical modes of forensic, deliberative, and celebratory speech, more contemporary analysts of speeches have emphasized the psychological impact of rhetoric. One such contemporary analyst, Fischer, speaks of speeches as identifiable in terms of "motivational" modes. According to his typology, the discourse at hand would be considered "reaffirmatory" or even "purificatory" rather than merely "affirmatory" or "subvertive."[12] That is, Jesus' words here are addressed specifically to his seventy(-two) ambassadors, but also, via the evangelist, to

10. Max Turner, "Spirit of Prophecy," 71. Turner insists that the verse is "much more easily interpreted as the use of apocalyptic *metaphor* to describe the disciples' success than as a literal description of a vision" (ibid.).

11. Mack, "Elaboration of the Chreia," 48.

12. Fischer, "Motive View of Communication," 131–39.

readers who are in solidarity with these messengers. It is frequently the case that Luke's narrative makes a polyfocal address, as in, for example, the Sermon on the Plain, where paired beatitudes and woes speak both to followers and to those who are wavering. Here, however, the address is more focused. Though some of the address may speak indirectly to those who are uncertain about Jesus' power to vanquish the enemy, in the main it invites those who take common cause with the teacher to explore a substantial mystery in which they are participating. Does the casting down of the adversary vindicate and establish those who work in Jesus' name and whose names are written down in heaven? Or does the equation between Jesus' vision and the narrative work the other way around, so that the success of the seventy(-two) provides evidence of that downfall? In either case, Jesus has a word for these faithful, a word that implies both praise and the redirection of their focus, as they (and we) will soon understand. The vision has been offered as an interpretation of their success; yet this very word of interpretation needs interpreting. The full force of Jesus' vision is revealed or unpacked in the elaboration that follows.

The hieratic style of Jesus' vision-report is sustained in the elaboration. The word δέδωκα ("I have given," v. 19) lends his bestowal of authority a "performative" ring. All societies are aware of solemn moments in which a statement is intended not simply to describe what is happening but to actually cause a state of affairs: "You are now man and wife;" "*hoc est . . . corpus meum*" ("This is my body"). So here, Jesus' words are not simply indicative, stating that Jesus has in fact transmitted authority to the disciples; rather, the words ceremoniously bestow authority on the disciples as Jesus speaks them. Again, Jesus' public prayer in verse 21 is solemn, declared "in the Holy Spirit." These are followed by words in verse 22 that possess a character so exalted that they have been called an "aerolite" from John's Gospel. Finally, Jesus' private word in verses 23–24 extends the privilege of the seer to a group of initiates through striking parallelism and contrast. Jesus' extended discourse, then, is framed so as to assure the seventy(-two) that they, like Jesus, have had their *apokalypsis,* their "unveiling revelation" (v. 21), even though (or perhaps because?) they are infants and not the wise. Jesus, now the interpreter of the vision, explains to them both what he has seen (the downfall of Satan) and what they have seen (the banishing of illness and evil), for the vision and the mission are one. From the viewpoint of the faithful reader, what Jesus says to the disciples he says to other infants whose names are written in heaven.

Redirection or Extension?

A key question is whether the argument emerging in this elaboration redirects or furthers the initial vision. It has been seen that Jesus' response to the seventy(-two) performs a kind of apocalyptic redirection of the disciples' words, even while it declares that evil has been conquered. Standing on its own the vision has a polyvalent power, which is explicitly taken down only a few paths by the sequence that follows. This is the logic: the disciples rejoice that the demons have been subject to them in Jesus' name; Jesus' vision explains why this has happened; he proclaims their power over the enemy; however, they should not focus on this but on their participation in heaven; Jesus rejoices, as an example to them of the correct perspective, while extending the idea of the Father's authority and revelation to the simple; the line of authority from Father to Son to recipient is traced; and a final word of blessing is conferred on the disciples' eyes and ears. In the main, the elaboration furthers Jesus' *chreia*/vision-report; but it also trains the gaze of the disciples, and thus of the readers, on those matters inherent in Jesus' gnomic apocalypse that will lead them to maturity rather than to sheer triumphalism or useless speculation.

Luke 10:17–24, then, includes an embryonic but striking vision[13] as it opens, with the effect of arresting the questioners within the text, and the reader of the text, so that their attention can be redirected and deepened along certain lines. As we move on to the elaboration, it would appear that the visionary *chreia*

13. More developed (or intricate) narratives of falling luminaries are to be seen in *1 Enoch* 86, *Testament of Solomon* 20:16–17, and, as we will see in the following chapter, Rev. 12:1–8.

has been somewhat tamed. To use the analogy of a piano, the middle pedal (rather than the right damper pedal) has been applied, so that several of the overtone strings are selected, and allowed to ring freely, while other possible overtones are silenced. If Jesus' word in this setting is meant to take the disciples' eyes off the wonder of their authority over demons, we should not be surprised to find that the mysteries of Satan's blitzkrieg also do not take center stage. Those of a speculative mind may wonder exactly when this vanquishing of the enemy took place and how: the evangelist leaves this discussion, so to speak, to the seer John (Rev. 12).

Some have given a sociological explanation for Luke's redirection of the reader away from potential apocalyptic speculation. Hoffmann[14] argued that a major point of the Lukan discourse was to address a church that no longer performed mighty deeds but that still could rejoice in Jesus' main bequest—names written in heaven. To engage in such mirror reading from the other side, the argument could just as easily be directed to those who set great stock by mighty deeds and visionary experiences and to whom a relativizing word might be rather shocking but necessary for maturity. As we work on this unit from a rhetorical perspective, we indeed sense that a wise delimitation and direction of the prophetic word has begun even in verse 19. The "μῆτις-like response"[15] given by Jesus on hearing the exclaimed pleasure is interpreted so as to enlighten judiciously what is obscure and to direct the hearers along the well-channeled lines of the *gospel*, which is itself the greatest *apokalypsis*. Though a certain domestication or taming of the vision-report has been achieved in the elaboration, still the elaboration possesses its own sharp edge. Its emphasis on infants, its criticism of the wise, and its foundation on a tantalizing (if unexplored) vision of the Lord himself, have the potential to judge and transform anyone who is proud and who has ears to hear.

14. P. Hoffmann, *Studien zur Theologie der Logienquelle*, Neutestamentliche Abhandlungen 8, neue Folge, 2nd ed. (Munster: Aschendorff, 1972), 248–50.

15. That is, a response that demonstrates cunning rhetoric, so called after Mētis, the primordial mother of Athena; cf. Mack, "Elaboration of the Chreia," 66.

Intertextual echoes of Jesus' vision, such as Isaiah 14:12–15 and Ezekiel 28:2–10, strengthen this underlying *topos*[16] of the downfall of the "wise," as does the recapitulation of contrast themes met earlier in Luke's Gospel. Jesus sent out the seventy(-two) as "lambs among wolves"; they return as "children" victorious over "scorpions." We are left with the impression of an encomium with a twist. In the epideictic mode, this speech praises not "famous men" but the simple—by virtue of their connection with Jesus and the Father. It is to the Father that thanksgiving is rendered, leaving only a blessing and not a frank encomium for those whose eyes have seen and whose ears have heard. The *chreia*, complete with its elaboration, is therefore epideictic in tendency but speaks with a deliberative accent, directing those who would follow Jesus to turn to the Lord for their identity. Jesus is both seer and interpreter: his vision confers a derivative authority on his followers, an authority that is put into perspective in the elaboration. The mixed character of its mode means that a sympathetic reading of the passage could lead readers to concentrate on the particularity of Jesus (soteriology), but just as sensibly on the communion of Jesus' followers with this One who is in communion with the Father (ecclesiology), or even on the responsibility of heeding the words that have been spoken and putting them into practice (ethics). Strangely, though the message is "diffused," the words retain a striking and powerful quality. "Benediction" is, by its very nature, fulsome, and holds within it implications for theology, ecclesiology, and communal living. This depth, explored in the ensuing narratival and discursive elaboration, has been aptly "set up" by the polyvalence of Jesus' initial vision.

16. Ancients considered the various topics (Gk. *topoi*, Lat. *loci*) as the places where one finds raw material for arguments. Topics were classed, according to Aristotle, as "common," "material," and "strategic." Common topics had to do with the possible and the impossible, with facts of past, present, and future, and with matters of degree. Material topics are dependent on the subject matter of the speech-act, while strategic topics blend the positive and the negative in order to suggest their idea. Within the prophetic corpus of the Hebrew tradition, the downfall of the exalted but proud person appears to be a common, or perhaps a "material," topic, ready to hand for the rhetorician.

Embryonic Visions within an Allusive Narrative: Luke 1:5–2:40

In the case of Jesus' own brief vision-report, we have seen that vision may be used at the head of an argument in order to be explored in an epideictic discourse that embraces the disciples even while Jesus is kept in the spotlight. This reserved yet evocative use of vision-report in an initial position is consistent with Luke's overall method. Attention to the beginning of his gospel discloses that the form also is deftly used here, as Luke sets up his major themes and prepares for the textures and contours of the story that he will weave. An analysis of Luke 1–2 will disclose how vision, oracle, and narrative are intricately related; it will also provide an opportunity to reflect on two current and justifiably well-celebrated methods of analysis that take account of the layered character of texts. The first approach is the literary interpretation of Robert C. Tannehill, who recognizes three levels of connection with the text: the signaled primary level, the imaginative engagement of the reader, and the subversive exposure of ideology. Though appreciative of the latter two connections, he emphasizes the first, with great benefit to those who read Luke-Acts with him. The second approach, which we mentioned in the discussion of Acts 9:1–25; 22:1–22; and 26:1–24, has been devised by Vernon K. Robbins, who in a preliminary article reflecting on the various foci of literary/sociological/rhetorical critics proposed his method as a means by which different groups could communicate and exchange ideas.[17]

Robbins, in overtures to his colleagues, thus engaged in a salutary introspective analysis, urging scholars of Scripture to think about why we do what we do. From its initial appearance, his socio-rhetorical analysis was articulated not simply as a method but as a study in meta-criticism, a comprehensive method that initially proposed four levels of analysis: inner texture (analysis of the text itself); intertexture (the text alongside its implied comparative texts); social and cultural texture (the text in its world

17. Robbins, "Using a Socio-Rhetorical Poetics," 303.

and the world at large); and ideological texture (the exploration of self-interests in the text and the reader). Consideration of his earliest use of this method discloses that the unity of these levels was achieved in a crescendo toward the final, determinative texture—that of ideology. Subsequently Robbins added a fifth level, "sacred" texture, to the initial plan, thus affording the scriptural text a final reading commensurate with its genre.[18]

The appeal of Robbins's method has been its move toward self-disclosure, reflexivity, and a consideration of the text in the light of the readers' world: here is a truly postmodern approach. Robbins celebrates the openness of language, of the text, and of a method designed to "bring into sight, sound, and feeling aspects of oral and written communication that otherwise will remain hidden."[19] As a champion of voices that may be otherwise silenced, Robbins has gained a well-deserved hearing. It is also clear that Robbins welcomes discussion and amendment by others, as evidenced through the addition of the fifth level to his method.

Robbins's analysis of Luke 1–2, performed at a fairly early stage in the development of his approach, has been helpful to me in working out a rhetorical poetics to describe the use of vision-report in Luke's persuasive narratives. The several embryonic vision-reports within Luke 1–2 are themselves narratives within the larger Lukan story of beginnings, a story that itself forms part of the extended narrative known as Luke-Acts—and Luke-Acts, of course, appears within the traditional Christian collection of texts, the New Testament. For our purposes, it is the rhetorical power of narrative that is at issue, and three levels of narrative at that: the vision narrative within the infancy narrative, within the Lukan narrative. In concert with Robbins, I do not consider that mere attention to rhetorical tropes or form may adequately take account of this complex situ-

18. Sacred texture is clearly described in Robbins's *Exploring the Texture of Texts: A Guide to Socio-Rhetorical Interpretation* (Valley Forge, PA: Trinity Press International, 1996), 120–31.

19. Vernon K. Robbins, "Socio-Rhetorical Criticism: Mary, Elizabeth, and the Magnificat as a Test Case," in *The New Literary Criticism and the New Testament*, ed. Edgar V. McKnight and Elizabeth Struthers Malbon (Valley Forge, PA: Trinity Press International, 1994), 200.

ation. Moreover, a simple "poetics," or literary analysis, will also not suffice, since vision-reports that possess a rhetorical dimension cannot be apprehended as sheer artifacts. At the least, a delicate balance of literary and rhetorical analyses is in order: the search for an interdisciplinary approach is consonant with Robbins's several "textures." The following literary-rhetorical analysis of Luke 1:5–2:40 has been refined through ongoing appreciation of and conversation with Robbins, whose master method has been suggestive for me both in terms of advantages and possible pitfalls. The finer points of this dialogue will emerge especially in the closing analysis of the Magnificat, though points of contact may be seen throughout. My major interlocutor in the first section is, however, Tannehill, whose interest in narrative shape matches the primary concerns of this study.

The Shape of the Action and the Actors

Any analysis of a narrative requires in the first place a delineation of boundaries: where are the beginning, middle, and end? The decision to excise a particular rhetorical unit from a larger narrative depends on perspective and purpose. One could take a shorter passage (e.g., Luke 1:26–56), as does Robbins in his "test case," marking it off by the disposition of names and narrative agents. This shorter text is helpful for Robbins, considering his goal of orchestrating different kinds of analyses; consideration of a longer text on various levels would be unwieldy. On the level of inner texture, he justifies this separation of text from what precedes and follows because here Mary and Elizabeth engage each other and divine agents without the presence of any males.[20] This insight is interesting from a contemporary perspective but may perhaps tells us more about current concerns for female autonomy than about the text itself. What happens if we follow the lead of Tannehill[21] and look beyond one sce-

20. Ibid., 173.
21. Robert C. Tannehill introduces this passage with the following observation: "The Lukan birth narrative is a carefully composed literary unit . . . united both by an elaborate pattern of repetition and by a sequence of increasing disclosure of

nario, examining the whole of Luke 1:5–2:40 as an integrated but complex narrative within Luke's larger work? To examine this larger section is essential if we are interested in observing repetitive or contrasting patterns, the development of plot, and an overall integration of vision and argument: this cannot be done well with only a few verses. A structural chart (see figure 2) may be helpful in demonstrating how these parts make up a comprehensive whole.[22]

The chart plots a six-part narrative, with constant features and variations. In every subsection a mysterious or visionary moment initiates, furthers, or fulfills the action of the story. As seen in the layout, sections I and II exhibit a parallel (though not identical) disposition: time marker, frame and background, vision,[23] reaction, oracle, response (with a question), and a sign related to the question of identity. After the time marker (1:5 and 1:26), the episodes proceed to give the context for the action sequences, first

God's purpose in Jesus" (*The Narrative Unity of Luke-Acts: A Literary Interpretation* [Philadelphia: Fortress, 1986], 1:15).

22. The parallel features disclosed in this chart have been noted by many, of course, and have been schematized in various ways, normally in diptych but sometimes also in tripartite structures. For a table showing representative structures, including those suggested by Galbiati, Burrows, Dibelius, Lyonnet, and Laurentin, see Raymond E. Brown, *The Birth of the Messiah: A Commentary on the Infancy Narratives in the Gospels of Matthew and Luke* (New York: Doubleday, updated 1993), 248–49. Many of the parallel features in the chart offered here confirm their observations as well as the architectonic analysis of Charles Talbert, who plots two cycles (1:5–1:38//1:57–2:52), matching narrative details concerning the birth of John against the story of Jesus (*Literary Patterns, Theological Themes, and the Genre of Luke-Acts* [Missoula: University of Montana Press, 1974], 44). Frequently scholars have considered the awkward pieces that do not fit the proposed schemes as clues to Luke's redactional activity, but as Brown himself, who proposed a two-staged composition, admits, it is difficult to "propose an analysis that will do justice" to all the factors involved (*Birth*, 251). The chart offered here seeks to take the text as we find it, highlighting the typical visionary elements of each of the sequences, showing how the twin narratives are linked by an episode where John and Jesus "meet" *in uteri* and also making clear the asymmetry of the entire passage. Rather than a static doublet, 1:5–2:40 is dynamic, moving forward to a climax and preparing the way for the gospel about Jesus rather than a twin story concerning two prophets.

23. It might be argued that an angelic appearance does not constitute a vision, since a vision involves seeing another world (e.g., Rev. 4:1). However, the Scriptures seem not to make such distinctions, as seen in Luke's own designation of Zechariah's encounter with Gabriel (Luke 1:22) as a "vision."

Figure 2: Narrative Episodes in Luke 1:5–2:40

I *Zechariah and the angel* [John]
time marker (1:5a)
narrative frame, background (1:5b-10)
vision—seen (1:11)
reaction (1:12)
oracle (1:13–17)
questioning response (1:18)
identity sign (1:19–20)
frame (1:21–23)
fulfillment (1:24–25)

II *Mary and the angel* [Jesus]
link, time marker (1:26)
frame and brief background (1:27)
vision—speaks (1:28)
reaction (1:29)
oracle (1:30–33)
questioning response (1:34)
identity sign (1:35–37)
Mary's word (1:38a)
frame (1:38b)

III *Conjunction: Mary and Elizabeth* [John and Jesus]
link, time marker (1:39)
narrative frame (1:39–40)
"happening" (1:41)
oracle = reaction (1:42–45)
extended oracle = response (1:46–55)
frame (1:56)

IV *Birth and circumcision* [John]
link, time marker (1:57)
frame (1:57–58)
narrative (1:59–62)
(inscribed) oracle (1:63)
"happening" sign (1:64)
reaction (1:65–66a)
frame (1:66b)
extended oracle *re. Jesus* (1:68–79)
frame (1:80)

V *Birth and adoration* [Jesus]
link, time marker (2:1)
narrative frame A (2:2–5)
birth (2:6–7)
narrative frame B (2:8)
vision (2:9a)
reaction (2:9b)
oracle (2:10–12)—embedded "sign"
angelic response (2:13–14)
shepherds' response (2:15)
viewing the baby (2:16)
responses (2:17–18)
conclusions, frames B and A (2:19–20)

VI *Presentation: Simeon and Anna* [Jesus]
link, time marker (2:21)
narrative frame (2:21–24); n.b.: no fuss re. name
A/ background Simeon, narrative (2:25–27)
oracle and "report": "I have seen" (2:28–32)
reaction (2:33)
oracle (2:34–35)
B/ background Anna, response and confirmation (2:36–38)
frame (2:39//1:6 in I)
frame (2:40//1:80 in IV)

featuring Zechariah and then Mary. Both episodes are galvanized by the appearance of an angelic visitor, who must comfort against human fear. The angel speaks God's solemn word, provoking a questioning reaction, gives a sign confirming the oracle, and then the episode ends with a concluding frame.

A consideration of the details discloses key contrasts amid the symmetry, and parallels amid the lack of symmetry. In the first section a man is visited, in the second a woman. This feature of pairing a male and female together seems typical, almost programmatic, in Luke (cf. 2:25 and 36; 4:26 and 27; 4:33 and 38; 7:2 and 12; 15:3 and 8, and so on). In his second volume Luke will emphasize the falling of the Spirit on men and women, according to the prophecy of Joel. Pertinent to this present study, with its interest in the visual and the auditory, is that Zechariah is struck by a *vision* of the angel standing at the "right side" of the altar, probably an indication of God's favor;[24] Mary, in contrast, is visited in her home but seems most startled by the angel's *word*. Curiously, the priest Zechariah is judged for not recognizing the identity of the angel Gabriel (1:19), while Mary is not faulted for asking a similar question. So far as the action of the second episode is concerned, the angel's identity seems irrelevant (though it is shared between narrator and readers, 2:26); instead, the dialogue focuses on the identity of Jesus, appealing to his title, his putative name, and his mysterious calling. Zechariah, in his visitation, is given no opportunity to respond to the angel because of the imposed sign of muteness that marks his disbelief (compare the stronger judgment in 2 Macc. 3:29). Mary, however, questions but then believes, declaring, "Here am I." Both Zechariah and Mary are given a promise about a baby that is fulfilled. Through all these parallels and marked contrasts the two episodes are woven together. Moreover, they form part of an ongoing story, since the sign given to Mary by the angel serves as the fulfillment of Gabriel's word to Zechariah as well as Gabriel's word to Mary:

24. Precedents that may be compared and contrasted to Luke's story include Josephus's *Antiquities* 12.282–83, where the priest Hyrcanus, also in the midst of duties, hears a voice, and 2 Macc. 3:22–30, where scourging angels appear in the temple precincts.

Elizabeth has conceived, and the plan of God is in the process of fulfillment.

Though the characterization of Mary certainly benefits by contrast with Zechariah, Luke is nonetheless careful not to overplay his hand here. We are struck by the careful "build up" of *ethos* for Zechariah and Elizabeth (1:5–6), as also Simeon (2:25–26) and Anna (2:36–37), as compared to the unadorned and almost sparse introduction of Mary in 1:26. This is surely not because Mary, the "most blessed" one, is unimportant to the evangelist; rather, this move seems calculated to prevent the major burden of Gabriel's message from being outshone. This heroine is typified by her lack of assumption and her adaptability to God's purpose. So she is fittingly introduced with simplicity. As with the Baptist, her role is to point to the Messiah, the "One to come who is mightier" (Luke 3:16).

In contrast to episodes I and II (the announcement of the two births), the last three episodes are not ordered symmetrically in terms of their subjects, John and Jesus. Though episode IV (the birth and circumcision of John) and episode V (the birth of Jesus) match each other in some respects, V is longer, and is completed by yet another episode (VI), which extends the narrative of Jesus into the scene of his circumcision and presentation. So it is that though readers are "cued" to see parallels and clear links between the stories of two babies, they cannot help but notice that the lion's share of the narrative is devoted to the significance of the second child. Even the material focused on John (episode IV) includes an extended oracle that points forward to that other child who is about to be introduced (1:68–79): Zechariah primarily rejoices in the fulfillment of God's purposes in his nephew, relegating the oracle about his own son to a poignant afterthought.

The central episode III is essential to the development of the narrative in that it explicitly joins the scenarios of Jesus and John through a series of events that they share through their mothers. It is interesting that Luke places this merging sequence early in the unfolding drama and so establishes the interconnection in a structural as well as a conceptual way. The section occupies a programmatic and dramatic position, verifying the promises that have been given to the two houses and preparing for the stronger emphasis that will be given to Mary's son. Despite its power, the episode is, quite literally, domestic. The name of the town is deemed insignificant to the narrative (1:39), and we hear nothing of the presence of Zechariah, though the event occurs in his house: the two women meet indoors, in the private domain to which they are accustomed. What is revealed within it comes not through the ordinary means of apocalypse or vision-report (no angelophany, oracle, or symbolic portents) but through the most intimate means possible: a sign felt only by Elizabeth, though its significance is sounded forth in her oracle and in Mary's extended responsive prophecy.[25] Yet the homey atmosphere and details—the "moving" of the baby, the greeting of two women relatives in their time of seclusion, Mary's continued stay with Elizabeth, presumbably to help her elder cousin during pregnancy—are strangely described according to the traditional rhythm of a solemn apocalyptic scene, where a "vision" is followed by an interpretation. The babe leaps, Elizabeth is filled with the Spirit, and she utters a loud cry that interprets what is happening. Frequently the significance of Elizabeth's responsive interpretation has been overshadowed by the poetic Magnificat, which immediately follows, though of course in the Roman Catholic and Orthodox communities verse 42 has held a special place of honor. Let us pause for a moment to consider how Elizabeth's "report" accents what has happened, what is happening, and what is yet to occur.

In terms of intertextuality, Elizabeth's "mighty cry" recalls two dramatic episodes: the welcoming and joyful cry of the Israelites as the ark of the covenant is brought into the camp, a portent of victory against the Philistines (1 Sam. 4:5); and the great cry of the symbolic woman Zion, whose voice shakes the ground and who is transformed before the eyes of the seer "Ezra" as a city

---

25. The variant that ascribes this canticle to Elizabeth complicates our reading. On the evidence of the manuscripts, the debate, the internal evidence, and the moderate consensus for Mary as the best reading, see Brown, *Birth*, 334–36. We will not argue the case here but will adhere to the traditional ascription of the canticle to Mary, whose youth and gender provide a typical Lukan counterpart to Simeon, the other "singer" of this extended episode.

in the process of being built through suffering (2 Esdras 10:27). Only the first is probable as a historical precedent for Elizabeth's action, since 2 Esdras most likely postdates the infancy accounts. Yet these two episodes show us the two typical cultural contexts of the "mighty cry": war and childbirth.[26] Both contexts are apposite to Elizabeth's prophetic word, which emphasizes the "fruit of the womb" (both hers and Mary's), which remarks upon the gestation period of faith (1:45) and which recognizes the import of this incognito parousia, this unseen coming of the King to his own. The entire episode is pregnant with joyful retrospection and anticipation—"blessed is she who believed, for there will be a fulfillment of what was spoken" (1:45). Elizabeth's oracle also gives voice to the unborn John, interpreting his joyful response to the coming of his unborn cousin and expectant aunt. Mary has come to honor Elizabeth, but it is Mary and her babe who receive the honor from the elderly and honored kinswoman. The unborn John "knows" the import of this event, and Elizabeth serves as voice of interpretation. Her notes of victory and of impending joy are extended in Mary's celebratory hymn (1:46–55, discussed in detail below) before we return to the "narrative framework" (1:39//1:56).

Episode IV continues the story about John yet highlights the promise regarding Jesus: Zechariah's loosened lips direct the hearer away from John toward God's purposes in his more exalted cousin. As we have noted, his priestly words of thanksgiving and blessing (1:68–79) point forward to the events of episodes V and VI. Like the previous episode III, no actual vision is seen, but rather a significant "happening" takes place: just as Elizabeth's womb indicated God's action among the people, so now the return of Zechariah's speech reveals that the divine purpose is being enacted in these events. The return of his speech, moreover, meets a public response similar to that of a crowd that has witnessed a mighty act of God: "Fear came over all their

---

26. To these intertextual echoes might also be added the intratextual gospel traditions of demonic "spiritual warfare" (Luke 4:33) and of Jesus' fruitful death throes (Luke 23:46//Matt. 27:50//Mark 15:37 and parallels), which herald, like maternal labor, the new age of the Spirit.

neighbors, and all these things were talked about" (1:65; cf. 5:9, 26; 7:16; 8:37).

Episode V is clearly the climax of the piece. Here the scene musters not simply one angelic visitor but an angleophany and an accompanying angelic host. Here, too, we witness the birth of the long-awaited child, indicated even by the arrival of the other child, and we hear of multiple responses to this great event. The vision of the angel and angelic attendants is punctuated by references to glory—glory that shines around those witnessing the vision (2:9) and glory hymned by the angels in solemn praise (2:14). Yet the real focus is not on the celestial glory, nor the angelic visitation, but on the One whom they are announcing: the newborn Messiah in his strange circumstances (a "Lord in a manger"). The oddness of this "sign" is emphasized through repetition: "in bands of cloth . . . in a manger" (2:7); "in bands of cloth . . . in a manger" (2:12); "in a manger" (2:16). Moreover, the recipients of God's revelation do not meditate at all on the glorious angelic vision but on the child, who emerges as the "vision" par excellence. It is on him that both Mary and the shepherds reflect; the shepherds play prophet to Mary, who treasures their words, and the shepherds return "praising God," presumably in voices that any person meeting them could hear. This final vision of the newborn brings the episode to its conclusion, resolving the narrative tension and matching the words embedded in the angel's announcement. The heavenly choir, a host of interpreting angels, declares what has been seen: "On earth, peace."

That the child himself is the most complete revelation of God is implied also by Simeon's "report" in the subsequent section, the denouement of episode VI. The vision-report ("My eyes have seen your salvation . . . prepared in the presence of all peoples") is spoken to God in a solemn benediction overheard both by those attending Simeon and by the reader. The rhetorical impact of this embedded report is strong, since it is verified by those who hear/read it as a sincere word to the Lord not to be doubted. What Simeon reports is then confirmed by Anna, who "speaks about the child to all who were anticipating the redemption of Jerusalem" (2:38). The use of the word "all" is universal enough to move outside the story frame and so embrace the ideal reader who stands at a different spot in salvation history yet who also may be hopeful that "redemption is drawing nigh" (Luke 21:18). In episodes I through V Luke has set up and followed through with a pattern of prepared "vision" or revelatory "happening" followed by reaction or oracle and response. Again in episode VI the elements are all there except for a vision or miracle proper to that section: yet Simeon's words rivet our attention on the child, and suggest that for him—and thus for the pious reader—the presentation of the child marks a great epiphany. Thus episode VI continues and augments the tendency of episode V, downplaying angelic vision while centering on the astonishing appearance of the child himself, the salvation of the Lord prepared before all, the light to the Gentiles, and the glory of Israel.

In all, we read this six-part story in the same way we might listen to a fugue. Two major themes, that of the forerunner and the Savior, are woven together as one, with the addition of supporting submotifs, so that the canon arrives at a climax where all voices come together, indicating Jesus as the one preceded, promised, proclaimed, and finally presented for adoration and wonder. There is grandeur and joy in the story but also a hint of darkness and woe as Simeon's blessing comes to an end (Luke 2:35). The whole narrative is well framed, beginning with a pious but barren Judaean couple walking in all the ordinances and ending with Mary and Joseph who have performed everything according to the law, now returning from Jerusalem to Galilee in the presence of a child who is full of promise. We come to closure, but not full closure, because the "fugue" functions as an introduction to a work that possesses several great movements; throughout the Gospel of Luke we will hear much more about John and his greater cousin, whose births and destinies are linked yet not symmetrical. The final verse provides a suitable sense of an ending coupled with an openness, a signal of further divine action in the world: "The child grew and became strong, filled with wisdom; and the favor of God was on him" (2:52).

The Argument: To Be "Hebrew" or "Greek"—Is That the Question?

The outlined structure of these two chapters shows how deftly Luke makes use of visions, oracles, and vision-reports: such unusual occurances emerge naturally in the narrative, in the same way that dreams interlace the Joseph stories of Genesis. Though at first glance they appear to be simply a part of the atmosphere, they are potently instrumental in their roles as they quietly initiate, direct, amplify, and interpret the narrative. First, there is the vision of Zechariah's angel by the censer. This vision occurs in the holiest place, the inner sanctum of the temple, and the only detail of the visitation, its locale near the instrument of incense, calls to mind the prayers of the people. This theme of faithful prayer is underscored by the angel's word and pictured in the human recipient Zechariah, who is himself a priestly representative as well as a needy individual conceived after the model of Abraham and other childless righteous ones.

What about the vision of the angel who enters Mary's house? Certainly the focus of this episode is on the angel's word. Yet his action, though not emphasized, holds significance. It is unusual for a greater to come into the domain of a lesser: is there a rhetorical or persuasive purpose here? Let us recall Luke's point concerning God's visitation in a similar rhetorical situation, Acts 11–12, where there is constant use of the verb εἰσέρχομαι, "to come, enter," and where Luke makes repeated reference to the entry of a holy one into the house of Cornelius. The reader likewise is affected by two significant happenings: the sign of the somersaulting baby, which precipitates Elizabeth's identification and confident praise; and the phenomenon of the freed mouth, by which John's position in the drama is verified. There is also the grand (though not extravagantly narrated) vision of angels praising God and the final concentrated focus on the child. Since we here are faced with narrative rather than outright polemic, we may expect that the argument will be underlying and suggestive.

Luke's persuasive message is formed as vision, oracle, and story line converge with several interconnected themes: the initiating

actions of God toward the pure in God's house and toward the
humble in a human house; the recognition of the child by one in
the womb and by a chorus of angels in the night sky; the unlikely
movement of shepherds toward a humble city lodging; and the
anticipation of a holy man and woman that they will greet a special
child in God's house. These are all poignant details by which we
can trace the rhetorical dimension of the text. There is a kind of
tension here as God *responds* to the deserving but fallible righteous and God *initiates* action that brings honor to those who
are humble but surprisingly pure of heart. The narrative details
match the dark word of Simeon: this child is set for the falling
and rising of many in Israel.

What happens when we examine the actual speeches or spoken
oracles of the story, those places where we might expect the rhetoric
to be made explicit? How do these speeches confirm or enrich the
implicit argumentation discerned in the visions and the overall
narrative? Let us consider, as an example, Mary's speech known
as the Magnificat. These verses, well celebrated in the memory of
the church and structurally prominent in the central section of the
outline we have traced, beckon for special attention. Indeed, they
have received such scrutiny in contemporary scholarship. Typically, two windows of approach have been used to view Mary's
words, approaches that might be labelled the "biblical" model
and the "classical" model.

Tannehill examines this speech-act by reference to a Hebrew
or biblical model of speech, the praise hymn, which consists of
a call to praise followed by reasons.[27] Interesting features that
emerge from Tannehill's perspective include the movement from
a bi-polar pattern (Mary-God) to the tri-polar (humble-proud-
God), an awareness of the inner rhythm of the hymn, and attention to the arrangement of verbs, which discloses two strophes
(vv. 46–50 and 51–55.) The strophes end similarly (vv. 49b–50
and 54b–55) with references to God's mercy and faithfulness to
Israel. In Tannehill's view, the first verse is individual in focus,
the second corporate, so that what Mary articulates now is seen

27. Tannehill, *Narrative Unity of Luke-Acts*, 29.

in the light of whole peoples. Within the context of Luke's story the Magnificat works powerfully, as the particular situation of a young expectant mother, archetype of the lowly, is extended by the biblical imagery and the structural arrangement to embrace all of God's disheartened people: Mary is rendered "an emblem or paradigm of God's saving work which is now beginning" even as "the Magnificat . . . provide(s) an initial characterization of the God whose purpose shapes the following story."[28]

Another window into the speech is provided by comparison with the classical model of the "complete" argument. Vernon Robbins[29] cites one of his graduate students, "Rose," who applies this model by adopting "I praise" as the proposition, with God's action as the rationale for this. Such a beginning is a little odd since the mixing of agents for proposition and reason defies normal logic. How can "I praise" be a proposition that requires a rationale, when praise is by nature a responsive expression of delight?[30] Nevertheless, a certain "argument" may be discerned, since Mary's hymn is not simply a hymn but a kind of hymnic theodicy with affinities, of course, to Hannah's praises in 1 Samuel 2:1–10. The outline on page 128 attempts to take account of both the hymnic and polemical nuances. Seen this way, the argument is a complex *enthymeme*[31] predi-

28. Ibid.

29. Robbins, "Socio-Rhetorical Criticism," 176.

30. Walter Brueggemann has called attention to the ideological danger of exhorting to praise without giving reasons in the section entitled "Doxology without Reason" in *Israel's Praise: Doxology against Idolatry and Ideology* (Philadelphia: Fortress, 1988), 89–119. Surely the ancient rhetoricians display keen insight into human nature when they point out that an encomium loses its power when it is predicated on careful argumentation—someone or something praiseworthy simply elicits our praise without calculation.

31. An *enthymeme* is an argument in which a supporting statement, or reason, is given, but a major premise is not declared. If all premises were made explicit, the *enthymeme* would be rendered a syllogism. Here is a prosaic example: "God will slay the wicked because God is righteous." Here a conclusion is made ("God will slay . . .") supported by a reason ("because . . ."). However, the *enthymeme* leaves undeclared its fundamental premise, that righteousness includes the execution of justice; indeed, it leaves undeclared a further premise, that capital punishment is just. A complete syllogism would be phrased as follows: "Righteousness includes the execution of justice; capital punishment of the wicked is just; God is righteous; therefore God will slay the wicked." Frequently the disclosure of an undeclared premise (or premises)

I Introduction	"my soul rejoices . . ."	46–47
II *Narratio*		
Proposition	"God regarded" = blessed me (= Israel)	48
Reason	"for he has done great things for me"	49
III *Confirmatio*		
Paradigm	"His mercy is on those who fear him"	50
Contrary	"He has scattered the proud"	51
Examples	"put down the mighty, exalted the low"	52
	"filled the hungry, sent the rich away"	53
IV Conclusion	"He has helped his servant Israel"	54
(citation)	"As he spoke to our fathers . . ."	55

cated on two undeclared premises: the major premise is that God is holy and merciful; the minor premise is that this holiness and mercy involves the judgment of the proud and exaltation of the humble. Here is further evidence that Kennedy's depiction of "radical Christian rhetoric" may be misconstrued. It would seem that reasonable praises are as foundational to primitive Christianity as unsupported assertions. The benefit of comparing Mary's speech to the classical model is that the piece thus emerges as a wholly integrated argument. In comparison with Tannehill's two-strophe approach, the distinction between individual and corporate blessing is not accentuated: from start to finish, Mary gives voice to the humble in Israel. Moreover, since the premise rather than the proposition involves the ecstasy of Mary—her God-directed joy and thanksgiving—the focus of the speech is on Israel's righteous and merciful God, while hearers are implicitly urged to join in.

These lines of argument are confirmed by the position of the speech within Luke's overall narrative. The proposition concern-

---

in an *enthymeme* demonstrates the shared presuppositions of a community. Again, some *enthymemes* reverse the premise and conclusion (as frequently happens in the Psalms), thus calling attention to the premise and setting up the conclusion as an anticipated condition or result: "God is righteous, therefore he will slay the wicked" (e.g., Ps. 26:1; 30:1; 75:1; 136:1). This form of *enthymeme* is also sustained in New Testament argument: "The Holy Spirit will come upon you . . . therefore the child . . . will be called holy" (Luke 1:35).

ing God's "regard" or "blessing" is prefigured in the action by
Gabriel's initial word at 1:28 ("Greetings, you who are highly
favored"), and is reiterated both at 1:42 ("blessed are you") and
1:45 ("blessed is she"). Similarly, the themes of God's concern,
God's character, and God's action are maintained and recast in
the subsequent episodes. Zechariah describes them as continuous
with God's promise "that we, being delivered from the hand of
our enemies, might serve him without fear, in holiness and righteousness before him all the days of our life" (1:74–75 RSV);
Simeon pronounces them fulfilled in the presented child, who is
"for glory to thy people and . . . for the fall and rising of many in
Israel" (2:34). Though the words breathe promise (with a dark
edge) to Israel, the central subject is that of the divine Promise
Maker and Keeper.

Attention to this approach directs us away from the benefit to
Israel and toward a consideration of God's character. But is this
an argument or a celebration? This would depend on whether the
reader hears an accent on the major or minor premise. Is God's
holiness and mercy being celebrated in Mary's voice? Or is Luke,
qua Mary, arguing for the startling actions of God, the upset of
the status quo. These seem to be false alternatives. If we attend
to the possibility of applying different models, the text is more
fully explored: various classical models may demonstrate the
polemic, and the "Hebrew" ones may demonstrate the themes
of victory or praise. It is important to note the typical blending
of modes in New Testament rhetoric so that there is always at
least an undercurrent of encomium, with God as the celebrated
object. Again, as we have noted, Hebrew wisdom and prophetic
pieces are predisposed to judgments and polarities (e.g., Ps. 1),
and this dynamic is sustained in much New Testament teaching
(e.g., the Sermon on the Plain, Luke 6:20–49). The rhetoric of
duality and reversal is therefore consonant with Old Testament
conventions and complicates the lines of rhetoric as we try to
understand Mary's speech in terms of classical, Greco-Roman
rhetoric. It would seem that the polarities make for a judicial
speech that cuts both ways: both condemnatory and acquitting
arguments become operative. Even while the simple are raised up,

the specter of judgment falls over the mighty. In terms of mode, the mood is *both* judicial and epideictic, arguing for vindication and condemnation even while it retains a flavor of praise and celebration. Luke's familiarity and comfort with the biblical tradition of dualism seemingly modifies the classical pattern, which typically concentrates on one rhetorical *telos* or goal. The appeal to authority as part of the conclusion, rather than as a feature of the main argument, is also typical. Whereas in the complete speech citation of authority occurs as part of the proofs, in the Magnificat (as in the elaborated *chreia* of Luke 10:17–24) the appeal to authority completes the argument: "as he declared to our fathers, Abraham and his seed forever." It is of interest, however, that the actual declarations of God to the ancestors are only gestured at, leaving the hearer of this hymn (or the reader, implied in the communal "us") to supply the necessary authoritative word. What might have been a heavy-handed playing of a trump card, "the prophetic word," is transmuted into an invitation. Readers are called to enter the imaginative and recollective world of Mary, Elizabeth, and their kinsfolk, remembering with them the mighty acts and poignant promises of God. For they too may benefit from the mercies promised to Israel, to Abraham and his seed.

So it is that Luke 1–2 emerges as a grand orchestration of sight and sound that narrates its story with force. The visions, or unusual "happenings" in scenes I, II, and III, initiate their more explicit oracles, while in IV and V the signs point toward the child who will come into full view in scene VI. This complex story incorporates within itself a startling declaration: this child is set for the falling and rising of many in Israel and as a light beyond these boundaries. God is acting in a new and surprising way, using the humble and weak, including the rabble (shepherds) and the traditionally pious, in the action. What God is doing and about to do will have an effect on everyone without exception; thus the reader is directed to "sit up and listen." Luke's use of vision and sign, culminating with the "vision" of the baby, provides a stirring overture for the marvellous story that will follow, but it remains subtle enough not to "steal thunder" from the

greater events of Jesus' ministry, teaching, transfiguration, suffering, death, resurrection, and ascension. In their initial place
in the Gospel, these embryonic visions are perfectly suited to
their function, initiating the action, interpreting the acts of God,
and focusing the attention of the reader on the one who is, in
his very person, what God is saying to Israel and to the nations.
The unassuming nature of the brief visions is helpful in paving
the way for the momentous story that Luke will relate as the
Gospel progresses. Similarly the open quality of these "visions"
and "signs" is also helpful in drawing various readers into the
narrative, inviting them to reflect on the "favor of God" that has
come to bring truth and peace. Indeed, the narrative is construed
so as to issue a gentle encouragement for readers to enter into
the anticipation, the adoration, and the thanksgiving of the actors in Luke's drama. Exemplary of this is the general reference
to "God's promises" at the end of the Magnificat and Simeon's
poignant oracle regarding "the thoughts of many hearts" that
will be "apocalypsed" (2:35, ἀποκαλυφθῶσιν).

When all is said and done, and when even the readerly imagination is exposed and interpreted, faithful readers come near the
end of this sequence and hear Anna speak to them, too, as those
who are looking for God's redemption. As with a formal speech,
which in its initial moments establishes a sympathetic and compelling *ethos* for the rhetor so that the audience will listen with
alacrity, so in his opening scene Luke invites the reader into the
meaning and progress of his narrative by the use of "open" and
suggestive visions. The contemporary reader is perhaps hampered
in responding to this invitation because we are less comfortable
with the vision-report than an ancient readership; even so, Luke's
winsome voice sounds its welcome, disarming even the resistant
reader.

Showing Our Cards

The very openness of the vision-report and the narrative present the introspective analyst with a difficulty, however. How do
we assess the very different ways of reading this text? How do

we account for significant variations that occur even when several readers do their work from within the same methodological framework? Do multiple readings signal that our readings are totally idiosyncratic? How do we prevent the suspicion that the assigning of meaning is arbitary? I continue to maintain that there are cues in a text that the hearer or speaker does well to heed. We recall again the insight of process theology that some textual cues are more "open" while others are more directive; nevertheless, the text itself provides the "lures"[32] for the interpreter who knows that a text may have a range of meanings but that some readings do violence to the text. From this perspective, one of the roles of the sympathetic reader is to respond to the indications of the text's language, be it relatively open or closed. Such a reader is concerned not to impose her or his own agenda on the text and careful to use criteria in analysis that are congenial to the text and not merely imported from an extraneous agenda. This is not to say that a hermeneutics of suspicion has no fruitful role to play; yet it must not be granted a hegemony by which the text is simply used for the purposes of a hostile and violent readership.

The advent of postmodernism has meant that more and more critics have let down their guard and refused to own the epithet "neutral." The "showing of cards" may be an aid to learning to play the game, or alternately, an excuse for irresponsible abandon. In speaking of my desire to hear the text and not to use the text as a pretext for my own new text, I have declared my stance according to the canons of postmodern scholarship. More and more scholarship is moving from a show of neutrality to a demand that we show where we are coming from. But I wonder if this demand is always a fair or fruitful one. Could the scholar, having declared where she or he is "coming from," feel liberated to do whatever is desired with the text? It seems that this is the approach of, for example, C. Keller,[33] who offers a "midrash" on Revelation 12 such that it makes an explicit appeal to those who opt to be "creative" while refusing outright to engage oth-

32. Pregeant, *Christology beyond Dogma*, 45.
33. Catherine Keller, "Die Frau in der Wuste: Ein feministlisch-theologischer Midrasch zur Offbarung 12," *Evangelische Theologie* 50 (1990): 414–32.

ers who come at the text from a different angle. If postmodern disclosure is used as grist for such a "sorting job," isolation and the impoverishment of discussion will be the result, rather than enriched conversation.[34]

It is true that neutrality in reading is impossible. We have also learned from Gadamer and others that pre-understanding may in fact be helpful. Nevertheless, it may be that we should not scorn too quickly the generation immediately preceding us, which spoke of the need to distance one's agenda, so far as possible, in reading the text. Neutrality may be a fiction, but like some legal fictions (e.g., "equality"), it stands for an important insight that we may be wise not to scorn wholly: there are at least two discourses going on in the act of reading, and I want to hear the voice/voices of the text or author before I speak my piece. Twenty-first-century scholars may be unable and unwilling to revert to the "safety" of dispassionate discourse, as in the "modernist" period; however, unless a special measure of courtesy is used along with contemporary frankness it is likely that the deepest conversations will be preempted or stifled.

Discussion of the ideological texture of the nativity narratives has led us, as might be expected, to consider our own commitments. We began with the driving concern of Vernon Robbins to help organize the different methods so that we can hear each other speak. His aim is an important one, given the present atomization and the tendency of scholars in one pursuit to ignore or even disparage the work of others. Robbins has suggested that others may

---

34. Vernon Robbins cites the work of Jane Schaberg (*The Illegitimacy of Jesus: A Feminist Theological Interpretation of the Infancy Narratives* [New York: Crossroads, 1987]), which suggests a new arena of intertextuality for the Jesus episode, namely, the Hebrew and Greek stories of rape and overpowering of virgins, hitherto neglected. These texts may be in some ways helpful. My problem with Schaberg's use of these texts, however, is my suspicion that ideology has been granted a hegemony here. Schaberg herself cannot argue that Luke actually presented a miracle of miracles in God taking a bastard child and raising him to the status of Messiah. Yet she urges that there are subtle clues that Luke is aware of this tradition and that it is lurking in his narrative: we seem to be moving back behind the rhetoric of the story, in Schaberg's view, to the rhetoric of an earlier historical tradition. But is it not much more likely that we are seeing our own reflection in the well of the text? Is it the rhetoric of the early first century or that of the late twentieth that is attracting our gaze?

want to reorder his proposed textures to mirror their own interests. He has himself moved on to offer a final "sacred" texture in order to complete the possibilities of approach.[35] His own understanding is that these textures are not hierarchical, but complementary, and in his hands the method works toward this interconnection.[36] It may be, however, that a five-tier method, presented at a time when a hermeneutics of suspicion is au courant, predisposes the analyst to treat the sacred as an unusual and separate category only discernible in explicitly religious texts rather than as a quality fully integrated at every level of many texts. Indeed, it is often the case that those engaged in ideological and sociological readings see their approaches as the real material readings that explain the cultures or worldviews from which our texts have issued. Robbins is concerned to acknowledge that "every theology has a politics"[37] and so presents his method progymnastically[38] as a corrective and amplification to more restrained methods. In the hands of those less enamored with literary analysis, less open to multiple

35. Robbins's excellent Web site on his socio-rhetorical method describes sacred texture as "a texture that is intertwined with each of the other four textures (inner, inter, social/cultural, and ideological), and refers to the manner in which a text communicates insights into the relationship between the human and the divine" (http://www.religion.emory.edu/faculty/robbins/SRI/defns/s_defns.html [accessed July 18, 2006]). For a clear introduction to the various textures as Robbins has finally established these, see his *Exploring the Texture of Texts*.

36. See, for example, the movement toward "sacred texture" in Robbins, "From Enthymeme to Theology in Luke 11:1–13," in *Literary Studies in Luke-Acts: A Collection of Essays in Honor of Joseph B. Tyson*, ed. R. P. Thompson and T. E. Phillips (Macon, GA: Mercer University Press, 1998), 191–214. Here Robbins uses the category of "abductive reasoning" to show how the rhetorical moves may "interweave theology and Christology in a manner that creates not only a new social, cultural, and ideological world, but also a new theological and christological world for the reader" (ibid., 214).

37. Robbins, "Socio-Rhetorical Criticism," 194.

38. In speaking about the constraints of other more "modest" methods of reading, Robbins comments: "Their goal has been to bring its narrative story world into view. Ironically, as they did this, the world in which the [book] emerged as a social product . . . vanished from sight. . . . The challenge before us is to establish an environment that brings together the narratorial and social dimensions of language in texts. Socio-rhetorical criticism has such a goal in view" ("Introduction to the Paperback Edition," of *Jesus the Teacher: A Socio-Rhetorical Interpretation of Mark* [Philadelphia: Fortress, 1992], xxiv).

readings, and less in tune with the tranforming possibilities of the Scriptures, the method may be used in such a way that the first three textures are subsumed under and orchestrated toward the "real" point: who gains and who loses in the ideology of the text. In such cases the "sacred" texture may likewise be wholly lost, since political questions frequently exert their wonted hegemony as the reader asks, "Do I like this power-game?" If the visceral response is given in the negative, appreciation of the sacred texture becomes moot.

Robbins has suggested that we engage in both "subjective" and "objective" analysis, bringing together in a deliberate and designed way the horizons of the ancient worlds and ourselves. Can this really be done, or is the task too hard? Will we think we are engaging in carefully controlled analysis, all the while importing our own (albeit honestly delared) agendas? Can subjective and objective analysis really exist together in a grand scheme? Or are they better done separately to meet different goals? The old question of what a text meant and what it means comes to the fore here—as well as what it might mean to us as we reconfigure its meaning. I am reminded of Tevye's celebrated proverb in *Fiddler on the Roof*—"a bird and fish may love each other, but where will they make their home?" Robbins is interested in bringing together different partners in conversation. This is important. It may, however, be better to limit ourselves at most times to modest projects, even while controlled interdisciplinary discussion is useful. A metacritical examination of various methods may help us get our bearings. Two methods in conjunction may be mutually enlightening. But as for a whole tapestry and typology on the text, combining method with meta-methodological concerns—can we really sort out the threads?

Structurally Central and Suggestive Visions: The Transfiguration Accounts

We have seen, in the embryonic visions of Luke 10:17–24 and 1:5–2:40, how a narrative may be deftly shaped by the judicious placement of even a brief vision-report. Jesus' evocative words at a key point in the first narrative provide a springboard not only for the elaborated discourse that follows them but also for the several readers who will make creative use of their polyvalent character. Included as part of the story that underscores the mission of Jesus' disciples in solidarity with their teacher, the collaborative possibilities opened by the vision seem apt. While the purposes of the author are not here infinitely malleable, Jesus' visionary words and the interpretation that follows them invite the reader to consider various ways in which the downfall of the Adversary and a mission in solidarity with the Christ might be connected. It is as though, in a literary mode, various readers travel on the road with the seventy(-two) to their various destinations and end by hearing Jesus' communal blessing.

In the nativity sequence the visions are less dramatically introduced but emerge rather naturally within the narrative, serving to catalyze the action, further direct it, and bring it to a stunning (though not fully cadential) climax. Over against the expanded oracle of Jesus, which directs the reader to concentrate on the gifts bestowed on the followers, the focus of the nativity visions is quite clearly on the Christ himself, even when the figure of his precursor cousin is in view. At the same time, even the ordinary and domestic areas of life (shepherds' fields, woman's womb, stable and home, the moment of hearing this Gospel read) are seen as hospitable and pervious to the presence of a God who enters the human realm.

We move on to consider a more extensive vision-report that is placed strategically in all three Synoptic Gospels: the transfiguration. The delimitation of these passages (Mark 9:2–8; Matt. 17:1–8; and Luke 9:28–36) is somewhat difficult, since the "journey down the mountain" (not described in Luke's narrative) provides a kind of commentary on the transfiguration passage in the other two Gospels. Indeed, in Matthew's version, verses 9–13 are introduced as the authoritative "interpretation" of the apocalyptic event that the disciples have witnessed. We will, however, concentrate mostly on the transfiguration itself, which by all accounts is a vision-report.

Some debate might be entertained concerning exactly which of the details of this episode are visionary: are we to take as "vision" the appearance of Elijah, Moses, and the cloud, or the entire luminous experience, including the altered Jesus as well? Matthew clearly labels the entire sequence visionary when he has Jesus requiring the disciples to tell no one "the vision" until an opportune time (Matt. 17:9). Clearly, however, this is a vision-report with a difference, since part of what is seen is continuous with the presence, teaching, and practice of the rabbi who has been with them for some time. In every case the continuity is underscored: Matthew's wording of the heavenly voice recalls the entire career of the "well-pleasing" Messiah from the baptism until this point (Matt. 17:5//3:17), Luke portrays the Master in prayer, and Mark has the bewildered disciples address their teacher as "rabbi." The effect of this strange vision-report, we will see, is to fuse vision and ordinary life, glory and suffering, so that readers discern what is obscure to be the true reality into which those who are intimate with Jesus are called to enter.

The transfiguration is thus depicted as a key moment in Jesus' own ministry, and in the apprenticeship of his disciples. Meditation on this scene has been a powerful source of spiritual growth for Christians throughout the ages. The New Testament itself pays special attention to this tradition concerning Jesus not only in the three Gospel accounts, but (possibly) in the Fourth Gospel's emphasis on glory,[39] probably in the reflections of 2 Corinthians 3–4, and certainly in the commentary on this episode in 2 Peter 1. This predilection to use the transfiguration as a springboard for spiritual rumination is seen beginning in the second-century Ethiopic *Apocalypse of Peter* and the docetic *Acts of John*, carrying through to the writings of Origen (*Commentary on Matthew*), Ephraim

39. John 1:14–17 declares: "[W]e beheld his glory, glory as of the only Son from the Father. . . . From his fullness have we all received. . . . The Torah was given through Moses; grace and truth came through Jesus Christ." This proem to the Gospel may well reflect the transfiguration in the same manner that John 1:29 reflects the baptism of Jesus without narrating it, that John 6:31–59 adopts eucharistic language in the absence of a Last Supper narrative, and that John 20:17 implies the ascension, though this is never detailed.

of Syria ("Sermon on the Transfiguration"), pseudo-Macarius (the homilies), pseudo-Dionysius, Symeon the New Theologian, and Gregory of Palamas, champion of the "hesychasts."[40] The developing written tradition concerning the "uncreated light" is amplified by the visual: scenes of the transfiguration were depicted as early as the fourth century.[41] In iconography this episode took a special place of honor.[42] It would seem that these ancient writers with ink and paint took their cue from the narrative, with its emphasis on salvation history, striking revelation, intimacy with Christ, and concentrated prayer. In recognition of this long-standing tradition, we will, during the course of this literary-rhetorical reading, take account from time to time of what those before us have both observed and celebrated as possessing a transformative potency. Here we follow the indications of the vision-report, which brings together different eras (Moses and Elijah with Jesus and the disciples), prescribing a communal perspective.

Structure and Apocalypse in Mark and Matthew

We begin our reading, according to the conventions of contemporary scholarship, with the "simplest" account, that of Mark's Gospel. As always with Mark the placement of the event is key to its understanding. The overall structure of Mark's Gospel can be visualized as two "mountains" of revelation. The first mountain

---

40. Hesychasm (literally, "the practice of quietude") attained its greatest popularity in the late thirteenth century. It was a tradition that involved meditative repeated prayers, bodily postures, and quiet attention to God, looking for God to illumine body and spirit by the "uncreated light" seen also on Mount Tabor.

41. We refer to the Brescia casket, a fourth-century artifact in the Museo Civico Cristiano (Brescia, Italy), that has imprinted on it a transfiguration scene with intriguing details, including the revelatory "hand of God." For a photo and a description, see Andreas Andreopoulos, *Metamorphosis: The Transfiguration in Byzantine Theology and Iconography* (Crestwood, NY: St. Vladimir's Seminary Press, 2005), 106–8. For commentary on the casket as a whole, on which may be seen several theophanic scenes with "the hand of God . . . representing the glory of God," see the thorough work of Catherine Brown Tkacz, *The Key to the Brescia Casket: Typology and the Early Christian Imagination* (Paris: University of Notre Dame Press, 2002), 93.

42. On the continuity of themes from the gospel accounts into the "rhetoric" of the iconographers, see again Andreopoulos, *Metamorphosis*.

comprises roughly chapters 1–8, where the question "Who is this Jesus?" is given the answer "He is the Messiah." The answer for this question is anticipated throughout the first half of Mark's Gospel, and is given a clear response at the climax of the section by Peter (8:29). The second mountain comprises roughly chapters 9–16, where the question "What kind of Messiah is he?" is initially answered by Jesus' own reproof of Peter, as the Lord teaches that he is "a Messiah who must suffer and so enter into glory" (cf. 8:31). This suffering dimension is then dramatically played out in the ensuing way to the cross. The transfiguration event comes just after this double "hinge" or "valley" (8:27–38) between these two great structures (1:1–8:26; 8:39–16:8). Peter has been both commended for his insight into Jesus' messiahship and challenged to accept (and emulate) Jesus' true nature, as one who suffers and so is glorified. It is immediately after this interchange between Peter and Jesus that the narrator signals the "kingdom" or "rule" of God has already "come" with power in Jesus, whose glory is made manifest in the transfiguration (9:1). Although all is not yet restored, the veil is pulled back for the disciples so they can see the significance of this one to whom they must listen. What Cyril of Alexandria notes about the Lukan account applies equally to Mark's narrative: when the three saw the glory of Jesus and Moses and Elijah, the kingdom of God had come even at that point for them.[43]

Mark's Gospel sounds several notes that are particularly evocative. First, the whole episode is encircled by the repeated word "alone" (μόνους, v. 2; μόνον, v. 8). Jesus initially takes the three disciples up with him alone; at the conclusion of the vision they see Jesus alone. This is a revelatory event that will shape their entire discipleship, as they encounter a teacher who appears in nearly indescribable glory. Though they call him "rabbi" (9:5), soon they will learn through the heavenly voice that this one is a fulfillment of two figures connected with faithful Israel: the Suffering Servant of God (Isa. 42:1–4; 49:1–6; 50:4–11; 52:13–53:12)

---

43. Cyril of Alexandria, *Commentary on Luke*, Homily 51, cited in Arthur Just, ed., *Luke*, Ancient Christian Commentary on Scripture (Downers Grove, IL: InterVarsity, 2003), 158.

and the visionary Son of Man (Dan. 7:13–14, 26–27), whom the Almighty glorifies as a representative of God's saints. Thus glory is firmly anchored to suffering, as the conversations both preceding (8:31–38) and following (9:9–13) have insisted. It is interesting that in Mark the episode of glory is sketched very briefly; almost as much time is given to Jesus' lesson after they leave the moment of luminescence, prepared by the divine word, "Listen to him."

Matthew's "vision" (ὅραμα, 17:9) follows the same contours as that of Mark, though the texture is thick with prophetic and apocalyptic echoes recalling great revelatory events of the past. Twice his narrative is pierced by the expostulation ἰδού ("Behold!" 17:3, 5). Indeed, the entire episode has the "rhythm" of an apocalyptic vision, as can be readily seen in comparison with such other visionary episodes as Daniel 10:4–11 or 2 Esdras 9:38–10:37. Here, like the ancient seer, the apostles see a wondrous sight, one whose face "shines like the sun," the major luminary of the sky. This glowing one is greater than the angel observed by Daniel or the Zion-Woman who terrifies Ezra, both of whose countenances are described as "like lightning" (Dan. 10:6; 2 Esdras 10:25). After beholding this wonder, the three hear a divine *bat qôl* ("the daughter of a voice"), an echo of God's own word on earth.[44] At this, they fall on their faces in awe, like many a visionary (Dan. 8:18a; 2 Esdras 10:30a), and are touched and raised up (Dan. 8:18b; 2 Esdras 10:30b), for God has something for them to do. Finally, on the way down the mountain (Matt. 17:9–13) Jesus assumes the role of the interpreting heavenly being, a messenger frequently encountered in visionary literature. During their descent together he explains the meaning of what has been revealed, so that the evangelist comments: "then the disciples understood" (17:13). It is, however, the full Matthean narrative of the cross, and beyond that the resurrection, that provides the interpretation of their vision.

44. The central importance of God's word in this pericope (as in Matthew generally) is confirmed by the chiastic analysis, offered (with reserve) by Dale C. Allison and W. D. Davies in *A Critical and Exegetical Commentary on the Gospel according to Saint Matthew*, 2 vols. (Edinburgh: T&T Clark, 1991), 2:684.

Textural Layers in Luke

Let us focus especially on Luke's account of the transfiguration,[45] which is the most "ekphratic"[46] of the three accounts even while it is replete with literary and rhetorical details consonant with a particular understanding of salvation history. The Lukan account is at once the most "scribal" in its element of extravagant intertextuality and the most allusively emotive of the versions. This dual strength may be seen in the unique use of the term "glory" (δόξα, 9:31, 32), which is redolent both of key scriptural passages and of the mystical theme of intimacy with God. Coupled with repeated reference to the cloud (twice in v. 34, once in v. 35), this term δόξα recalls vividly the appearance of God's glory (kābôd), which led the Hebrew people by day and by night through the wilderness. The Shekinah, that ineffable "presence" of God, was discerned by the Israelites in the cloud of glory, both as a protection and as a guide, during their sojourn in the wilderness. It also had the effect of irradiating the face of their leader Moses after he had been in intimate contact with the Lord, both on Mount Sinai and in the "tabernacle of meeting." This detail of the narratives is commented on by later writers, including the rabbi Paul in 2 Corinthians 3.

Emphasis on "glory" also recalls, for any reader who is aware of Jewish tradition, the cultural practice of those who throughout the centuries have commemorated this time of Israel's intimacy with God in the wilderness by erecting tabernacles during the Feast of Booths. The reference to splendor also sets in motion echoes of a postexilic tradition that emerged from a reading of Ezekiel, who by means of a vision revealed that God's glory was not confined to one place, not even to holy Jerusalem, but was movable (as it were) on a celestial and fiery chariot-throne. Ezekiel's insight (that

45. Note that the verb μεταμορφόομαι ("I undergo metamorphosis, I am transfigured") is omitted in Luke's account, though it is found in Matthew and Mark. One may speculate that Luke avoids a potentially distracting term with unfortunate overtones for a Gentile audience acquainted with Ovid.

46. Ekphrasis is the rhetorical term used for the construction of a vividly portrayed scene and is similar in function to the demonstratio, visio, and a figure sub oculos (see p. 34, n. 9).

God was still with the faithful exiles) fed the vision of mystical rabbis, who, meditating on Ezekiel 1, themselves glimpsed the *merkabah* (the throne of glory), the heavenly courtroom, and the attending Angel of God who presided over the sacred torah. This mystical tradition, largely oral and certainly esoteric in nature, is witnessed to in the later Enoch literature (e.g., *3 Enoch*). So, then, the term "glory," in its Lukan connection with the imagery of "clouds" and "tents," sets off a host of echoes, intertextual and intercultural.

In Luke 9:28–36, the evangelist depicts a rabbi taking his inner group of disciples to a holy place to pray. They call him "Master," but through this event he will be revealed as greater than any mystical rabbi, indeed, greater than even the law-giver and the prophets. The initial time marker of the narrative suggests that we are to expect something new—this event occurs on about the eighth day, which early in the Christian tradition had become the symbol of resurrection and new creation.[47] The other Gospels detail the "sixth" day, perhaps to recall God's creating power (so Origen, Ambrose, and John of Damascus) but probably also to recall Moses' reception of God's word after the mountain had been covered in glory for six days (Exod. 24:16). In Luke, the "Master" (Ἐπιστάτα, v. 33) enters into significant communion with Moses and Elijah, figures associated with powerful revelations of God's power and poignant moments of intimacy. Moses, we remember, spoke with God "mouth to mouth"; Elijah was visited by God's still small voice in a time of despair. Alone in Luke's narrative we hear that these two great servants of God talk with Jesus about his own approaching death in terms that clearly recall God's de-livering power in past times—Jesus is being strengthened in order to accomplish his ἔξοδος ("departure," literally "exodus," 9:31), his redemption of the people, in Jerusalem. Side by side with this

47. Some have also discerned an allusion to the eighth-day celebration of the Feast of Tabernacles (Lev. 23:36). On the developing significance of the eighth day, see Basil of Caesarea, *Hexaemeron* 2.8; PG 29:52ab, and Ambrose, *Exposition of the Gospel of Luke* 7:6–7, in Just, *Luke*, 159. Also helpful is the collection of ancient commentary on pp. 145–322 of John Anthony McGuckin, *The Transfiguration of Christ in Scripture and Tradition* (Lewiston: Edwin Mellon, 1986).

recollection of numinous biblical scenes is the Lukan description of the disciples, who, though they do not understand all this, are themselves embraced in glory. While they are afraid, the cloud of glory, the mysterious presence of God, envelops them too, and they are left with the sound of the Father's voice ringing in their ears: "This is my beloved Son, my chosen, listen to him!"[48]

Yet another detail of Luke's account calls attention to its intertextual nature as well as its subtle theologizing. We have seen already that Matthew considers the event to be visionary in nature, placing the word ὅραμα (vision, 17:9) in the mouth of Jesus as he gives retrospective instructions to his disciples. Luke gives no such label to the episode but signals its visionary nature through touches associated with *merkabah* mysticism, extravagantly picturesque language, and the use of ἰδού ("Behold!" 9:30).[49] Then, too, there is Luke's unparalleled description of the visionary disciples as being "overcome with sleep" during the transfiguration vision (9:32). This reference to sleep seems to function on different levels, creating reverberation within Luke's own text and within the corpus of biblical and parabiblical material. Its most simple echo occurs on the level of what Vernon Robbins calls "inner texture," linking the passage with Jesus' agony in the garden, at which time also Jesus contemplates the coming ordeal and the disciples are found sleeping, hampered by their human inability to pray in constancy with their Master.[50]

48. It is interesting to note that the earliest depictions of the transfiguration in the tradition of Jewish iconography tended to represent the voice (or glory) of God, with its directly revelatory implications, by means of a hand descending from the heavens (on this, see Andreopoulos, *Metamorphosis*, 106, 118), perhaps reflecting the accent of Matthew's Gospel. This feature was lost in later iconography as Jesus became the utter focus and means of revelation: perhaps the referential nature of the divine voice/hand has the tendency to place the observer in an objective role, whereas emphasis on the glory of God in Christ, illuminating all in its path (as in Luke's gospel), more readily embraces those "outside" the text or the icon.

49. The parallel use of ἰδού in Matthew and Luke, though not in Mark, might be considered a "minor disagreement" that would challenge the four-source theory of synoptic development, in which Matthew and Luke should not agree together against Mark in those cases where the triple tradition is in view. However, since we have here to deal with a vision-report, it is entirely likely that Matthew and Luke have adopted this term independently as a conventional means of presenting the vision.

50. Subsequent readers of the Gethsemane account (Luke 22:39–46) may have intuited a common thread here, associating revelation with sleep and Jesus' coming

Prayer and sleep are associated with vision in various and con-
tradictory ways in biblical literature, perhaps because both are
"liminal" activities, that is, activities on the "edge" of human
experience. Often fervent prayer and/or sleep are the conditions
by which a vision may be seen (e.g., Gen. 15:12; Job 4:13; Zech.
4:1), so that the end of the dream sequence is signaled by the
dreamer awakening and responding to the vision (e.g., Gen. 28:16;
Jer. 31:26; Matt. 1:24). However, at Isaiah 29:10–11 a deep sleep
is said to block the revelatory moment: "The LORD has poured
over you a deep sleep: He has sealed your eyes [the prophets]; he
has covered your heads [the seers]. For you this whole vision has
become nothing but words sealed in a scroll." So then, that the
disciples were sleeping when they saw Moses and Elijah (Luke
9:31–32) would seem at first blush to confirm the opinion of J. S.
Hanson, who refuses to distinguish between "dream" reports and
"vision" reports but coins the term "dream-vision report."[51] Yet
the situation is more complex than this. For it is as the disciples
become "fully awake" that they see the real object of visionary interest: "his glory" and the "two men standing with him." It appears
as though Luke is aware of the complex dynamic in apocalyptic
literature that makes use of both positive and negative aspects of
sleep in association with prayer and revelation.

For example, in Zechariah 4:1 (a prophetic text with affinities to
the genre of apocalypse), the angel is said to revive the prophet as
though waking someone from sleep and then reveals more to him.
Concerning this dynamic of sleeping and awakening in Zechariah
and its relationship to "what is real," Steven Tuell comments:
"This could mean that the vision . . . came in a dream. However,
the language . . . suggests that the prophet may have intended a
comparison: being summoned by the angel at the beginning of
the vision was *like* being awakened from sleep. For Zechariah,
the world of God's revelation is not less, but more real than the

---

ordeal with God's grace to comfort. The angelophany to Jesus alone, attested in later
manuscripts at Luke 22:43, matches the strengthening function of Moses and Elijah
at the transfiguration and likewise renders the sleep of the disciples as a narrative
commentary on their blindness to the crucial moment.

51. Hanson, "Dreams and Visions," 1408.

waking world. Entry into the visionary state was not like falling asleep, but like waking up!"[52] Visionary texts thus exploit both associations of sleep with the revelatory, sometimes depicting the seers as receiving visions in their sleep but sometimes speaking about the visions as inducing a coma from which the seer must be revived. This second dynamic is seen in Daniel 8:18; 10:9–10; and 10:19; as in 2 Esdras 10:30–31; 12:3b–10; 13:13b–21; and *1 Enoch* 14:24–15:1, where the seer is either asleep and wakens to be further instructed or struck down by the weightiness of the vision and needs to be revived before he can receive an interpretation, explanatory oracle, or explicatory vision. The revival and instruction of the seer is sometimes followed by mediating prayer and a priestly function for others of the faithful community who have not been privy to the revelation.

In Luke these tendencies are combined. The disciples begin by praying with Jesus, then aptly "sleep" while presumably they see an initial vision of the three in glory (though the omniscient narrator describes these things to the reader at this point), then awaken to "see" the vision in all its glory, with Jesus firmly established in the central position. Not all visions, then, are dream-visions. By reference to the conventions of apocalyptic vision-reports, we might speculate that authors who report waking visions intend that these should be taken very seriously, for they correspond to the time of deepest revelation and clear instruction. The three disciples, in Luke's account, are privy to a mystical and stupefying vision; they then are fully revived so as to understand the theological significance of what they are seeing. This pattern is followed by a dramatic surprise—the disciples are transformed from spectators or "seers" to actual participants in the numinous and "fear" as they enter "the cloud" (9:34). Though unique among the synoptic accounts, this entry into the world of the vision is no creative anomaly of Luke: in Exodus, Moses is illumined by

52. Steven Shawn Tuell, "Haggai-Zechariah: Prophecy after the Manner of Ezekiel," in *Thematic Threads in the Book of the Twelve*, ed. Aaron Schart and Paul L. Redditt, Beihefte zur Zeitschrift für die alttestamentliche Wissenschaft 325 (Berlin: de Gruyter, 2003), 282; see also Carol L. Meyers and Eric M. Meyers, *Haggai, Zechariah 1–8*, Anchor Bible 25B (Garden City, NY: Doubleday, 1987), 229.

his sight of the glory of the Lord. In apocalyptic texts, seers may
tour the heavenlies and may even be transformed by their sojourn
there, as in *1 Enoch* 71:11, where "Enoch" is transformed in the
presence of the heavenly hosts and perhaps even renamed "Son of
Man."[53] Luke, then, had to hand a general tradition of transformation by contact with the sacred and describes the transfiguration
as enveloping the three mortals who beheld it.

This intriguing personal dimension of the text is denied by
John Paul Heil, who, in a relatively new monograph on the transfiguration, argues that the third person plural pronoun (αὐτούς,
Luke 9:34) refers to the duo of Moses and Elijah rather than to
the three apostles.[54] That is, Moses and Elijah, rather than the
three followers, are seen as "entering the cloud." Heil gives lexi-
cal and contextual reasons for his exegetical decision but also is
highly dependent on an appeal to the genre of "pivotal mandatory
epiphany." That is, he considers the transfiguration event to be a
visionary epiphany with *transitional* status, not important in its
own right. Thus its sole purpose is to lead to the main teaching,
which focuses on Jesus, the one who will die a humiliating death
and who is the model for those who would follow God. Neither
Moses nor Elijah suffered such a death; only Jesus' path signifies
"a profound affirmation of the totality of the human condition,"
a path and affirmation that cannot "escape" but must exhibit "the
courage to embrace rejection, suffering and death."[55] The "enter-

---

53. The dating of this transformation passage in *1 Enoch* is uncertain and may not,
in fact, predate Luke. However, it is clear that the tradition of seers being transformed
by their mystical visions was established by the time the New Testament was written,
since Paul makes ironic reference to it in 2 Cor. 11:13–15. Similarly, *merkabah* practice,
though not texts, may have been established by early Hasmonean or even late Herodian
times. On this, see Ithamar Gruenwald, *Apocalyptic and Merkavah Mysticism* (Leiden:
Brill, 1980); Alan Segal, *Two Powers in Heaven: Rabbinic Reports about Christianity
and Gnosticism* (Leiden: Brill, 1977); D. Dimant and J. Strugnell, "The Merkabah
Vision in Second Ezekiel (4Q385 3)," *Revue de Qumran* 14 (1990): 331–48; Edith
Humphrey, "Why Bring the Word Down? The Rhetoric of Demonstration and Disclosure in Romans 9:30–10:21," in *Romans and the People of God*, ed. S. Soderlund
and N. T. Wright (Grand Rapids: Eerdmans, 1999), 129–48.

54. John Paul Heil, *The Transfiguration of Jesus: The Narrative Meaning and Function of Mark 9:2–8, Matthew 17:1–8, and Luke 9:28–36* (Rome: Editrice Pontificio
Instituto Biblico, 2000), 267.

55. Ibid., 319.

ing into the cloud of Moses and Elijah" enables the disciples to
fix their attention on Jesus alone.

Heil's emphasis on the figure of Jesus and the importance of
suffering is commendable. However, his exegetical move here is
counterintuitive, since the sentence does not make it clear that
Moses and Elijah are in view as the subject of the infinitive "to
enter" and it would be bizarre to detail the fear of the disciples
upon the disappearance of Moses and Elijah if the evangelist were
trying to call attention away from these two. Clearly, the sense
of the numinous is in view in Luke's telling of the story and is
significant, alongside the clear message about Jesus' person and
role in redemption. The most natural reading of the sentence is
that the three were afraid because of their own intimate contact
with the cloud. This adds a new dimension to the narrative, though
clearly the central figure of the story is Jesus "alone." To limit
the significance of this episode rigidly, however, is a pedestrian
move that does not appreciate the polyvalent potential of vision-
reports, a characteristic that we have seen throughout this study.
The artistry of Luke is such that he can allow the overtones that
accompany a vision-report to be sounded even while he carefully
directs the imagery toward a main end. His is the skill of a pianist
who judiciously uses the sustaining damper pedal to afford the
music a great depth and seamless quality without muddying the
main line of the tune. Luke is able, through the vibrant imagery
of this passage, to settle attention on Jesus even while he allows
the uncanny nature of the event to make its mark, including this
strange detail, that the disciples themselves "enter" into the glory
that they behold. Subsequent iconography and commentary on the
passage confirm a reading that both fixes the spotlight on Jesus
and affords the disciples a touch of glory, borrowed, as it were,
from their Master.

Sustaining a Rhetorical Tradition

In subsequent readings of the Lukan passage, the glory on
Jesus' face is understood as also transforming his disciples. They,
like Moses and Elijah, are illumined by the divine presence. Note

that it is only in Luke's Gospel that the luminescence is associated with Jesus' Old Testament interlocutors as well, who also appear "in glory" (9:31). As Ambrose puts it, "It was a luminous cloud that does not soak us with rainwater or the downpour of storm, but from dew that sprinkles the minds of men with faith sent by the voice of almighty God."[56] Peter speaks, "not knowing what he said," for there is no need to set up booths of dwelling; the disciples themselves are to become tabernacles of the divine presence through what Jesus is about to accomplish. Evident in the declaration, the transfigured face, and the glory cloud is the divine visitation by which God has gathered up those who are "with Jesus." The vision established both the unique identity of Jesus and the identity of the human players in the drama (apostle, prophet, law-giver) who live in the light of that mighty one.

From Luke's perspective, it would seem that the three are detailed both for their apostolic particular role in the formation of the early church and as stand-ins for the ongoing Christian community. So much is going on, as in a mediaeval landscape, that it is necessary to take stock of what we have seen and heard. Let us collect the images and themes: intimate prayer with God; communion with the faithful (as represented by Moses, Elijah, and the three); the careful recollection of God's law and revelation in the past; the reminder of God's redemption of Israel, pointing forward to the liberating cross; the personal gathering up of the disciples into the glory of God; and the centerpiece of the whole drama, Jesus, alone before them, with a divine oracle directing actors and readers to heed him, the chosen one. The final sentence ("they . . . told no one . . . in those days anything of what they had seen," 9:36) brings together vision, word, history, and mystery in an almost programmatic fashion.

In the Lukan account of this episode we see an artful use of the vision-report, demonstrably aware of the potential of vision and oracle, centrifugal and centripetal forces, innertextual and intertextual connections, and the force of culture and social

56. Ambrose, *Exposition of the Gospel of Luke* 7:19–20, cited in Just, *Luke*, 161.

conventions in the hearing and re-envisioning of a text. Luke's position of the passage differs from the Markan position but is equally as powerful. In Mark (followed, with some differences, by Matthew), the transfiguration heads the second great body of material, suggesting an answer to the question: "What kind of Messiah is this?" In Luke, the transfiguration occurs just before the great "journey" sequence by which Luke organizes much of Jesus' teaching material: Jesus, having been strengthened for the "road out" (literally, *ex-odos*), gives his disciples one last object lesson (9:37–43) and hard lesson on his fate (9:44–50) and then "sets his face" toward Jerusalem (9:51). The glory of the transfiguration, and its darker import, casts its glory and shadow on all that will occur in the rest of the Gospel until Jesus reflects on the meaning of his life as he journeys to Emmaus: suffering is the sine qua non for glory (24:26).

The rhetorical power of the episode, unleashed by Luke, is further demonstrated both in Paul's letters and in the Petrine tradition of the New Testament. Paul comments on the work of the Holy Spirit in the transformation of the host of believers (2 Cor. 3:18)—their very gaze on the Lord, or perhaps on the image of the Lord in each other, is used in order to transform them increasingly into glory (μεταμορφούμεθα). In the same context Paul speaks about the common beatific vision of all who are in Christ in terms that recall the transfiguration but that also picture enlightenment as a present gift by which the church can be assured of God's final re-creation and resurrection: "For God who said, 'Out of darkness let light shine,' has shone in our hearts to the end that we should have the light of the knowledge of the glory of God in the face of Christ Jesus" (2 Cor. 4:6).

Similarly, the first chapter of 2 Peter offers a scriptural commentary on the transfiguration of Jesus. The epistle writer tells us that for the apostles this sight of the transformed Jesus "confirmed" or "made sure" the "prophetic message" of the Old Testament; it is to the apostles' testimony concerning this Jesus, recorded now in the New Testament Scriptures, that his readers are directed, because the apostolic witness functions as "a lamp shining in a dark place." By way of Jesus, the Sun of Righteousness, the community, together with the prophets and the apostles, is to understand the revelation of God. Yet the light is conceived here not only as cognitive but also as transformative. The great glory and honor of the "Father" is shared by the "beloved Son" (1:16–17). It is because of this great *apokalypsis* that the epistle considers those in Christ as "by God's divine power . . . *called* into his own glory" (1:3) so that they might become "partakers of the divine nature" (1:4). Both Peter[57] and his addressees are envisaged as having their own imitative "exodus" to undergo (ἔξοδος, 1:15) as prelude to an "entry" (εἴσοδος, 1:11) into the kingdom (εἰς τὴν βασιλείαν) of God. So the faithful are pictured as following in the pattern of the Messiah, seen in Luke 24:26: it is "necessary . . . to suffer . . . and to enter . . . into glory."

The epistles of 2 Corinthians and 2 Peter, in concert with Luke, exploit the combined power of vision and interpretive word to encourage, confirm, and exhort, as well as to instruct. Indeed, both letters stress the Christian notion that God now has revealed a common vision to the community, rather than a privileged vision, coupled with a common *evangel* that interprets what has been seen. Yet another book of the New Testament declares that God has finally *spoken* by means of his express *image* in the "Son . . . who reflects God's glory" (Heb. 1:2–3). The letters of 2 Corinthians and 2 Peter, seemingly taking their cue from the transfiguration episode, would agree. In the person of the Messiah, word and vision are pictured as meeting with perfect equity.

"We have the prophetic *word* made more sure . . . as a *lamp* shining in a dark place." (2 Pet. 1:19)

"For the God who *said* . . . has *shone* . . . in the face of Christ." (2 Cor. 4:6)

---

57. The apostolic name is intended here as a reference to the letter's named narrator, not as a comment on authorship.

4

FIRING THE IMAGINATION

Visions with Embedded Propositions

(REVELATION 11:15–12:17; 1:12–3:22; 4:1–5:14)

O ur survey of various vision-reports in the New Testament until this point largely has been confined to authors who very likely understood the Greco-Roman conventions of speech craft, while they also were informed by prophetic and apocalyptic forms from Hebrew literature, including vision-reports. While in their writings these two worlds may at times collide, our analysis of visions adjacent to or within arguments has yielded a surprising result—reports of visions regularly function in a natural rather than an overbearing manner in the rhetoric of New Testament speeches or narratives. Frequently they sit relatively easily within their argumentative contexts and contribute to speeches conceived after the various classical modes. Moreover, they compel but rarely force a closure to the argument at hand; rather, they deepen or even complicate the rhetoric by virtue of their polyvalence. We move at this point to the furthest pole of our spectrum toward "open potential," as we consider the Apocalypse, a book composed almost entirely of allusive visionary language and seemingly far removed from the rational, discursive mode of Paul, more perplexing than the implicit rhetoric of Luke's repeated narratives, and less univocal than the transfiguration episodes.

Over three centuries ago, Robert Boyle, a chemist and apologist for Christianity, depicted the disdain for Hebrew oratory that was common in an age much influenced by the classical sensibilities:

> Their Dark and Involv'd Sentences, their Figurative and Parabolical Discourses; their Abrupt and Maimed Way of expressing themselves which often leaves much place to Guesses at the Sense; and their neglect of connecting Transitions, which often leaves us at a losse for the Method and Coherence of what they Write; are Qualities, that our Rhetoricians do not more generally Dislike, than their Practice.[1]

Boyle himself did not share the prejudice of his age against Hebrew rhetoric, yet he was obliged to excuse the infelicities of visionary style by reference to the "genius of those times."[2] It has only been in the last seventy years or so that our own day has emerged from this academic allergy to "parabolical" and mysterious discourse; so attention has turned, once again, to the final book of the canon. Certainly the prophetic and the "apocalyptic"[3] breathe a different air from classical rhetoric—so different, in fact, that some may question whether violence is done to the book of Revelation when we compare it to the classical models of speech. The rhetorical dimension of visionary genres such as apocalyptic, however, has

1. Robert Boyle, *Some Considerations Touching the Style of the Holy Scriptures* (London: printed for Henry Herringman, 1661), 158–59, as cited in *The Hebrew Bible in Literary Criticism*, ed. Alex Preminger and L. Greenstein (New York: Ungar, 1986), 217–18.

2. Ibid., 218.

3. On the movement away from the use of this adjective-qua-noun, see the introduction to Edith Humphrey, *The Ladies and the Cities: Transformation and Apocalyptic Identity in* Joseph and Aseneth, 4 Ezra, *the Apocalypse, and* The Shepherd of Hermas, Journal for the Study of the Pseudepigrapha: Supplement Series 17 (Sheffield: Sheffield Academic Press, 1995); and on the dangers inherent in it, see the helpful article by Robert Webb, "'Apocalyptic': Observations on a Slippery Term," *Journal of Near Eastern Studies* 49 (1990): 115–26.

been demonstrated in such studies as E. Schüssler Fiorenza's commentary on Revelation[4] and J. J. Collins's articulation of apocalypses as having an illocutionary function.[5] More recently, scholars collaborating in a Society of Biblical Literature group have been bold enough to investigate the "rhetorical dimensions of apocalyptic discourse,"[6] and Tina Pippin has responded passionately to what she regards as the pernicious rhetoric of gender in a book that is "not a safe space for women."[7] Like the Gospel narratives, apocalypses are not well comprehended as sheer artifacts, for they aim to persuade.

However, what is the best way to study the rhetorical and literary impact of this book? The seer John surely differs from those New Testament authors for whom we can make constraining arguments concerning their self-conscious use of classical devices and rhetorical forms.[8] Most would assume that the Apocalypse displays either a natural or a contrived Semitic atmosphere and so must be considered in terms of Hebrew models of disputation and proclamation. Two contrasting points may be made here. First, it has been argued cogently that the classical species have a heuristic value, even when applied to "alien" texts: see

4. Elisabeth Schüssler Fiorenza, *Revelation: Vision of a Just World*, Proclamation Commentaries (Minneapolis: Fortress, 1991).

5. John J. Collins, *The Apocalyptic Imagination: An Introduction to Jewish Apocalyptic Literature* (New York: Crossroad, 1987), 32; also in the revised *The Apocalyptic Imagination: An Introduction to Jewish Apocalyptic Literature* (Grand Rapids: Eerdmans, 1998), 41.

6. Carey and Bloomquist, *Vision and Persuasion*; Watson, *Intertexture of Apocalyptic Discourse*.

7. Tina Pippin, *Death and Desire: The Rhetoric of Gender in the Apocalypse of John*, Literary Currents in Biblical Interpretation (Louisville: Westminster John Knox, 1992), 80.

8. Even in the cases of Paul and Luke some critics have demurred, wondering whether these two were informed by classical rhetoric or considered the Aristotelian categories inadequate. For a helpful discussion of the problem, see W. Wuellner, "Jesus' Sermon in Luke 12:1–13:9," in *Persuasive Artistry: Studies in New Testament Rhetoric in Honor of George A. Kennedy*, ed. Duane F. Watson, Journal for the Study of the New Testament: Supplement Series 30 (Sheffield: JSOT Press, 1991), 93–110. Wuellner seeks here to consider a sermonic passage in terms of rhetoric, without ignoring the literary genre and without specific reference to "Aristotelian" rhetoric. He finds promising the "motivational" categories of Fischer, "Motive View of Communication," 131–39.

the practice of Yehoshua Gitay in analyzing Hebrew prophecy, where he cites Quintilian: "men [sic] discovered our art before ever they proceeded to teach it" (*Institutio Oratoria* 7.10).[9] Second, although classical strategies may illuminate an alien text, it is important to ask which critical spectacles are more suited to a particular job of observation. In light of these observations, the classical model will be (advisedly) applied to our passages, even while care is taken to consider other ways of understanding the rhetorical strength of the Apocalypse. Analysis can in fact show that classical categories are not incongruent in a study of the Apocalypse's rhetoric. Rather, the Apocalypse is revealed as a work characterized by cultural syncretism, and as such it demonstrates competence in both Hebrew[10] and Greco-Roman conventions. A rhetorical analysis of the Apocalypse (or parts of it) may thus be guided, in part, by comparison of its speeches to Greco-Roman rhetoric. However, we will also go beyond the concerns of original exigency, species of argument, formal components of argumentation, and striking ornamentation to ask questions associated with the "new rhetoric"[11]—questions of persuasion and "practical" force, oral sensibility, communal assumptions, and performance.[12] Since the genre apocalypse is strongly marked as a "literary" form, our rhetorical analysis must be at every step accompanied by appreciation of aesthetic, dramatic, and structural devices.

9. Yehoshua Gitay, *Prophecy and Persuasion: A Study of Isaiah 40–48*, Forum Theologiae Linguisticae 14 (Bonn: Linguistica Biblica, 1981), 39.

10. The quest for typical Hebrew rhetoric is complicated by the fact that there are no living examples of Hebrew rhetoric or any "handbooks" or theoretical writings comparable to the instruction of the anonymous writer of the *Rhetorica ad Herennium*, Aristotle (*Ars Rhetorica, Rhetorica ad Alexandrum*, attr.), Quintilian (*Institutio Oratoria*), Cicero (*De Inventione*), Hermogenes (*Progymnasmata*), and others. We must make our own observations by comparing the various prophetic and apocalyptic written works and extrapolating from these what the oral conventions must have been that informed such writings.

11. Perelman and Olbrechts-Tyteca, *New Rhetoric*.

12. For a lucid taxonomy and consideration of various methods, see W. Wuellner, "Rhetorical Criticism and Its Theory in Culture-Critical Perspective: The Narrative Rhetoric of John 11," in *Text and Interpretation: New Approaches in the Criticism of the New Testament*, ed. P. J. Hartin and J. H. Petzer (Leiden: Brill, 1991), 170–85.

We begin with Revelation 11:15–12:17, a bewildering sequence that juxtaposes the suffering of God's people, the fall of the adversary, and the victory of the Arch-Martyr, the Child/Lamb. We will then consider the messages to the seven churches in Revelation 2–3, which are carefully construed so as to introduce major themes and promises of the Apocalypse. Finally, we will engage in a reading of chapters 4–5, a throne-room vision designed to move the reader to worship rather than to engage in argumentation. Where our earlier examples of vision-report were governed by word and only punctuated by vision, here the opposite obtains: vision predominates, punctuated by key declarations or propositions. Among the three examples, differences are also found in the precise relationship of narrative to discourse, the overall mode of speech, the formation of the discourse, and the specific place that the vision occupies within the implied argument. These features confirm our conviction that a delicate balance of rhetorical and literary analysis is required.

Rhetoric, Action, and Declaration: Revelation 11–12

The quest to bring a rhetorical perspective to bear on a narrative found in the Apocalypse is immediately deflected by a host of substantive and methodological questions. What voice shall we use to speak about this book? How can we retell and redemonstrate its sounds and sights? Do we hear or use the voice of a classical (i.e., Greco-Roman) rhetor? Do we hear or adopt the accents of a Hebrew prophet? And what about orality and textuality? How do we study rhetoric in a text, in *this* text? Is the argument in the story, or does argument interpret the story? Do we see a pastiche of sources skillfully interwoven by a scribe? Do we listen to and behold an integrated narrative designed for an effect? Do we see a fantastic mystery that invites us to experience by proxy the first experience of a visionary? Are sights or sounds primary? And which sights and sounds? What tools can we use, which spectacles or cornet to see and hear most plainly? And having heard and seen, what difference does this make to us? Will the text move us in a similar or different way than it did its "original audience"? Can we responsibly consider ourselves as members of its implied audience, that is, the larger potential audience suggested by the world of the text?

As is customary in rhetorical study, the first step is to isolate a suitable unit for analysis. Such a preparatory move, though helpful in delimiting the task, unfortunately risks damaging the character of an extended narrative so that its overall rhetoric is obscured. With the Apocalypse the situation is even more complex, since the book presents itself as a macro-genre[13] and as such employs a wide variety of rhetorical and literary strategies suited to its various moments. With full recognition of the challenge that this visionary narrative represents, I propose to consider a passage from the central portion of the Apocalypse. This selection (Rev. 11:15–12:17), like the entire book, presents us with a daunting but intriguing juxtaposition of narrative and declaration, symbol and argumentation. Contrary to the usual prescription for rhetorical analysis, I have deliberately chosen a section that will not present itself by consensus as an easily determined unit. In terms of the literary structure of the Apocalypse, some will see the unit as overriding a fundamental division of the book into two halves: chapters 1–11 and 12–22.[14] Some might argue that the passage finds a more natural and poignant ending with 13:1, where the dragon takes his stand on the shore of the sea. Yet 13:1 does not possess the character of a full cadence, since the dragon's marginal position sets in motion the events of the chapter that it heads; in harmonic terms it is a "deceptive" progression, from dominant to minor submediant, rather than a "perfect cadence," which ends with the tonic, or "home key," chord. We might as well face the artificiality of our scholarly excision of passages. This is a lesson directed to us by every grand narrative, including the Gospels and Acts, but most forcibly by the Apocalypse, which proceeds by intercalation and the knitting together of parts. The section

---

13. This book contains conventions of the apocalypse, prophecy, and the epistle, not to mention numerous subsidiary genres such as the "edict," mythological narrative, various forms of hymns, imprecations, and the like.

14. Structure will be considered more carefully below.

11:15–12:17 has been chosen for internal reasons that will become apparent, but also so as to push deliberately against the constraints of rhetorical analysis by unit and to acknowledge the fundamental "knit-together" quality of this arch-narrative. We will begin with a bird's eye view or "tour" of the terrain that tries to capture the impact this passage might have on an imaginative ideal reader.

First Tour

A trumpet sounds—not just any trumpet, but the one played by the seventh angel, the final herald of a dramatic series. At any time the sounding of a trumpet would be compelling, but at this point in John's vision the sound is particularly imposing. Let us flash back to the earlier chapters of the Apocalypse and recall that the series of events heralded by the seven trumpets has been interrupted by the events of chapter 10 and half of chapter 11. Not only has there been a rupture of the sequence but we have been kept deliberately in suspense by the angelic acknowledgement of that rupture and the promise of its resumption. At 10:6 the mighty angel swears with great solemnity that the delay[15] has come to an end and that the seventh trumpet, the last one, will soon be sounded, marking the revelation of the mystery of God (10:7)—an event expected by God's prophets. As we witness John eating the little scroll, his commission to prophecy, his measuring of the temple, and the drama of the martyred and ascended witnesses, we nurture in the back of our minds the solemn declaration of the angel: we are anticipating the sounding of this trumpet, the revelation of this mystery. There is a faint rumbling, a gentle portent at 11:14, as the "third woe" (that is, the seventh trumpet) is announced—and then that trumpet sounds!

Given the promise, the suspense, the announcement, and the auditory jolt, we are predisposed to sit up and take notice: at last, the mystery of God! Nor are we disappointed. Great voices (φωναὶ μεγάλαι) in heaven proclaim it: "The kingdom of this world

---

15. Contrary to popular opinion, and American hymnody, the angel does not predict the end of "time," though the term for chronological time is used (χρόνος), but an end to the period of delay.

has become the kingdom of our Lord and of his Messiah, and he will reign forever and ever" (11:15b). In response to the mystery, the attendants in the heavenly throne room fall from their own thrones and worship God on their faces in chorus (11:16). They render thanks to the One of many names, who has great (μεγάλην) power, because he has begun to reign, has been victorious over nations, and has brought the time of judgment for all, great (μεγάλους) and small (11:17–18). Still more arresting sights and sounds ensue: the heavenly temple opens, and the holiest object, the mysterious ark, is seen accompanied by appropriate fireworks and rumblings—and great (μεγάλη) hail, presumably rained down on the earth (11:19). Everything is described in these superlative terms. If we are of a biblical mind set, we may be reminded of the pyrotechnics on Mount Sinai that prefaced the giving of the Torah. Whatever our competence in biblical literature, we are prepared for significant events. We are peering into the holiest of holies, and if we have read the Apocalypse sequentially we will call to mind that at the finale of the seal sequence similar celestial disturbances signaled the appearance of the seven angels with trumpets (8:5).

This dramatic throne-room scene (11:13–19) functions, then, both as a fulfillment of earlier promises and events and as an elaborate introduction to the drama of chapter 12. The solemn pronouncement of the mystery of God, that is, the arrival of his rule, has opened a new chapter in our hearing and seeing: anything can happen now! Again, we are not disappointed. Just as the ark had appeared in the heavenlies in 11:19, so now appears another great (μέγα) portent (12:1) without further introduction. This queenly figure, accompanied by sun, moon, and stars, cries out in a wordless but pregnant voice and is opposed by another sign, a great (μέγας, 12:3) dragon, who sweeps and stoops and seeks to devour (12:4). The woman's newborn son is rescued to heaven, and the woman herself flees to a safe place in the wilderness (12:5–6). More lore is divulged concerning this dragon: there is war in heaven between the dragon of many names and the angels so that the dragon is cast out (12:7–9). There follows another great (μεγάλην) pronouncement from heaven (12:10–12), which, stripped of its oracular solemnity, has this to say: "Exactly *now* has come the kingdom of God because of the victory—so act accordingly! But beware, for that dragon is not quite finished!" Yet again we are subjected to the sights and sounds of persecution and war: pouring water, swallowing mouths, whirring wings, pursuit, rescue, and ongoing rampage (12:13–17). The tumult is more than literary: no longer are we mere observers of the drama, but we find ourselves encoded there, rhetorically addressed by virtue of our position on earth (12:12b) and actively embroiled in battle, if we consider ourselves bearers of the "testimony of Jesus" (12:17).

Here, then, are the sights and sounds of our chosen narrative: long-awaited pronouncement (11:15), response and sign (11:16–19), triptych of persecution and battle (woman and dragon, 12:1–6; war in heaven, 12:7–9; dragon and woman's children, 12:13–17), and interpreting declaration (12:10–12). Both the declaration and the final part of the triptych usher the reader into the drama, for the second part of the declaration implicates us ("those on earth," 12:12b), and the final verses of the sequence bring the battle to our level (12:13–17). Suddenly we are no longer listening to John's story and hearing voices in heaven; we are a part of it all, willingly or by compulsion. The καιρός ([specific or critical] "time," 11:18) of the arriving kingdom, depicted in the drama and the proclamations, emphasizes that the dragon's καιρόν (12:12) is short and calls us to our own moment of crisis. Are we dwellers of heaven or of earth? Who is truly great? How are we implicated in the battle, in the suffering, in the judgment, in the victory? The rhetoric of the unfolding layers of vision-narrative manipulates our perspective from heaven and into the holiest place (upward and inward), then down to earth and into our own situation, holy or otherwise. Similarly the strange argument of the spoken declarations gives voice to the speechless woman and her children—blood ends in victory and martyrdom itself speaks out (c.f., τὸν λόγον τῆς μαρτυρίας, "the word *of* their witness/martyrdom," 12:11). Now has come salvation, therefore rejoice!

Sights and Structure

Let us look more carefully at the structure of the narrative before going on to consider the actual argument of its embedded speeches and the overall rhetoric of the narrative. On all counts, the events of chapters 11 and 12 have been considered as (a) central and key sequence(s). Some see chapter 11 as concluding the first half of the Apocalypse, while others place these chapters in the center of a series.[16] Of course, no "structure" traced in a book by readers is a final decision, and the form that is afforded to a piece may vary with perspective. The discernment of structure in a composition is for the purposes of understanding the piece better, and some variation is therefore to be expected among readers unless the writing signals its structure by means of titles and subtitles. This is particularly true of books that obscure their lines of composition, such as the Apocalypse. Close attention to the "sections" of this work will demonstrate that the author has cunningly "inserted" a subsequent sequence into the previous one, as with the "trumpet" sequence that is "contained" within the last seal (8:1–2) or the "bowl" sequence that is "contained" in the sounding of the last trumpet.[17] Again, the seer uses the technique of "intercalation," that is, short "displaced" passages that are transposed into the next section and so link sections together. These merging techniques make

16. This chapter is seen as the beginning of the second half of the drama by Adela Yarbro Collins, *The Combat Myth of the Book of Revelation*, Harvard Dissertations in Religion 9 (Missoula, MT: Scholars Press, 1976); and Henry Barclay Swete, *The Apocalypse of John* (London: MacMillan, 1906). However, the following scholars place it in the center of a series: N. W. Lund, *Chiasmus in the New Testament* (Chapel Hill: University of North Carolina Press, 1942), 327–28; J. G. Gager, "The Attainment of Millennial Bliss through Myth and the Book of Revelation," in *Visionaries and Their Apocalypses*, ed. P. D. Hanson (Philadelphia: Fortress, 1982), 146–55; Alan James Beagley, *The "Sitz im Leben" of the Apocalypse with Particular Reference to the Role of the Church's Enemies* (Berlin: de Gruyter, 1987); and Elisabeth Schüssler Fiorenza, "The Composition and Structure of the Book of Revelation," in *The Book of Revelation: Justice and Judgment* (Philadelphia: Fortress, 1985), 159–80. For a convenient charting of several representative structures, see Humphrey, *Ladies and the Cities*, 82–83.

17. Though there is an interruption in the narrative (section "D" described below), there are plenty of textual cues that 11:15–19 continues at 15:5–6.

the quest for subparts difficult, though as readers we will want to manage the kaleidoscopic effect of the visions by looking for sequences that begin and end, even if the overtures and closures are softly blurred.

My preference—with a bit of fine tuning—is the structuring suggestion of Schüssler Fiorenza, who understands the whole of the Apocalypse as a set of interlocking brackets, ABCDC′B′A′,[18] with the central episode marked by the appearance of "the little scroll" (roughly designated as chapters 10–14, with a brief intercalation at the beginning of chapter 15). Large structural chiasms are common in antiquity and may well have served as a mnemonic device for epic poetry; in written works, however, the effect is to enshrine the central piece (in our case, D) in a series of "hedges." The central piece provides the clue to the work's most powerful meanings, which the reader is obliged to strive to understand. One travels to the center through a set of complex ideas and episodes, and then travels out from the center to a conclusion of sorts. For an apocalypse this is an apt structure, because apocalypses are characterized by mystery.

In this structure the section labeled D may be viewed as the "holy of holies" of a literary temple, that inner core that is to be taken very seriously. This little scroll stands in the middle of the larger epic flow of the Apocalypse: introduction (A), promises (B), seals and trumpets (C), bowls (C′), fulfillment (B′), epilogue (A′). So then, D "interrupts" this larger drama but also retells the story and so comments on it from a heavenly perspective, casting light on the implications of God's dealings with his enemies, the earth, and his people. At the very center of this central section is chapter 12: the gravity of this chapter is signaled at 11:15 by an aural prelude, the intercalated seventh trumpet. So then, chapter 12 takes on not only a structural but also a thematic centrality. Its own detailed format can be outlined as follows:

18. Schüssler Fiorenza, "Composition and Structure," 175; and Humphrey, *Ladies and the Cities*, esp. 97–100.

Introduction   Two portents, 12:1–3
  A Woman persecuted and flight, 12:4–6
    B War in heaven, 12:7–9
      C Declaration, 12:10–12
  A′ Woman persecuted and flight, 12:13–16
    B′ War on earth, 12:17 (and continuing in 13:1)

Earlier commentators on this passage, and studies concerned with a history-of-religions approach, consider the various sources that John used, such as the presence of the Leto-Python-Apollo motif[19] juxtaposed with the Hebraic myth of the expulsion of Satan. Our interest here is in the juxtaposition and the overall effect. In a full chiasm, the reversed return to B′ and A′ has the effect of bringing the sequence to completion, or closure. Here, however, there is a modified chiasmic structure (ABCA′B′)[20] that opens up the sequence for a "to-be-continued" effect at 12:17 and 13:1. However, the interlacing of A and B, with C in the center, still achieves the typical effects of a chiasm. That is, it connects the major sections A and B (the primordial battle and the plight of God's people) and calls attention to the central term, C. John's manner of introducing the narrative suggests that this is not simply a vision vouchsafed to him but an indication of the way things stand: unlike other visionary sequences, it is not his usual "I saw (and behold)" that we read but the impersonal passive ὤφθη,

19. See esp. W. Bousset, *Die Offenbarung Johannis* (Gottingen: Vandenhoeck und Ruprecht, 1906); Yarbro Collins, *Combat Myth*; and Yarbro Collins, "Feminine Symbolism in the Book of Revelation," *Biblical Interpretation* 1 (1993): 20–33.

20. Antoninus King Wai Siew (*The War between the Two Beasts and the Two Witnesses: A Literary-Structural Analysis of Revelation 12.1–14.5*, Library of New Testament Studies 283 [New York: T&T Clark, 2005], 125–26) objects to this imperfect chiasm, suggesting a different structural reading that places vv. 7–12 (labeled "The War in Heaven") in the central portion of a chiasm (which in itself forms part of a larger concentric pattern). Given the kaleidoscopic nature of John's visions, different perspectives will yield different patterns: we should not assume that structural suggestions can be "reified." His reading has the advantage of concentrating on the places where action occurs, and it elucidates an interesting parallel between the "escape" of the child and the "escape" of the mother. However, it neither distinguishes between the forms of conflict (persecution vs. battle) nor notes the shift in genre between vision and oracle. In particular, it does not observe the embedded nature of the proclamation in vv. 10–12 and the significant manner in which this statement subtly interprets the actions in heaven and on earth.

"*There was seen* a sign in heaven."[21] Notice also how at the end of the passage (B') the war motif is imported into the struggle between the dragon and the woman, thus firmly linking the two sequences: "Then the dragon was angry with the woman and went off to make war on the rest of her offspring" (12:17).

In the midst of this complex narrative comes the declaration (C). The declaration has itself a threefold structure of statement, explanation, and response. God's reign has come, since the accuser has been conquered. How has this happened? Through the blood of the Lamb and the word of testimony. So then? Rejoice, or be woeful, depending on one's situation "in heaven" or "on earth." The odd interaction of this victorious declaration with the surrounding rehearsal of visionary conflict is notable. Two visionary sequences—the dragon and the woman, and the heavenly conflict with Satan—are skillfully spliced together and sandwiched around the declaration. Moreover, the conflict leads to victory, where it is followed by a declaration of victory; the declaration itself is slightly bifurcated by the concluding woe, and the conflictual imagery is resumed in the narrative, leaving a sense of open endedness. The open endedness is accentuated by the sequences that follow the chapter under discussion. John goes on in chapter 13 to picture the ravages of the dragon's beast and the judgments of God on those who join the beast. We are led to ask: why this sequence? What is the relationship of the declaration of victory and the interconnected description of conflict? What is the effect of this juxtaposed ongoing war and the confident declaration of closure? Clearly, the "victory song" (12:10–12) is no simple declaration, but through its structure and careful interweaving with the narrative it becomes a commentary on the ongoing war. There

21. David E. Aune suggests that the passage is not to be understood as a vision because of this change in introductory formula ("Intertextuality and the Genre of the Apocalypse," in *1991 Seminar Papers*, ed. Eugene H. Lovering Jr., Society of Biblical Literature Seminar Papers Series 30 [Atlanta: Scholars Press, 1991], 156). This conclusion seems to ignore the overall framework of the Apocalypse, in which these are things seen by John from his heavenly perspective established in Rev. 4 and reaffirmed at 10:1. Nevertheless, the "appear" formula is not indifferent and has a particular rhetorical effect. See also Leonard Thompson (*The Book of Revelation—Apocalypse and Empire* [Oxford: Oxford University Press, 1990], 38), who notes the difference but nonetheless considers these to be visions.

is an argument of sorts implied through the unusual juxtaposition of two narratives and the chiasm.

Sounds and Fury: The Implied Argument

How should the words of the loud voice be understood, then? Is this a victory song? Should we take the form-critical route and compare it to victory hymns of the Hebrew Bible? Notable similarities to this form would include the key word "for" (ὅτι, vv. 10b, 12b). This connecting word introduces the reason for rejoicing, followed by a description of the mighty deeds and the summons to rejoice. Compare, for example, Psalm 98 (97 LXX):

> Sing to the LORD a new song,
> *for* [LXX ὅτι, Hebrew *kî*] he has done marvelous things.
> His right hand and his holy arm have worked salvation for
>   him. . . .
> Shout for joy to the LORD, all the earth.

Here the purpose clause, like many of those found in the Hebrew Bible, gives the reason for unqualified joy. We have seen already that the positioning of the declaration within John's rhetoric at 12:10–12 is more ambivalent, though joy is enjoined. Moreover, the declaration itself concludes with a woe, which is unprecedented. Though the victory songs in the Psalter may warn[22] the enemies of the victor against resistance, they never highlight the power of the adversary who has been (or is to be) vanquished.

Analysts have, of course, pointed out this anomaly already. Those concerned to fit the declaration into a particular hymnic form have adopted the method of Procrustes by lopping off the woe found in verse 12b. See, for example, John J. O'Rourke, who assumes that the passage was originally a Semitic hymn, a pure paean of joy and praise, later modified by John.[23] Other analogies to the declaration might be drawn with profit, notably similarities

22. Thompson (*Revelation—Apocalypse and Empire*, 90) includes warnings as typical of victory hymns but does not comment on the difference here.

23. John J. O'Rourke, "The Hymns of the Apocalypse," *Catholic Biblical Quarterly* 30 (1968): 409.

to the songs of Zion or to the enthronement songs of Israel. A parallel to the latter form is especially tantalizing given the presence of the following themes and topics in the declarations and adjacent narratives of 11:16–18 and 12:10–12: the anointed one, the quelling of raging nations, the ascent to the throne of a destined child, the reference to covenant, and a strong injunction to acclaim the King.[24] While the intertextual echoes (esp. Ps. 2 and 110) are clear, consideration of the enthronement psalms as a parallel to this declaration has one drawback: Typically, enthronement songs have an atmosphere of security and envisage an ongoing, settled rule of YHWH. This is lacking in our declaration.

However, there is a point of contact between the rejoice-woe contrast and Hebrew literature. It is interesting to note that psalms frequently conclude with a studied dualism (Ps. 1:6; 2:11–12; 99:8–9; 110:6–7; etc.). In the royal psalms such dualisms highlight the sense of security and justice. In Revelation 12:10–12 the impact of the dualism is more complex, giving a sense of peace with one hand ("rejoice") as it takes away security with the other ("woe"). Thus the dualism, shared here with other pieces, takes on a unique function. Our frustration in the quest for a genre against which to compare this passage leads to contemplation on the purpose of finding generic labels. There is no such thing as the "Platonic" form of a Gospel or an enthronement psalm: to some extent, every passage or larger piece is sui generis, containing idiosyncratic elements or distinct combinations of elements. "Genre" is a heuristic concept, not a "thing" in itself, for we determine genre by comparing several pieces of literature that have marked similarities and making an abstraction. Even in the case of a piece that defies clear classification, comparison remains helpful in discerning the work's remarkable rhetorical technique, organization, and effect. In the book of Psalms, it may be remarked that there are both unequivocal hymns of praise with an epideictic purpose; there are also mixed psalms, such as the "songs of Zion," that combine epideictic praise with deliberation—a call to agree with the speaker and join in praise

24. On coronation rites and the possible exigency of enthronement hymns, see, among others, Roland de Vaux, *Ancient Israel: Its Life and Institutions*, trans. John McHugh (London: Darton, Longman and Todd, 1961), 102–7.

as well. The impact of Revelation 12:10–12 is neither simple nor combined in genre but provides the reader with an enigma. That is, the two impulses of "praise" and "woe" work against each other, requiring the reader to question which "shoe" fits.

Perhaps further insight may be gleaned by considering the identity and role of the "loud voice in heaven" that makes the declaration at 12:10. Klaus Peter Jörns considers the voice to be identical with the loud voices heard already (e.g., at 11:15 and 11:19), that is, the choir of the martyred under the throne who unendingly praise God and the Lamb.[25] Such a view leads us back to classing the declaration as a hymn, a hypothesis that seems to have been adopted by the NRSV translation, which renders the word λέγοντες (literally "saying") as "singing" at 11:17. David Aune offers a more compelling suggestion: the voice functions *alongside* the voices of the elders and other speakers in the heavenly throne room and thus plays with these actors the conventional ceremonial of the court so as to ascribe ultimate power to the King of Kings.[26] Here, the liturgical meets the political, as is to be expected in an ancient piece.

In offering this hypothesis, Aune links the voices to the ceremonial prostrating of the elders, the decision-making function of the Ruler when called on by plaintiffs, and the argument *e consensū omnium* ("from the consensus of all") made by the throngs of beings who concur in the acclamation of the King. The attendants' words of acclamation comment on the action of the Ruler and the events that are taking place, acting rather like the chorus in a Greek drama,[27] a chorus composed of a single leader and multiple voices speaking antiphonally. Aune argues that the effect of this heavenly court ceremonial, the pure and holy panegyric of the heavenly throne room, renders earthly imperial ceremony a mere parody of the real thing.[28]

25. Klaus Peter Jörns, *Das hymnischen Evangelium: Untersuchungen zu Aufbau, Funktion und Herkunft der hymnischen Stücke in der Johannesoffenbarung*, Studien zum Neuen Testament 5 (Gütersloh: Gerd Mohr, 1971), 91.

26. David E. Aune, "The Influence of Roman Imperial Court Ceremonial on the Apocalypse of John," *Biblical Research* 18 (1983): 5–26.

27. Ibid., 14.

28. A detailed and fascinating discussion of irony in the Apocalypse is to be seen in the work of Harry O. Maier, *Apocalypse Recalled: The Book of Revelation after Christendom* (Minneapolis: Fortress, 2002).

Aune, in treating the book of Revelation generally, refers to the rites of *consecratio* (the deification of a ruler), *accessio* (the enthronement), and *adventus* (the visitation of a subject people by the ruler or his emissaries), all of which would have been well known to the audience of Asia Minor. Shouts of acclamation, both spontaneous and ritualistic, accompanied such rites and included the naming of the ruler, reasons for his greatness (which included, by the way, salvation), and the recital of his mighty deeds. It seems to me that the act of *adventus*[29] is most helpful in understanding the power of 12:10–12. Nor is its impact wholly lost on a late twentieth-century audience, which may not have much present memory of such ceremony but has encoded in its art, film, and literature what is appropriate for the arrival of royalty. Already in chapter 11 we have been prepared by the heavenly angel to receive the victorious ruler. Indeed, in 11:15, after the sounding of the seventh trumpet, we hear a victory announcement from heaven and the answering acclaim of elders, who address God in the second person. In a piece that sounds remarkably like the *adventus* welcome speech,[30] the elders thank the heavenly Ruler on behalf of a larger group of subjects, eager for benevolent judgment. Here again, in chapter 12, the same expectation is created. Though there is no direct second-person address to God, we can visualize an attendant announcing to all within reach of his mighty voice that the ruler is at the door: "*Now* have come the salvation and the power and the kingdom and the authority." He then goes on to explain the benefits of this rule (in this case, the emancipation of the subjects) and describes the heroism of the king and his army: all of these are topics of the *adventus* speech but are here narrated in third person and directed toward the subjects rather than in homage to the ruler. The proclamation closes fittingly in a call to rejoice. Like the encomium of praise, this epideictic declaration

29. For a consideration of later *Adventus Augusti* coinage, openness of the text, and the possible reinterpretation of the Apocalypse in Hadrian's time, see Larry Kreitzer, "Sibylline Oracles 8, The Roman Imperial Adventus Coinage of Hadrian and the Apocalypse of John," *Journal for the Study of the Pseudepigrapha* 4 (1989): 69–84.

30. See Sabine MacCormack, *Art and Ceremony in Late Antiquity* (Berkeley: University of California Press, 1981), esp. 8, for a description of the *adventus*.

introduces the matter, narrates the reason for it, praises the achievements of the ruler, and concludes with a call to honor him:

Introduction   ("I heard a loud voice," 10a)

   Narration

           Proposition: ("Now have come the salvation and the power and the kingdom. . . and the authority . . ." 10b)

      and

           Reason: ("for the accuser of our brethren has been thrown down . . ." 10c)

Achievements

           Victory: (*felicitas*; "But they have conquered him by the blood of the Lamb and by the word of their testimony," 11a)

           Humility: (*pietas*; "for they did not cling to life, even in the face of death," 11b)

Conclusion

           Call to rejoice: ("Rejoice, then, you heavens and those who dwell in them,"12a)

           [anomalous woe contrast ("But woe to the earth and the sea!" 12b)]

A direct appeal to the *adventus*, however, like the hypothesis of a victory hymn or of an enthronement psalm, cannot account for verse 12b, the declaration of woe, and the subtle interaction of the hymn with the battle/persecution narrative. However, if we agree with Aune and Maier that John uses the classical motifs and forms in an ironic manner in order to disestablish the pretending, earthly, empirical powers, then the reason for the exceptional "woe" of verse 12b becomes clear. Here the court ceremonial and symbolism function to undercut their imperial correlates even while they acclaim the true Ruler. To recognize God's rule is to understand that the fury of the dragon and his imperial representatives is inevitable, but short lived. The establishment of the true, arriving Ruler involves the judgment of the pretender and his minions, so that the epideictic tenor of the declaration takes on forensic overtones.

The symbolism and echoes of rhetoric, then, may function in an inverse as well as in a direct way. If the declaration of 12:10–12 is merely seen as a projection of Christian worship or simple reapplication of Hebrew praise songs on the events of heaven, then we would be hard pressed to explain the thrust of 12b. Similarly, it is difficult to see a place for the *adventus* within a picture of ongoing war and persecution. If, however, the rhetoric functions by also parodying the activities of the earthly locus whence it is drawn, then the subtlety of John's artistry, both literary and rhetorical, can be better recognized. The *adventus* of the true Messiah, the true King of the cosmos, is greeted by true ceremony (worship and prayer) and with joy; the diabolic *adventus* of the dragon is a source of woe, even though the Pretender will have his short-lived day of ceremony (13:4). We are asked through the direct and indirect rhetoric to consider which rule is truly "great."

Some, like Fischer, have analyzed rhetoric by asking questions about how speech motivates its readership. In terms of his motivational modes, the declaration of 12:10–12, as it stands in its completeness and in connection with the surrounding visionary narrative, is both affirmatory and subversive. The overall direction of the rhetoric is not to reaffirm or redirect hope but to establish that hope while subverting usual categories. John speaks to those who see themselves as marginalized (in the desert with the refugee woman) and allows them to hear the heavenly heralding of a King. Similarly, he intimates that there will be a righteous marginalization (11:10, 18) and imminent condemnation of the pretender to the throne. The loud voice in heaven, as a component within the twin narratives of the woman and the war, enacts an *adventus*, arguing in encomium style for the honor of God, the Lamb, and his martyrs while at the same time declaring judgment on the accuser and those linked to him in woe. This is a double game, a delicate and subtle game of praise and parody.

The apocalyptic throne-room vision, with its drama and embedded declarations, announces and indeed argues for the establishment of the kingdom. Paradoxically, what could be seen as an argument against the fact of God's rule is redirected as a reason for it: the earthly rampage of Satan is the demonstration of God's victory, and the fall is linked inversely with the effective blood of the Lamb and the martyrdom of the faithful. This passage of the Apocalypse argues that things are not as they seem: martyrdom and death equal victory; the very fury of Satan's earthly activity signals that God is already the Victor. Whereas Luke connects the same topic of Satan's fall in Luke 10:18 to a successful and dramatic ministry, here the sign of God's rule is a fugitive and exiled queen, that is, a host of martyrs. In terms of argumentation, John's visionary logic is convoluted yet powerful: Rejoice because of your seeming failure; rejoice because of death, for death implies life. The Lamb is a Lion, the fugitive is a queen, and the dragon is already judged as he rampages.

John's subversion of the political and spiritual status quo is seen not least of all in his playful but sharp application of the trope of "assumption" in the chapter under discussion.[31] The unnamed Christ-child is "assumed" into heaven during the vision of 12:5, when the readers already know that this "king" has come to victory not by eluding death but becoming the slaughtered Lamb (Rev. 5). John thus takes a swipe at the imperial cult: "You want an emperor? You want a king who will rule all the nations? You want a man so bound for greatness that his end is apotheosis? Well, it isn't Caesar. Here is that one destined to rule the nations with iron. But he rules from the cross!" The ongoing power of this juxtaposition is demonstrated by the medieval adaptation of the glory/cross theme, in which Jesus is depicted as a king ruling from his cross of execution (e.g., *The Dream of the Rood*[32]).

An even darker note is intimated, here at 12:12, as at the end of the Apocalypse (e.g., 18:4; 22:11). This note sounds the insistent question: to rejoice or not to rejoice? Where are you standing, where are your loyalties? Have you a part of those in the heavens, or those on the earth? Are you called to joy or to woe? Perhaps, such a polarizing dualism is too stark, and the vision calls Christian readers to see both the woe and joy together, and not the one separately from the other, as appropriate expressions for their ambiguous situation. Like the angel with the little scroll (10:2), the faithful community has a foot in two worlds. The imagery and rhetoric of the Apocalypse

31. For a close reading that details John's unusual and polemical use of the assumption/ascension motifs in chaps. 11 and 12, see Edith M. Humphrey, "Which Way Is Up? Revival, Resurrection, Assumption, and Ascension in the Rhetoric of Paul and John the Seer," *ARC: The Journal of the Faculty of Religious Studies, McGill University* 33 (2005): 328–39.

32. This celebrated Old English poem may be found in its original language in Michael Swanton, ed., *The Dream of the Rood*, Manchester Old and Middle English Texts (New York: Barnes, 1970).

move in two directions at once, depicting the frightening prospect of the faithful in the precarious time of three-and-one-half (11:3; 12:6, 14; 13:5) but also calling, like the prophet Elijah, for an end to hobbling and for the taking of a stand. As Leonard Thompson has noted, in the Apocalypse the boundary markers are soft, and so the question of identity is ever present.[33]

A Double-Edged Sword

We have seen, in this analysis, the benefits and limitations of a structural analysis, a form-critical application of hymns or psalms, and various rhetorical perspectives, classical and motivational. Though no method can do it justice, the power of the text, in both its narrative and speech, is manifest. We should conclude by noting that potency and potential carry with them their own dangers. The peril of the double-edged sword of parody is but one illustration of the difficulty we encounter in reading "open" texts.

My husband and I have a running argument about the relative virtues of Metaphysical poetry (17th c.) versus Restoration poetry (Pope, Dryden, etc.). I prefer the metaphysical poets to those of the restoration, because the technique of parody "cuts both ways." At times, such works as the "Dunciad" or "Absalom and Achitophel" come perilously close to impugning the ideal that is being inversely connected with the object of ridicule. Is it appropriate to use non-creation imagery to parody an enemy, and can the practitioner of this fine art really avoid marking the positive image by his literary weapon? The irreverence of parody is necessary for the mark to be made—but what if the sword falls back and destroys the ideal against which the antitype is being compared? Irony and parody are not tools to be used by the novice, nor can they be appreciated by the novice. So then, if we note that in the Revelation Christ "wears the clothes of the emperor,"[34] we may find ourselves wondering about the Emperor who is truly venerated in the Apocalypse—does

33. Thompson, *Book of Revelation*, 8.
34. See Ernest P. Janzen, "The Jesus of the Apocalypse Wears Emperor's Clothes," in *1994 Seminar Papers*, ed. Eugene H. Lovering Jr., Society of Biblical Literature Seminar Papers Series 33 (Atlanta: Scholars Press, 1994), 637–61.

he also wear no clothes? The answer to this is that the text itself deconstructs the image, and the Lion-Lamb in fact does wear no clothes: that is the point.[35] Nevertheless, parody, of all types of discourse, requires hard work on the part of the hearer.

Polyvalence, rather than linear discourse, prevails in the Apocalypse: the oracular but argumentative declarations interact equally with the narrative to make their mark. We are not dealing with a mustering of words and ideas to create a logical presentation of a case (judicial, deliberative, or epideictic) but with the combination of argument and evocative symbolism within an open narrative. In this type of text even more than others it is the role of the hearer/reader to trace the images and reconfigure them. However, the creative methods congenial to our own postmodern situation may carry their own dangers if controls are not constructed along with the new readings. Such exploitation can take the form of resisting the text's own cues as to which symbols are interrelated, or that of going far beyond the bounds of the story in a search for more palatable images to transform the pictures of the Apocalypse. That is, the critic is faced with Scylla and Charybdis: she or he may flatten the polyvalence, or read it idiosyncratically, or even engage in a combination of such actions. We do well to heed the advice of Jacques Ellul: "It is necessary . . . to go back from the text to the symbol, and not to study the symbol more than the text."[36] Such a procedure will at least predispose hearers/readers to commune with the implied speaker/narrator, whether or not they like what is spoken/written. Such a reading of the whole text and a careful response to its paradoxical images are not automatic. The reader, with John, is called to eat and to digest a bittersweet scroll. The Apocalypse, and 11:15–12:17 in particular, is about the use of power and about deep issues of identity. The hearer/reader is given a bittersweet word and left to

35. For a trenchant discussion of the seer's irony, consider Harry O. Maier: "Rehearsing in order to reverse, enthroning so as to decrown, setting up only to knock down, Revelation unmasks the masquerade of tyrannical political power and urges its hearers to walk a more costly way" (*Apocalypse Recalled*, 199).

36. Jacques Ellul, *Apocalypse: The Book of Revelation* (New York: Seabury, 1977), 35.

sort out the issues. The words of the book include a declaration of victory amid ongoing conflict, its pictures include the portent of a refugee queen who is both fleeing the demonic and protected by a divine hand.

What, in the end, is the reader to think about this ambiguity and about the queen and her besieged race? Do they disappear without a word from the scene at the end of chapter 12,[37] or does she reappear in more glorious garb, finally empowered to speak? Atypically for an apocalypse, the reader is not given an explicit interpretation of the visions in chapter 12, except that suggested by the embedded declaration in 12:10–12. The voice from heaven gives its oblique commentary and accentuates the conflictual symbolism; the hearer and beholder is left to find his or her voice but offered a compelling sight and sound at the conclusion of the drama, "Behold, I am coming soon" (22:20). "The Spirit and the Bride say, 'Come,' and let whoever hears say, 'Come'" (22:17).

Edicts of Closure or Letters of Promise? Revelation 1:12–3:22

The messages to the seven churches in the Apocalypse are chapters that, unlike the rest of the book, regularly are used in preaching, presumably because they have been considered less daunting and mystical than the other portions. Preaching and Bible study of this sequence have frequently concentrated on the historical and social details that can be gleaned concerning the named cities, following the same approach as has been customary in exposition of occasional Pauline letters: "what the text meant" is to be established, and only then can application ("what the text means") be discerned. In commenting on the approachability and explicit historical situation of this section, Hemer (following Swete[38]) remarks: "Here is the key to the easiest lock in an admittedly difficult

---

37. Pippin, *Death and Desire*, 76.

38. H. B. Swete, *The Apocalypse of St. John*, 2nd ed. (London: MacMillan, 1907).

text."[39] As a resource for historical background, Hemer's work is unparalleled, and his approach (which he designates "audience-criticism")[40] does not exert a hegemony that would supplant other types of reading. It is indeed the case that an understanding of the first-century milieu of the Asia Minor churches is essential to a full-blown appreciation of the first rhetorical impact of this section. Nevertheless, the messages to the churches, as we shall see, are not simple "letters," nor can they be read solely in historical terms without reference to their unusual literary context—they are, after all, an early sequence in a series of *visions,* and so their symbolic and allusive character must not be lost in a mistaken attempt to read them as we would other New Testament epistles. We cannot assume that attention to historical context alone gives us the tools to "capture" the message. As much work has already been done in terms of the characteristics of the various cities, weight will be given here to the more general social constraints of rhetoric and to the ambiguities and depth of the visionary setting in which these jewels are encased.

In approaching the words to the churches, yet another move must be avoided. Already we have noted the difficulty of excising apt passages for the purpose of literary-rhetorical analysis from the knit-together narrative(s) of the Apocalypse. We might be tempted to treat these written transmissions of John in isolation, even though they are based on visionary pronouncements of the glorified Son of Man. Surely here we have ready-made speech-acts, neatly divided for our analysis. In terms of our adopted structure, this section stands fairly discretely as the B′ portion of the larger chiasm. However, attention to the beginning of the Apocalypse will show that this book is not to be conceived simply in terms of chiastic structure but also as having a forward movement. That is, though one can find a mysterious center at 12:10–12, this core does not obviate the dramatic moments of a work that picks up momentum through increasingly intense series of sevens until the

39. Colin J. Hemer, *The Letters to the Seven Churches of Asia in Their Local Setting,* Journal for the Study of the New Testament: Supplement Series 11 (Sheffield: JSOT Press, 1986), 1.
    40. Ibid., 210.

New Jerusalem is reached. Since the messages to the churches "set up" much of the action of the Apocalypse, it will not do to treat them as discrete passages separated off from the rest of the visionary narrative. We might point out here, as well, that though John's Apocalypse takes the form of a complex of visions, there is nowhere any talk in the initial chapters concerning John "dreaming" or about him "waking from a dream." The lively quality of the Apocalypse engages the reader from the very beginning, where the genre apocalypse is conjoined with the conventions of the letter and John links himself to those who are also "partakers in the trial and the reign" (1:9). Here is a series of vision-reports that will neither permit mere observation nor encourage the recipient to wallow in mystic stupor and speculation (cf. 22:8). Rather, the visions embrace their readers, presenting to those who may hear the Spirit's voice and allowing them to see spiritually what John heard and saw when he was "in the Spirit [but not asleep] on the Lord's day." This is clearly a series of waking visions, directed to those who must, on hearing and seeing, awake. The form and structure of the messages to the churches cohere with this major purpose, where aesthetics are shaped for the purpose of forceful, even jarring, rhetoric.

Turning to See the Voice

Elsewhere I have shown how the references to the New Jerusalem and various women figures in the messages to the churches suggest themes that are more fully explored as the Apocalypse comes to its climax.[41] However, the most obvious indication that the seven messages are integrated within the whole is found in the person and description of the Son of Man in 1:12–20. This

41. Hints of the faithful woman figure, New Jerusalem, are to be seen in 2:7; 3:4, 12, 21, while intimations of the faithless woman figure are darkly nestled in the center of the seven pronouncements, the message to Laodicea, at 2:20. See Edith M. Humphrey, "A Tale of Two Cities and (at least) Three Women: Transformation, Continuity, and Contrast in the Apocalypse," in *Reading the Book of Revelation: A Resource for Students*, ed. David L. Barr (Atlanta: Society of Biblical Literature, 2003), 81–96.

opening epiphany exerts its influence over the next two chapters[42] and, indeed, over the entire Apocalypse. The epiphany of the One like the Son of Man concludes with a reference to the possessions proper to this "Living One": he has the keys of death and hades, he holds the seven stars in his hands, and he walks with prerogative among the seven churches (1:18, 20). These details of intimate connection with the churches head several of the letters (2:1b; 3:1b, 7b) and establish a pattern that connects the letters firmly to the speaker, whom the reader has "seen" through the Christophany vouchsafed to John. Indeed, the identity between the speaker and the message is so complete that John startles us with his remark—καὶ ἐπέστρεψα βλέπειν τὴν φωνὴν (and I turned to *see* the voice). John's turn of phrase, like the Lukan tag of Paul's call as a "vision" (Acts 26:19), has been taken by some as a mere case of *katachrēsis* (the use of a term in an eccentric context). John's unusual wording is not wholly unique: precedents may be found in the Hebrew prophets, who "saw" God's word (Isa. 2:1; Amos 1:1; Mic. 1:1; Hab. 1:1). However, both in Acts and in the Apocalypse the link between the divine word and the One revealed is so strong that the conflation may bear theological significance. Paul heard the Lord Jesus and thus was blinded; John must turn to see the all-powerful Voice.[43] The seven messages that ensue will

42. J. Ramsey Michaels argues cogently for the function of 1:19 as a programmatic statement indicating the narrative technique (i.e., hermeneutical pattern) of the Apocalypse rather than its structural organization. See Michaels, "Revelation 1:19 and the Narrative Voices of the Apocalypse," *New Testament Studies* 37 (1991): 604–20, esp. 614. In this case, "that which you have seen" is equivalent to "that which is," so that the role of the knowledgeable narrator becomes essential. Michaels paraphrases 1:19 as follows: "Write now what things thou hast seen and *what they signify*" (ibid., 606). If the interpretation of "what has been seen" corresponds in John's understanding to what "really is," then it may also correspond to what *is not*, as with the parodic inversion of 1:19 and 17:8 (ibid., 614). Apparently within the seer's understanding there remains also the element of what may not (yet) be signified openly. Thus the vision is narrated alongside interpretation, with surplus unsignified elements. It is in the "what you have seen," as well as in what is left unspoken, that the mystery continues, complicating the expressed interpretative word.

43. J. H. Charlesworth has argued that John here christologically "remints" an established Jewish tradition of the hypostasized heavenly Voice (cf. Word, or Wisdom). His case in "The Jewish Roots of Christology: The Discovery of the Hypostatic Voice," *Scottish Journal of Theology* 39 (1986): 19–41, is firmly critiqued by David E. Aune,

similarly incorporate image with sound, imploring the churches to pay heed and turn.

In the seven messages to the churches the introductory reference to the Son of Man takes on a participial or pronominal form ("the one *holding*"; "the one *who* died"; "the one *who* has") that hearkens back to the details of the epiphany. These phrases of identification follow the initial third person formula Τάδε λέγει ("Thus says," 2:1b, 8b, 12b, 18b; 3:1b, 7b, 14b)—consonant with the *praescriptio*[44] for the Roman edict formula on which the seven proclamations seem to be based, at least in part.[45] Where these introductory phrases do not refer to the actual possessions of the speaker (as in 2:1b, 12b; 3:1b, 7b) they describe him in an honorific manner (e.g., 2:8b, 18b; 3:14), a feature found in the classical edict formula. This convention, of course, establishes the *ethos* of the speaker as in longer speeches, so that the solemnity of

---

who counters that a pre-existing Jewish tradition is not demonstrable (*Revelation 1–5*, Word Biblical Commentary 52 [Dallas: Word, 1997], 88). Aune (*Revelation*, 87) reminds us of the Masoretic and Septuagint readings of Exod. 20:18 ("the people saw the voice/sound"), of the Septuagint reading of Dan. 7:11 (though not in Theodotian) in which Daniel "beheld the voice," and of Philo's commentary on such peculiarities. Charlesworth goes beyond these examples, suggesting that "apocalyptists [including John] forced metaphors until they become conceived as hypostatic creatures" ("Jewish Roots," 37). Even though Charlesworth provides only a putative case for an early *belief* in the hypostatic Voice, the Hebrew/Jewish material to John's hand and the seer's own climactic identification of the Logos (Rev. 19:11–16; cf. 1:16) invite us to see this as more than a figure of speech and thus to capitalize the "Voice."

44. The *praescriptio* was the initial term of an imperial or magisterial edict, in which the title and name (or titles and names) of the one issuing the declaration are given, followed by a verb of declaration ("he says"). Aune explains that the difference between such an edict and a formal letter is that the recipients of a letter are "formally addressed by proper names" during the introduction while the recipients of an edict are not (David Aune, "The Form and Function of the Proclamations to the Seven Churches [Rev 2–3]," *New Testament Studies* 36 [1990]: 201).

45. David Aune discusses the numerous forms to which scholars have appealed as they describe this sevenfold section, which is clearly a "mixed genre." In working through not only the *praescriptio* but all the rhetorical moments of the seven parallel passages, he amplifies and refines the original argument of Gunnar Rudberg ("Zu den Sendschreiben der Johannes-Apokalypse," *Eranos* 11 [1911]: 170–79). Aune thus offers a compelling argument that this passage should be recognized as John's polemical application of the genre of the Roman imperial edict. He also recognizes the Τάδε λέγει as an echo of the Septuagintal "Thus saith [the Lord]," as we will discuss below (see Aune, "Form and Function.")

the words will be marked and the instructions heeded. All these details suggest that we should not consider the seven speech-acts in the first place as "letters" but as "edicts" or "pronouncements," solemnly spoken and transmitted in written words that signal authority as in, for example, a papal encyclical. The introductory formula, coupled with the closing reference to the "Spirit," is the literary equivalent of the imperial seal.

The link to orality is thus stronger in this sequence of seven than in some of the narratives we have considered. Yet the genre "apocalypse" is clearly connected with this writing in a way that is more marked than one of its predecessors, the "prophecy"—scrolls written on in heaven are opened and read for the privileged, are eaten, and the like. Apocalyptic seers are told not simply to transmit God's message by word but either to seal up what has been written (Dan. 12:4) or to make clear God's word in writing (2 Esdras 14:45). Sometimes, as in 2 Esdras, both concealment and publication of the mysterious word are enjoined (14:45–48). In the case of the book of Revelation, the emphasis is on the open nature of the heavenly scrolls. After all, these edicts to the churches issue in the unsealing of the seven-sealed scroll in the hand of the Lamb. However, the Apocalypse also sounds the note of mystery: consider the "shout" of the seven thunders, which John is told to "seal up" (10:4).

The Mystery

This sense of mysterious concealment is also created during the sequence of the seven words to the churches, a characteristic that runs against the grain of the edict formula. We should expect, if these letters were to be understood as single-minded pronouncements, that there should be no ambiguity, and also that the persuasive element would be strongly subordinate to the element of command.[46] Certainly there is an element of "straight-talking" in the edicts, particularly at threatening moments of the discourse,

---

46. Aune remarks that "the authority of the ruler . . . means that the inclusion of the persuasive element is almost entirely voluntary rather than necessary" ("Form and Function," 201).

that is, the sections where demands are made of the hearers. Yet there is a bizarre humility associated with the Ruler so that the seer can countenance the picture of one knocking on the door and wooing back a "first love." This very characteristic is, it seems, associated with the mystery of his identity, a mystery that will be gradually and reverently disclosed as we travel through the apocalypse. The "Lion," the sovereign nature of the Speaker, is not disclosed without the human and humble aspect of the Lamb. It would seem that John the Seer follows the same logic as the "Messianic mystery" of Mark, not willing to make absolute claims for the Christ until his full character is made known. Like their speaker, the seven words to the churches have a dual nature—they are both edicts that command and love letters that speak words of promise.

So it is that, during the christological predicates of the seven messages, the "speaker" is never explicitly named, though he is given an associating and polyvalent title at one point.[47] The honorary references to this exalted one mount as we move through the edicts, so that by the time we get to the final word to Laodicea there is a crescendo of allusive epithets: "Thus says the 'amen,' the witness/ martyr, the faithful and true [one], the beginning of/ruler over the creation of God (ἡ ἀρχὴ τῆς κτίσεως τοῦ θεοῦ)" (3:14b). In terms of structural integrity, Aune's remark is apt: "the cumulative effect of these titles and characterizations is to unify the seven proclamations as pronouncements of the exalted Christ who appeared to John in 1:19–20."[48] Yet the sections are unified in mood as well as structure. That is, there is a tone of mystery even while the epideictic creeps into the overall deliberative genus of the proclamations. Though we must "turn," here we have to do with no simple summons to obedience, as from a master to subjects. Rather, these pronouncements intimate the sublimity and intimacy as well as the authority of the one making the decree: in their mounting enthusiasm they seem designed to move the hearers to praise. Yet even while the

47. Aune points out that "he is identified as the Son of God" at 2:18 (ibid., 190). However, this phrase is still ambiguous, applicable to angel, Israel, or Messiah, as has been frequently pointed out with reference to the Gospels.
48. Ibid., 193.

praise is heightened and the emotive stakes are raised for the readers there is still no outright declaration of the speaker's identity. As Jane Austen's Marianne (*Sense and Sensibility*) says of her relationship to Willoughby: "it was every[where] implied, but never professedly declared." So here the identity of Jesus is everywhere implied but not yet declared, but for a worthier reason. The full identification of the hero is left until we have met the great Martyr, the slaughtered Lamb, and understood his intimate relationship with the people of God. It is not until the final and great Christophany of chapter 20 that we will move beyond the intimations of the Voice to hear the articulation of Jesus' "secret" name, inscribed on the thigh, finally and absolutely announced: "King of Kings and Lord of Lords." Sound, sight, and inscribed word merge in this climactic and unequivocal revelation.

Forward Motion

So it is that this initial visionary episode (chapters 1–3) sets up a hunger that is meant to be satisfied in the final chapters, setting the seven edicts over against the conclusion in a promise/fulfill-ment dialectic.[49] Consider the following parallels:

1:12–16//19:11–16	description of Jesus
1:18//20:2–3	keys
1:17//21:6	Alpha and Omega
2:7b//22:2	tree
2:11b//20:6	life, no second death
2:17//19:12; 22:4	name
2:28b//22:16 (cf. 21:22–23)	star, moon
3:4–5//19:14 (cf. 19:8)	fine white linen
3:12//21:2, 10, 12–14	New Jerusalem, God's glory
3:21//20:4	sharing the throne

One of the initial "promises" is the intimated identity of the "one like a Son of Man," who is disclosed, by the end of the Revelation,

---

49. On the general relationship between the beginning and the ending sections, see Schüssler Fiorenza, "Composition and Structure," 175–76, and Humphrey, "Tale of Two Cities," 82–85.

to be *himself* τὸ Ἄλφα καὶ τὸ Ὦ (The Alpha and the Omega) and the great Lord: "they shall see his face and his name will be on their foreheads" (22:4). The identification of the faithful with the Son of Man is such that in chapters 2–3 the predicates of the sender are not totally subordinated to the *paraenesis*. Not only do the descriptions of the Son of Man attribute authority to him but they also break out of this mold. Even as attention is fixed on the glory of the one who "walks among the candlesticks," "died and came to life," "has the sharp two-edged sword," "has eyes like a flame of fire and feet like burnished bronze," "has the seven spirits and the seven stars," and "opens and no one shall shut,"[50] so too the potential glory of God's people is intimated. She shall "rule with Him," "have a place on the throne," "have a crown," and receive "the morning star." Yet this is not an automatic reward, as the dark and direct words to Laodicea make clear. Aptly, and with an echo of dominical signature to the synoptic parables, the series ends with the recurring coda ὁ ἔχων οὖς ἀκουσάτω τί τὸ πνεῦμα λέγει ταῖς ἐκκλησίαις ("Let the one who has ears hear what the Spirit is saying to the churches," 3:6).

As with the central mystery of the book of Revelation (12:10–12), here the reader finds himself or herself inscribed, personally addressed, but addressed also from within the context of the believing community. The believer with spiritual ears is personally issued a summons and promised a mystery, both of which are the common property of those who "hold to the word of God and the martyrdom of/testimony to Jesus" (μαρτυρίαν Ἰησοῦ, 1:2, 9; 12:17; 19:10; 20:4). What is named and not named, and the manner of naming, are the major means of establishing this dynamic of revealing while concealing. So it is that the one who holds the keys is pictured both as shutting doors by sovereign edict and opening doors of promise by the gentler route of persuasion. The rhetorical impact of the imagery of the seven messages is to establish interconnected

---

50. The proclamation to the Laodiceans (3:14–21) is the exception that proves the rule, swerving from the propositional form, using three descriptive names that clearly establish authority, and ending with a reference to the enthroned status of the speaker. The hearer is not enticed to worship here but alternately chastised and wooed: mystery flees before *paraenesis*.

conditional promises punctuated by warnings. The implications of these are played out in both the darker and the more glorious passages of chapters 18–22.

Scruples for Today

Throughout this discussion of the identity of the church and of Christ, of promise and of judgment, it is inevitable that some have been uneasy with, if not directly resistant to, the gendered language used by the seer. It has become a truism in postmodern circles that symbols not only speak about reality but also shape it. It is also true that symbols, because of their potential for many meanings, may be hijacked or robbed of their deepest impact by the unscrupulous or the ideologue. It must be acknowledged that the gendered imagery of the Apocalypse can be and has been abused. But a sympathetic reading of the visions will acknowledge that this book paints its pictures not only for women but also for men—indeed, for both together as a group, and not separately. There is as much scandal for the male reader of the Apocalypse, who is called to picture himself in a female role, as for the female reader, who is called to embrace both a complete dependence on God and a call to "reign" with Christ. It is not as if Revelation were concerned with an elaborate chain of being, from God through angels, through males, through females, down to the inanimate created order. John twice is forbidden to do obeisance even to the mediating angel (19:10; 22:9), and at the end of the Apocalypse all, "great" or "small," find a level place before the throne of God and the Lamb (19:12; 20:11). Those who have read the Apocalypse solely for gender have recoiled from the imagery that they find there. But if the Apocalypse is read more fully we see a complex network of associative metaphors: bride and queen are cast as strong as well as humble figures. The woman in chapter 12 is mother, martyr, and warrior; likewise the bride in chapter 21 is a fortified city. As these figures are subordinate to God, so they retain strength over against their detractors. Though the book, in word and picture, is concerned with power, it does not concern itself in the first place with empowerment but with suffering and reliance on a mighty God. Readers of our time may have difficulty not only with the choice of imagery but also with the unveiling itself: are the extremes of lowliness and authority, realism and hope, too disturbing to our constitutions?

The Center, the Circle, and the Margins: Revelation 4–5

As we come to the end of our survey of passages on the "open" end of the spectrum, we settle on chapters 4–5 of the Apocalypse. These visionary passages of the heavenly courtroom and its worship are potent examples of a symbolic literature that has a deep effect even while it leaves a "surplus of meaning" that cannot be fully "cashed out" but continues to tantalize the reader. Here the visionary and the oracular combine to sketch a portrait of the unseen and as yet unknown realm. Yet the purpose of this "exotic" vision is not to tantalize or lead to speculation, as might well be the case with the stupefying visions of the celestial realms in *1 Enoch* (e.g., 14:8–25 or chapters 17–36) and as is certainly the case in much gnostic literature. Even while the visionary details of Revelation 4–5 baffle, they are carefully circumscribed by a trained attention on the throne and the Lamb. Moreover, their ultimate purpose is directed deftly by heavenly voices and hymns that interpret the kaleidoscopic images assaulting our imagination. We will first consider the overall action of these two chapters and then analyze the particular role of the acclamations and hymnody that punctuate their dramatic flow.

An Astonishing Entrance

The cosmic vision begins as John is invited, through an open door, to "come up here" into the throne room of heaven.[51] The

51. Scholars associated with the Society of Biblical Literature Apocalypse Seminar divided apocalypses into two major categories—those with an emphasis on history (I), and those with an otherworldly journey (II). Normally the New Testament Apocalypse has been classed in terms of the first category, though here at 4:1 we see an embryonic interest in the second major theme. For classifications and other details of this morphology, see Collins, "Morphology," 14–15.

initial action he beholds is not that of drama but of ongoing worship. Here is a scene of mystery: the Holy One attended by twenty-four noble elders—perhaps prophets and apostles representing the faithful. The worship is led by strange angelic, living creatures (cf. Isa. 6; Ezek. 1), who never cease their praises and who enjoin the noble faithful to fall down before the one on the throne because he is worthy of all honor. He is the creator and they are his creation. In this chapter there is a sense of timelessness, of ongoing and uninterrupted praise, of continual joy before the Creator for his mighty acts. The whole of creation meets in the vision of those strange beings, who are pictured as animate yet very foreign. The churches of God are represented here too, by the elders and by the seven lamps (cf. chapter 1), now seen by John as blazing before God's throne. This is a present, ongoing, solid reality: the sensitive reader grasps John's sense that the praises of the Almighty go on now, as the seer speaks of this.

There is also an intimation that this scene is too lofty, too removed, too strange for us to enter. We look, via John, through a window in heaven, at a vivid scene that can hardly seem permanent, at least from the human perspective. What does humankind know of such uninterrupted sight of God? John communicates this separation, inserting a complication into the plot. As he gazes at the one on the throne he becomes aware of a problem: there is an unread scroll, an unopened book of complete and utter importance, which no one is able to unseal. Here is the whole cosmos before God, and a book that promises to offer an explanation: all the pieces of the puzzle are there, but John does not know what to do with them. Struck by consonant dissonance, John weeps, despite the scene of praise around him. Here, it seems, is a blot on the perfect praise of God. Yet John is not rebuked or removed from the heavenly court. Perhaps we imagine that such perfection would be jealous of its own calm, and reject, ignore, or drown out a discordant voice.

Instead John is taken seriously. One who is intimate with God, an elder, responds to his grief, and says, "Don't weep!" This is not a dismissal, however, for he gives John a reason. John is not simply offered an alternative perspective, but a solution to an urgent problem. Yet the answer is not primarily a proposition. It is personal: "Behold, the Lion of Judah." When John turns, however, he sees that the Lion is the Lamb of God, the standing-slaughtered one. The vision implies a proposition, as well as a mystery, but does not yet declare it. Moreover, underlying any teaching about the Lion-Lamb is the unspoken proposition that the gulf between the throne room and earth, astonishingly, may be bridged. The vision goes on to sketch yet another connection between the two worlds: the twenty-four elders, representatives of the faithful, hold before the throne bowls of incense—that is, bowls filled with prayers—and the perfume and smoke of the incense goes up to God along with the songs of the saints. They pray and they sing praises to the Lion-Lamb. It is as though the prayers of longing and suffering are transmuted into an offering, consonant with the offering of the standing-slaughtered one:

> You are worthy to take the scroll and to open its seals, because you were slain, and with your blood you purchased humans for God from every tribe and language and people and nation. You have made them to be a kingdom and priests to serve our God, and they will reign on earth. (Rev. 5:9b–10)

By vision the seer includes redeemed humanity with him in the heavenly throne room, suggesting that the worship of heaven can be "interrupted" by human grief, that human sorrow can be offered as praise, and that the realm of nature can also, given voice by a human priesthood, enter into the new song of the Lamb! From the center of the circle to the margins, there is an integration of this multifocal vision. Yet the most profound effect of the vision is not to drive the reader to theological contemplation, or to the construction of propositions, or to the distillation of a theological "message." Worship, that other kind of "orthodoxy" ("right praise"), presses down on the reader as he or she is swept up into a "proxy" vision engineered by the rhetorical and literary skill of this unlikely seer. The worship is given a specific shape by the embedded declarations within this drama: the hymnody serves to interpret the scene as well as to stir the reader.

Interpreting Hymnody

As we consider the acclamations and songs within the dramatic context of chapters 4–5, it is clear that they are uttered in the mode of celebration; yet according to the overall rhetoric of John they are also instructive or paraenetic. A structural consideration of the two chapters and the disposition of the hymnic portions within the double vision shows the interconnections and the impact of this diptych:

Chapter 4	Chapter 5
A. Voice of instruction	A. Voice of interrogation "Who is worthy?"
B. εἶδον . . . "the sitting One"	B. Heavenly setting and complicated action
C. Heavenly setting and beings	C. εἶδον . . . the Lion . . . the standing-slain Lamb
D. Four beasts: "Holy . . . who . . ."	D. Twenty-four: "Worthy are you, for . . ."
E. Falling down	E. Many angels: "Worthy is he who . . ." [CODA: Multitude: doxological acclamation to "the Sitting One and to the Lamb"] Four beasts: "Amen"
F. Twenty-four: "Worthy are you, our Lord and God, for . . ."	F. Falling down

A general pattern is to be seen in the two sequences: both feature a voice, a heavenly setting, the injunction to "behold," a third-person acclamation and second-person hymn (accompanied by reasons), and humble *proskynesis,* or abject worship. The brief choral passages within the visionary diptych have proven notoriously resistant to form criticism. As with the declaration of 12:10–12, the second-person passages in these chapters (4:11; 5:9) are reminiscent of praise psalms with the *kî* or ὅτι clause—Brueggemann's "praises *with* reason"[52]—while the third-person participial clauses recall prophetic descriptions of the Almighty or

---

52. Walter Brueggemann, in *Israel's Praise* (89–119), contrasts the biblical passages that call arbitrarily for worship against the more characteristic psalms that give reasons.

imperial court ceremony where characteristics are used in praise. We have seen already that although "reasonable praises" have an august history in the Hebrew tradition, they also may function as *enthymemes*, or crafted arguments with an implied major premise. So with the reasons for praise here, which function so as to enjoin the reader to enter into joy. The first "argument" ("for you created all things," 4:11) is unremarkable and rather brief, calling attention to the creative power of God, because of which he ought to be worshiped. In contrast, the new song is more extensive and functions so as to establish the appropriateness for the worship of "the Lamb":

> *For* you were slaughtered and by your blood
> You ransomed for God
> Saints from every tribe and language and people and
>   nation;
> You have made them to be a kingdom and priests in ser-
>   vice to our God
> And they shall reign on earth. (Rev. 5:9)

The propriety of singing praise to the Lamb is connected not only with his mighty deeds (the redemption) but also with the identity of the worshipers themselves, as well as to their anticipated identity: "They shall reign on earth."

In terms of implicit argument, the hymns direct the hearer/reader to accept and celebrate the worship of the Lamb as a rightful component of the worship of the One on the throne. Christopher Rowland goes so far in his popular commentary as to suggest that "chapter 5 includes the coronation of the Lamb."[53] His assertion goes beyond the actual content of this chapter; Rowland does not actually demonstrate a coronation in his analysis, though we have seen the influence of the *adventus* conventions on the dramatic acclamatory celebration of 11:15–12:12. In Apocalypse 5, however, the acclamations do move the hearer/reader to praise the two major figures with one breath: a coronation of the Lamb is already assumed or it is implied in chapter 12 or it occurs offstage toward

53. Christopher Rowland, *The Book of Revelation* (London: Epworth, 1993), 77.

the climax of the Apocalypse as a whole. Here, in the diptych of chapters 4–5, there is a final goal in view: to link the unnamed One with the Lamb whose human name, Jesus, has been solemnly uttered in the opening narration of the Apocalypse. The heavenly vision accomplishes this through the explicit propositions of the second-person hymns, which begin with the One on the throne and then move to the praise of the Lamb. Through the double structure of the throne-room scene the reader is propelled forward to the final hymn, where their praise is combined.

Along with this symmetry, there is also an inverted order to be traced in the dispersion of the choral parts:

A	third-person acclamation	(4:8)
B	second-person praise hymn	(4:11)
B′	second-person praise hymn	(5:9)
A′	third-person acclamation	(5:11–12)

So then, the scene begins and concludes with the four beasts (4:6; 5:14); between these two brackets we hear the praise of the elders concerning the "Sitting One" (4:11) and a crescendo from elders, to *many* angels, to *every* creature (in the sequence concerning the Lamb, 5:9–13). Static parallelism and symmetry is thus enriched by forward movement and climax. The chiastic symmetry is capped by reference to "the new song" of the twenty-four and a concluding doxology, which incorporates the subjects of both chapters (5:13) and produces the rhetorical effect of acclamation *e consensū omnium*.

The four beasts, however, have the last word. If chapter 5 had been constructed in symmetry with chapter 4, the beasts should have spoken first on behalf of the Lamb (cf. 4:8). Instead, however, the four speak their one word—"Amen!"—at the end of the second sequence, completing a ring structure of endless praise.[54] Yet even here we do not reach the end, nor does the intuitive reader expect it. After all, a pattern of word and action

54. On this extension of Isaiah's trisagion ("Holy, Holy, Holy") into ceaseless praise, see Erik Peterson, *The Angels and the Liturgy*, trans. Ronald Wells (New York: Herder, 1964), 3.

has already been established: "*Whenever* the living creatures give praise and glory and thanksgiving to the One seated on the throne, to the One unto ages of ages, the twenty-four elders fall down . . . and worship" (4:9–10). This rising and falling cadence of chapter 4 serves as an apt final punctuation to the entire double sequence: the four beasts' *word* is merely penultimate and must be completed by the *vision* of the elders in prostration and worship. It is probably not insignificant that this final visual detail of the throne room is wordless and uninterpreted. We are left not with questions, propositions, and explanations regarding the mysteries of the heavenlies and its inhabitants, but with a comment upon the Lamb and the One on the throne who is to be adored. As Leonard Thompson remarks, "Worship is a radical equalizer that breaks down all boundaries in heaven and earth except that between the worshipping community and the two objects of worship."[55]

Yet are there, in the end, two in view? Attention yet again to the "names" or "titles" offered in worship, and to the sights and sounds, may help us here. As we enter with John through the open door we are initially met in the vision by the *sight* of One who is unnamed (4:2) or cryptically named by *antonomasia* as "the Sitting One." We then *hear* him acclaimed with the title "Lord God *Pantocrator*" (4:8) and described as one with "being" in past, present, and future participles (ὁ ἦν καὶ ὁ ὢν καὶ ὁ ἐρχόμενος). Away from celebration and back into the vision, we again *see* the "Sitting One" (4:10). The sequence closes, as we *hear* the acclamation of the one who is "Lord" and "God" because of his creative power.

Chapter 5 follows a different pattern regarding naming. The identity of the Christ is set up as a primary question, anticipated by the angel's titles ("Lion of the tribe of Judah, root of David") in verse 5, and mystified by the vision as John sees a "standing Lamb as though slaughtered" (v. 6). The identification is complete by this point, and the Lion-Lamb is standing, through vivid description, before the reader. Thus the hymn of 5:9–10 simply

55. Leonard Thompson, *The Book of Revelation* (London: Epworth, 1993), 69.

recounts the accomplishments of the Lamb without explicitly naming him. The coda puts together the glory of the Ineffable One with this second figure, and names the second as the Lamb (v. 13). Indeed, the conventions of the Hebrew psalm complicate our ability to count the figures of worship: could it be that the phrase "to the one seated upon the throne and to the Lamb" is a parallelism rather than an additive construction?

Double Vision

Careful attention to the initial description of the Lion-Lamb (5:6) may confirm this suspicion. John describes the position of this figure in a way seldom noticed, because, as with other mysterious details of apocalyptic vision, it is difficult to picture. This one is seen both ἐν μέσῳ τοῦ θρόνου (in the midst of the throne) and simultaneously ἐν μέσῳ τῶν πρεσβυτέρων (in the midst of the elders). Translators have taken an easy way out of this conundrum of two positions, understanding (as is grammatically possible) the first ἐν μέσῳ to suggest a stance *between* the throne and the four living beings (literally, "standing in the middle of the throne and the four living beings"). However, it is more likely that John pictures the Lion as in the midst of the circle, in the midst of the throne that is encircled by the beasts, and then also in the company of the elders. This "double vision" is consonant with the statements of Jesus in the seven edicts regarding his throne and with 7:17, which unambiguously speaks of the one who is "in the midst of the throne (τὸ ἀρνίον τὸ ἀνὰ μέσον τοῦ θρόνου) and yet a shepherd amid those who must be led. The Lion, who has the throne by birthright, also stands as Lamb amid his suffering people; though he has the right to sit, he is the standing-slaughtered Lamb. His lot is both with the One on the throne and with created kin.

Chapter 5 thus sets up intimations of a great mystery that will be unveiled through the continuing action of Revelation. This figure will be known as "the Lamb" (a complex and symbolic title) until chapter 19, where another title will be uttered ("The Word

of God," 19:13), along with a secret[56] name ("King of Kings and
Lord of Lords," 19:16). Finally, at the conclusion of his work, John
will revert to the human and personal name of "Lord Jesus" with
which the Apocalypse began. Through their complex of vision and
speech, chapters 4–5 set up a reserved and double mystery, which
becomes explicit as we travel through the Apocalypse—that the
standing one and the sitting one share a Name;[57] yet the standing
one also names the redeemed who will be a kingdom and priests.
Paradoxically, though the throne-room diptych assigns monarchy
to the Lamb, John also intimates in these chapters the *sharing* of
a throne.[58] The subsidiary message of hope offered to the faithful does not threaten to usurp the position of Christ but rather
amplifies it, as the hymn to the Lamb declares: "You are worthy,
because you have redeemed." Here centrifugal and centripetal
lines reinforce each other. At the end, the most allusive of visions
makes its deep impact in order to sway the imagination to grasp
that which is only with difficulty expressed in propositions.

56. It would seem that David Aune's explanation ("Roman Imperial Court
Ceremonial," 22) of a ruling title connected with the thigh "where the sword lays
[*sic*]" fully explains this image of the name on the thigh, though it is also consonant with the military imagery used here. Yet the reference to "thigh" often has
overtones of intimacy in the Hebrew Bible, is associated with the swearing of oaths
(Gen. 24:2), and is found in epiphanic passages (Gen. 32:25). We would agree with
Bousset (*Die Offenbarung Johannis*, 432–35) that this is rather the final disclosure
(at the point of triumph) of the authoritative name, secret until this moment. The
identification of the Lamb as King of Kings and Lord of Lords becomes the revealed
"secret" that this early Christian community treasured and that was closely related
to their identity. As Adela Yarbro Collins points out, this is the "specific location
of . . . epiphany" (i.e., Jesus and not Caesar) whereby "the divine [is] manifested
in human form." ("Insiders and Outsiders in the Book of Revelation," in *"To See
Ourselves as Others See Us:" Christians, Jews, and "Others" in Late Antiquity*, ed.
Jacob Neusner and Ernest Frerichs, Studies in the Humanities [Atlanta: Scholars
Press, 1985], 218).
57. See also the careful analysis and extended argument concerning the cumulative
effect of divine titles transferred to Jesus and the use of Old Testament language to
describe Christ in Jan Fekkes, *Isaiah and Prophetic Traditions in the Book of Revelation*, Journal for the Study of the New Testament: Supplement Series 33 (Sheffield:
JSOT Press, 1994), esp. 71–74.
58. Robert Hall, "Living Creatures in the Midst of the Throne," *New Testament
Studies* 36 (1990): 606–13.

On Danger and Depth

We have seen already that open language is fraught with danger. In our analysis of the polyvalent imagery contained in the "little scroll," we noted the double-edged sword of parody, which presents a particular difficulty in the reading of an open text. Similarly, the letters to the churches could be read in such a manner as to neutralize the warnings that they issue. In the hands of the unscrupulous there is also peril of misappropriating the juxtaposed images that run through the Apocalypse. Real harm has been, and can be, done by those readers/hearers who attend to the wrong side of the Apocalypse's strong and enigmatic images and assume to themselves a "diabolical" agenda. This procedure has been seen in our own day in the events at Waco and in the interpretation of the first seal, along with its poetic preamble, "Eden to Eden," by David Koresh.[59] In attending to the plight of Koresh and his followers, and the mistakes made by the government in the Waco fiasco, there has been an understandable scholarly sympathy for this writing; however, certain details in the commentary and the poem, coupled with Koresh's proffered "key" to interpretation (Psalm 45), suggest that Koresh had taken the wrong side of the power/weakness equation in the Apocalypse. It appears that he understood his own union with several (some of them juvenile) female members of the group as salvific. Moreover, he looked to the "passing away" of the "birds" (his followers) as a means to spiritual summer and as a passage to life through literal death. In the light of such a reading, Tina Pippin's aversion to the "sacrificial lamb" logic of the Apocalypse, that calls Christians to imitate the Lamb, is lucid.[60] Elisabeth Schüssler Fiorenza's antidote to such destructive appropriation of the symbolism is well known:

59. "Eden to Eden" is the poetic proem to "An Unfinished Manuscript by David Koresh on the Seven Seals of the Book of Revelation," which appears in full along with a scholarly commentary by James Tabor and J. Phillip Arnold in the appendix to James D. Tabor and Eugene V. Gallagher, *Why Waco? Cults and the Battle for Religious Freedom in America* (Berkeley: University of California Press, 1995), 187–211.

60. Pippin, *Death and Desire*, 102.

only in situations where people are legitimately crying out for justice will the Apocalypse elicit a fitting response.[61]

However, we must admit that the Waco episode transpired partly as a result of a marginalized group's reading this text—precisely the situation that should have prevented the misappropriation. Less obvious but still egregious examples of misreading abound in our present context (e.g., the *Left Behind* series), reminding us that it is not enough to be stirred by the potency of Revelation's complex imagery and logic. Rather, the book must be read vigilantly so that we are confronted with its own internal critique of ideology and the pursuit of power. Such a reading of the whole text and a careful response to its paradoxical images are not automatic. At 10:9, the reader, with John, is called to eat and to digest a bittersweet scroll. Those who move too facilely to the sweet will appropriate a vision of unreality or may even justify oppression by a shallow appeal to this book; those who taste only the bitter will continue to be suspicious of the final benediction to which the Apocalypse would lead. The invitation of the Apocalypse to its readership puts within our reach a force for life, but also a power that can be used against its nature. Our reading can take on the form of a wayward and self-destructive Frankenstein or that of a delightful "sub-creation."[62] How we read becomes a parable of how we live.

We have seen that the Apocalypse, and 11:15–12:17 in particular, is about the use of power and the strength of weakness, about what and who is truly great, and about deep issues of identity. We have heard that the Apocalypse, and especially the edicts to the churches, is about the identity of God's people, an identity "opened" by promise and bounded by warning. We have seen and heard that the Apocalypse, and especially chapters 4–5, is about the interconnection between this world and another—an interconnection that has as much to do with vulnerability as it

61. Schüssler Fiorenza, *Revelation*, 139.
62. This helpful concept, not to be confused with "co-creation," is borrowed from J. R. R. Tolkien, "On Fairy-Stories," in *Essays Presented to Charles Williams* (Oxford: Oxford University Press, 1947), and C. S. Lewis, *The Weight of Glory* (New York: Macmillan, 1949).

does with power—and that invites those who are lamenting to turn their voices to praise. At our end is our beginning. So it is that these "open" visions, studded with hymnic and oracular commentaries, urge us to receive imaginatively what was presented more polemically in Paul's "unvision" of 2 Corinthians 12. John's visions, punctuated by adoration, add depth to Paul's insight that "strength is made perfect in weakness." By means of the Apocalypse we may move beyond a paradoxical yet closely argued case through an open door.

CONCLUSION

Toward a Hermeneutics
of Imagination and Sympathy

Ours is a time in which the invitation of the "open door" narrative seems more congenial to readers than the bracing quality of an argumentative speech. Fantasy literature and cinema are currently in their postmodern heyday, while debate largely has degenerated to the level of publicized spectacle and sound bites. It would therefore be easier to speak simply of the aesthetic and entertaining qualities of vision without recourse to their polemical use, of which many readers may be viscerally suspicious. However, within the vision-reports of the New Testament there is a studied convergence of these two human activities, creativity and argumentation, which provides an opportunity for the critic to reflect on the myriads of rhetorical possibilities in writing, on the conventions of the past, and on contemporary habits of mind. We began this study by commenting on the use of the vision-report at dramatic and key points of various New Testament texts. Our analysis of several of these has confirmed the beauty, potency, and ambiguity that typically emerge when this literary form is used in different kinds of texts.

Reviewing the Texts and Their Impact

In the first two examples read, we analyzed how two New Testament writers employ the vision-report to complete what they have to say, whether in a polemical discourse (2 Cor. 12:1–10) or in a narrative that contains a sustained speech (Acts 7:54–60). Here we observed the careful use of intertextual and intercultural strategies: Paul blends classical rhetoric with the conventions of the Jewish apocalypse; Luke brings together the conventions of the apology with historical review and apocalyptic revelation. Moreover, both authors do not play their hand in a predictable manner but "play" with the conventions of the text and the expectations of their readers. Thus Paul musters *ethos*, *logos*, and *pathos* in an ironic manner, braving the dangers of parody, while teasing the reader with expectations of a vision-report that, in the end, simply does not deliver. Luke, in the same way, sets up an outrageous "defense" that turns into an accusation, thus leading his reader to expect the inevitable—the martyrdom of the cheeky yet angel-faced deacon. Again, Luke deftly reverses the normal shape of the revelation-interpretation so that the reader learns, even before the audience in the text, the identity of the Son of Man. Paul's humor and the subtle shaping of the narrative by Luke both engage the reader and tame the latent polyvalence of the vision, thus making the authors' cases in a convincing manner. The argumentation is explicit, even while we encounter surprises as we follow the polemic from beginning to end, and implicit points are often made in such a way that the logical flow is complicated and enriched. Though carefully coached to hear the arguments in a particular way, readers are nonetheless afforded a modicum of freedom because of what remains unspoken and because of the inherently open quality of the visionary genre.

Our second set of texts provided the opportunity to observe how repetition may be used within narrative to direct the implicit argument of extended narrative. These literary structures combine speech and vision-report in a more equal manner than the first set, where word dominated vision. Here speeches are wholly combined with the vision-report, so that word and vision are matched. Readers may be hard pressed, in this balance, to determine whether they are being convinced by a case or ushered into a story: both actions occur at the same time, so that readers are placed on the judge's bench and required to "decide" about what is true while they are also asked to suspend judgment and simply watch the narrative unfold. These texts in Acts (10:1–11:18; 9:1–25; 22:1–22; 26:1–24) are also complex in that they sustain a double focus, their polemic engaging both the characters within the text and a diverse readership. The repetition and complexity of the offered vision-reports create for the astute reader different levels of narration—arguments within arguments and even visions within visions. For the ideal reader who shares concerns with the characters in the text, a quiet invitation to enter the world of the text is issued. In particular, the repeated narratives of Saul's revelations coax the reader to wonder about how the divine light is continuing to make an impact on his or her world and to consider, with Paul, the best way to convince would-be followers of the Way to heed that light.

Repetition becomes a vehicle by which breathtaking action is relieved by a moment of narrative pondering. Events are stilled, and a deep impact is made on those who are receptive to the persuasive narrative.

In the third inquiry we considered texts that, through their vision-reports, highlight the importance of persons and worship. The expanded visionary *chreia* of Luke 10:17–24, the infancy sequence of Luke 1:5–2:40, and the transfiguration accounts (Matt. 17:1–8; Mark 9:2–8; Luke 9:28–36) combine in a studied way the themes of divine glory and potential human glory. In the first case, the vision is given "up front" and then its implications are teased out through an elaboration that, at its very end, opens up to embrace the hearers both inside and outside the text. In the infancy narratives, undeveloped visions and other revelatory events are placed judiciously alongside hymnody so as to grasp the imagination of the reader and set up the implicit argument that will be sustained throughout Luke-Acts: this child is the glory of Israel and the light of the Gentiles. In the transfiguration accounts (especially that of Luke) classical and Jewish traditions are combined in such a way that attention is settled on Jesus even while the whole of salvation-history and the hope of the faithful are also brought into view. Luke's complex interest in word and vision, history and mystery are here showcased, though the art is self-abnegating, calling attention away from itself to the main character. In this section, following Luke's cue, we looked to the history of Christian interpretation as the tradition, beginning with the New Testament epistles and continuing into commentary and iconography, and meditated on the curious and beckoning episode of the transfiguration. The personal and the doxological are not well considered in isolation nor do the various forms of this story engage the detached reader. Instead, the rhetoric of the narrative makes an impact on the gathered community at the same time that the intimation of a commonly shared *apokalypsis* urges the reader to move from individual criticism of the text to hearing and seeing it together with others.

The final texts examined were all excised from an elaborate vision-report, which assumes the genre and the name Apocalypse even while it tips the hat to other forms such as epistle and prophecy. Here vision dominates over word insofar as this is possible of a narrative that entrusts the words of God to its readership (Rev. 22:18–19) and is designed to confirm the identity of its main character as the "Logos of God." The imagination of the reader is stimulated by this wide-ranging and wild narrative, in which action, images, actors, sights, and sounds converge. Because of the flowing character of the work and the long-sighted perspective of the genre apocalypse, it was necessary to set the particular passages within an overview, taking into account the whole structure of the piece. There we saw that centripetal and centrifugal impulses work in cross currents and that symmetry is enriched by a forward movement that comes to a climax. At any moment the reader expects the narrative to come to a conclusion, but instead meets a "deceptive cadence." We are surprised to find ourselves forcibly jolted out of the role of spectator and placed within the canvas of the story. Several of the constituent forms of the vision-report make a double impact on the reader: for example, the ongoing use of hymnody not only leads to worship but also instructs by interpreting the unsettling signs that readers are seeing. In this book the analyst of rhetoric discovers how paradox can be powerful, and not simply disconcerting. Here, at the very place where we might have expected full reign of the reader, vision-report is matched with direct and indirect polemic, provided by embedded propositions. Thus the imagination, though stirred and unleashed, is still guided. One gets the sense of being ushered through an open door—the butler, though ever so discretely, is still doing his job even while the reader's gaze is drawn to the bejeweled door and to the glories that lie beyond.

These representative New Testament vision-reports all make their impact, then, through a combination of sign and word. We are reminded of the shrewd comment made by St. John of Damascus regarding the complementarity of word and image in the areas of divine revelation and human worship: "[T]ake away images altogether and be out of harmony with God . . . or receive them with the language and in the manner which befits them."[1] The Damascene was, of course, speaking about the importance of written word and physical objects in Israel's past and in the contemporary debate of his own day concerning the use of icons. However, his words seem an apt description of what we have discovered with regard to the vision-report, which combines images that appeal with immediacy and poignancy to the "sight" or the imagination with words that clarify and interpret what is being seen. In our present analyses we have moved from those vision-reports that rely heavily on the word toward those that put the weight on the visual and have seen that persuasion and argument may be discerned along the entire spectrum, from the explicit to the implicit. This ought not to be a surprise, since even pure visual art is seldom devoid of a polemic, despite the plea of some aestheticians—much less, then, would we expect to find writings (even those that incorporate visual imagery) that are sheer *objets d'art*. Though generalizations do not always match reality, it would appear that those vision-reports that concentrate on the

1. *Apologia of St. John Damascene against Those Who Decry Holy Images* 1, Internet Medieval Sourcebook, http://www.fordham.edu/halsall/basis/johndamas cus-images.html (accessed July 18, 2006).

verbal tend to impress on the reader a more precise argument, whereas those that work more through the imagistic make a deep impression by implication. At one end of the spectrum, the main appeal is to the "mind" and logical faculties of the reader (though the emotions are stirred by the vision), whereas at the other end, the images are propelled to the imagination and the heart (with the verbal directors ensuring that the shots do not misfire). So then, one gets the sense of a sharp and salty polemic with, for example, the speech of Paul and the narrative of Stephen's last words, over against a deep and compelling polemic with the world created in the Apocalypse—images, words, and all. We are speaking simply of tendencies, however, since it is also the case that Stephen and the seer Paul may create a hunger for the mystical in those who attend to the deeper notes of their polemic, while the allusive imagery of John the Seer is frequently pierced by devastating and pointed irony to be grasped by the quick of mind. That the transfiguration accounts, which blend word and image in near perfect balance, have provided "raw material" for both iconic art and liturgical prayer (not to mention the nonverbal tradition of hesychasm and mysticism) is not surprising.

Critical Issues and Ideological Challenges

Our analysis of vision-reports from the pole of rhetorical discourse to that of imaginative symbolism has shown that persuasion can take either an explicit or an implicit form and that sometimes these approaches can be combined. Moreover, the application of a blended literary-rhetorical analysis is helpful in taking account of all three moments in the writing-reading process: authorial intent (so far as it can be determined), the text in itself, and the elicited response or collusion of those who read. The adaptability and multiple forms that rhetorical analysis now has assumed is helpful, since the analyst can choose which of these concerns— historical, literary, or reader-response—to emphasize. Yet the variety of rhetorical approaches is a complicating factor, leading both to salutary introspection and a methodological navel-gazing that could paralyze. One critical issue recurring throughout this study has been to acknowledge that there is a false dichotomy between radical Christian rhetoric and carefully framed logic. We have observed how the vision-report joins, in different combinations, bald declarations of faith, enthymatic logic, and allusive or suggestive conceptual imagery.

This combination of authorial strategies has called for the use of different analytical tools. These reading strategies have opened up such features as surface structure, directions of plot and action, the use of irony and tonal subtleties, actantial interplay, characterization, the ubiquity of mixed forms, the judicious disturbance of anticipated literary and rhetorical patterns, and the coexistence of "Hebrew" and "classical" patterns. In many cases the discovery of the text has been associated with a discovery of the strengths and weaknesses of the various approaches to literature and rhetoric that are at our disposal. The application of classical categories to our New Testament texts, initiated by George Kennedy, Burton Mack, and myriad others, has confirmed the ease of some New Testament writers within the Greco-Roman world of rhetoric and literature and has shown their ability to make classical sets of conventions their own. The insights of motivational modes proposed by Fischer and heeded by Wuellner have been useful in disclosing the probable aims and impact of the speech-acts. The evolving and carefully construed work of Vernon Robbins has provided a very helpful blending of sociological and literary concerns while offering a big picture and a large arena in which methodological introspection and conversation can take place. It has also offered a precise tool for the thorough and close-up examination of a short text. The actantial model, surface structure analysis, and "reader-response" overviews have, alternatively, provided ways of looking at the overall action and impact of a larger body of selected text, helping us to grasp why these make the imaginative and rhetorical impact they do on many readers. The peculiar weaknesses of the various methods have been noted as we have used them. To take account of these is to adopt a sober attitude toward the various approaches and to refrain from supposing that any of these yields scientific or comprehensive results. Let us hear again and again the bon mot of Vernon Robbins: "The name of the game here needs to be perspicuity and humility."[2] A modest approach to analysis is required. This does not render the contribution of these various artistic methods negligible.

Another facet of the reading process that has been illuminated is that of ideological commitment and dissonance, both inside and outside the text. Attention to rhetoric inevitably leads to a discussion of the power plays inherent in an argument. The general move in our generation from a hermeneutics of neutrality to a hermeneutics of engagement is attended by both promise and peril. Some have supposed that engagement of the reader is identical to the hegemony of the reader and his or her concerns. It may indeed be the case that adherence to the myth of radical neutrality and attachment to the myth of readerly autonomy are merely different sides of the same coin and thus equally dubious. Vision-reports provide a hard case scenario by which we can sort out the difficulties as well as the strengths of the hermeneutical turn[3] that we are currently making. Such aspects as the Scripture's symbolic use of gendered language, its call to humility and self-sacrifice, and its insistence on divine authority are bound to elicit

2. Vernon K. Robbins, "The Present and Future of Rhetorical Analysis," in *The Rhetorical Analysis of Scripture: Essays from the 1995 London Conference*, ed. Stanley E. Porter and Thomas H. Olbricht, Journal for the Study of the New Testament: Supplement Series 146 (Sheffield: Sheffield Academic Press, 1997), 48.

3. The North American religious community is indebted to the insights of E. Schüssler Fiorenza, who highlighted the significance of this hermeneutical shift in her 1987 Society of Biblical Literature Presidential lecture, "The Ethics of Biblical Interpretation: Decentering Biblical Scholarship," *Journal of Biblical Literature* 107 (1988): 3–17. In this lecture, expanded into *Rhetoric and Ethic*, Schüssler Fiorenza laments that the academy has not actually moved beyond a "rhetorical half-turn" and calls for engagement and transforming praxis on the part of her colleagues. Not all may agree with her positive agenda, that is, the contours that she traces for a transforming hermeneutics; there may also be cause to be unnerved by her great optimism concerning the transformative potential of academia—particularly biblical scholarship—in the world (see, e.g., my response to Schüssler Fiorenza's project offered at the 2000 Society of Biblical Literature colloquium and entitled "The Hegemony of Liberation," http://www.edithhumphrey.net/response_to_elizabeth_schussler_fiorenza.htm [accessed July 18, 2006]). However, her critique of scientistic "value-free" inquiry, her queries regarding the clash between postmodernism and ideological commitment, and her insistence on a hermeneutic of imagination are equally salutary.

resistance from many contemporary readers. It is interesting to note how this inevitable resistance is sometimes granted the status of a desideratum or even a requirement for careful reading. The word "critical" in the phrase "critical reading" frequently slips from its technical to its popular meaning as the scholarly community considers what it means to read well. Our human propensity to dismiss those with whom we are in foundational disagreement is addressed by Theodore Stylianopoulos, who, in this time of hermeneutical shift, "calls for irenic disclosure of confessional and scholarly commitments in order to achieve honest, critical discussion of the points of convergence and divergence and, in the end, if necessary, to agree to disagree amicably."[4]

Perelman and Olbrechts-Tyteca do well to remind us that careful reading means acknowledging the richness of the text and our difficulty in apprehending it. One of the major burdens of their "New Rhetoric" is to recall the complexity of language and to acknowledge that hearing (and reading) is not a science but an activity fraught with danger:

> The meaning and scope of an isolated argument can rarely be understood without ambiguity: the analysis of one link of an argument out of its context and independently of the situation to which it belongs involves undeniable dangers. These are due not only to the equivocal character of language, but also to the fact that the springs supporting the argumentation are almost never entirely explicitly described. In establishing the structure of an argument, we must interpret the words of the speaker, supply the missing links, which is always very risky. Indeed it is nothing more than a plausible hypothesis to assert that the real thought of the speaker and of his hearers coincides with the structure which we have just isolated. In most cases, moreover, we are simultaneously aware of more than just one way of conceiving the structure of an argument.[5]

Perhaps it is the case that, without a speaker, the argument traced remains a mere facsimile, without any inherent value. Likewise,

---

4. Stylianopoulos, *New Testament*, 187–88.
5. Perelman and Olbrechts-Tyteca, *New Rhetoric*, 187.

without a reader, the text remains mute. (But what if there will always be a reader of a particular text?) However, the proponents of the "new rhetoric" remind us that our reconstructions of a text ought not to be posited so as to exert a hegemony. Such caution implies that an argument, in this case a specific argument in a New Testament text, has its own integrity, an integrity that may be fuller rather than merely belied through its polyvalent character.

One of the questions that any text poses to its putative readership, if we will but allow it, is: "Do we want to enter its world?" This question becomes particularly acute when the world of the reader and the perceived world of the text collide. We may be reminded of the poignant episode in the popular children's film *The Never-Ending Story*, where Bastian, on realizing that the realm of the story, "Fantasia," has impinged on his own "real" world, slams the book shut in horror: indeed, the hair on the neck of the child watching this film may also rise as the child-Empress of Fantasia suggests that Bastian himself is being observed by those children who live outside of his book, and outside the film, in a story world of their own. That film's shock, however, is resolved by suggesting that the reader is, in fact, the one in control, the complete and perfect creator who can name, bring back to life, and direct the action anew. This is a meta-narrative that delights our age, a notion that rings true to our search for authentic experience.

In fact, the biblical narratives, though they invite readers to participate, turn such a postmodern insight entirely on its head. Postmodernism is right to challenge the myth of neutrality—though a strategy of dispassionate observation may, from time to time, be a helpful literary and philosophical ascesis or discipline. It is true that any one human perception is limited and that there is no room in reality for the autonomous critic. Reading requires engagement. However, is there really any more room for the autonomous creator-reader? Reading the Bible with attention to the cues that it issues does not allow us to retain the fantasy that its world is dependent on us. Rather, we and our world are dependent on the world of the text—or rather on a larger reality that the Bible inscribes and represents. Like the icon, the biblical text frequently works by means of "inverted perspective," with the focal point of the text not outside of the text, but inside of it, below the surface rather than at the level of the reader. The effect is to thwart any reader who would adopt the objective stance and to embrace would-be readers. The voices in the text call and the sights beckon, asking us whether we want to enter so as to really see and hear. In the first place, that "entry" is not so that we can become absolute creators of the narrative but so that we can find a place of dependence within a story that is larger even than the sacred text we are reading, a story not of our own making. Graciously, however, the story suggests that those who enter it indeed are given the role of vital acting and do contribute to the shaping of that story. Vision-reports in the New Testament, which subsume their creative impulse to narrate under a sense of awe, model the kind of creativity to which the faithful reader is also invited.

This invitation to creativity may be more open than the pious reader can easily stomach and more frank than the reader who anticipates religious suppression might have expected; similarly, it may be less like a carte blanche than the postmodernist would desire. Alternatively, readers may be reluctant to admit the freedom of Luke in his retelling blends of Paul's story, surprised by the playfulness of Paul where they had expected a heavier hand and annoyed by the implied judgment of the Apocalypse when it concludes with polarized imagery:

> Let the unjust still do unjustly, and let the impure still be
>   impure;
> and let the just still do justly, and the holy still be holy. . . .
> The Spirit and the Bride say, "Come,"
> and let the one who hears say, "Come." (22:11, 17)

The New Testament vision-report invites entry into its fictive world; yet this fictive world depicts itself as subsumed by a larger and more solid world than that of the human imagination alone—and outside the gates of that larger world, the seer warns, is death.

History, Literature, Rhetoric, and Theology

It is at the level of the imagination that today's reader may most easily spy an open door. The use of (even dark) humor, which assumes perspectival vision, is similarly winsome to those who speak easily of worldviews and who consider all assertions to be shaped by bias. Again, in a day when autonomy can so easily devolve into loneliness, the insistence of the New Testament texts on community and communion, their celebration of a shared and sacred mystery, may prove inviting. The recovery of the importance of history, and the attachment of these vision-reports to various moments in history, may also open up a forgotten thesaurus for the rootless reader of today. The beauty and arresting juxtaposition of imagery and word may also commend these visions to the reader in terms of aesthetics and beauty. For those who do not despise innocence, there is also an appeal in the wide-eyed celebratory mode of some of the hymns and doxologies that accompany these visions. Much time has been spent in this current study demonstrating the studied wit and artless beauty, the richness of texture and jostle of life evidenced in these vision-reports. These are qualities to be appreciated, and invite what I have called a hermeneutics of receptivity among those who care to be borne away by the rhetoric of these texts.

Yet it would be both dishonest and inadequate to concentrate solely on those aspects of the text that lend themselves to appreciation and celebration. As rhetorical and serious pieces, the vision-reports (and the passages to which they are joined) also speak soberly and, to some, in an offensive manner. Attention to the undeclared premises of the *enythememes* and to the tendency of the narratives sounds darker and more alien notes than many would like to admit. There is the constant appeal to a larger, demanding meta-narrative, whose Author cannot be controlled. There is the constant theme of suffering leading to glory. Everywhere there is the assumption that authority may be invoked, though a response by means of love is preferable. There is the implicit judgment on the present state of humankind and the world and more explicit charges against blindness, lack of thankfulness, and egocentrism. The hope of a common vision does not pander to a search for what is utterly novel or wholly idiosyncratic. Such offenses, and many more, are greatly amplified and magnified so that they can be clearly heard and seen in the words and images of the vision-report. For those whose ideology is so defined that humor cannot be perceived, for those whose self-rule forbids the sway of the text's argument, for those who recoil at the idea that vulnerability may be more potent than power plays, the visions will, in their essence, remain mysterious, no matter how many times they are related.

Yet imagination remains the portal by which sights may be glimpsed and sounds heard as from afar. The reader may come to an unexpected point where, by chance, he or she notices something striking and is delighted by what a vision-report can "do" in the hands of a gifted writer. It may be that at first such a sensitive reader might consider this feature simply to be a peculiarity of the biblical text, just as art critics comment on the peculiar perspective of the icon and how one must not judge an icon by the canons of representational art but accept its inverse lines. This gift of surprise may encourage the autonomous and self-styled "critical" reader to let drop, at least for the moment, the protective hermeneutics of suspicion and allow the text to enter his or her world as an equal conversation partner, providing an intriguing hologram of past societies and past writers. To listen for all the overtones, to search out the multiple implications of the images and ideas, is, at the very least, enriching. The reader then becomes someone bigger than before the reading began. At best, however, such "inside" reading offers an even more radical transformation. For the New Testament vision-report, fully apprehended, does not leave its proxy seer, the reader, on his or her feet. Luke, Paul, the seer John, and others in their ranks, have, it seems, practiced the art of becoming transparent and of blending their voices with an orchestra whose theme is designed to celebrate Another. Their sub-creative visionary work has functioned for many as a conduit not to an equal, but to a senior conversation partner. To hear this voice and to turn to see this face is to be leveled immediately to the ground. The case is closed; and then, an open hand and an open door beckon.

BIBLIOGRAPHY

Allison, Dale C., and W. D. Davies. *A Critical and Exegetical Commentary on the Gospel according to Saint Matthew.* Vol. 2. Edinburgh: T&T Clark, 1991.

Andreopoulos, Andreas. *Metamorphosis: The Transfiguration in Byzantine Theology and Iconography.* Crestwood, NY: St. Vladimir's Seminary Press, 2005.

Aune, David. "The Apocalypse of John and the Problem of Genre." *Semeia* 36 (1986): 39–50.

———. "The Form and Function of the Proclamations to the Seven Churches (Rev 2–3)." *New Testament Studies* 36 (1990): 182–204.

———. "The Influence of Roman Imperial Court Ceremonial on the Apocalypse of John." *Biblical Research* 18 (1983): 5–26.

———. "Intertextuality and the Genre of the Apocalypse." In *1991 Seminar Papers,* edited by Eugene H. Lovering Jr., 142–60. Society of Biblical Literature Seminar Papers Series 30, Atlanta: Scholars Press, 1991.

———. *The New Testament in Its Literary Environment.* Philadelphia: Westminster, 1987.

———. *Revelation 1–5.* Word Biblical Commentary 52. Dallas: Word, 1997.

Beagley, Alan James. *The "Sitz im Leben" of the Apocalypse with Particular Reference to the Role of the Church's Enemies.* Berlin: de Gruyter, 1987.

Betz, Hans D. *Der Apostel Paulus und die sokratische Tradition. Eine exegetische Untersuchung zu seiner "Apologie" 2 Korinther 10–13.* Tübingen: Mohr Siebeck, 1972.

———. *Galatians: A Commentary on Paul's Letter to the Churches in Galatia.* Hermeneia. Philadelphia: Fortress, 1979.

Bousset, W. *Die Offenbarung Johannis.* Gottingen: Vandenhoeck und Ruprecht, 1906.

Bovon, François. *Luke 1: A Commentary on the Gospel of Luke 1:1–9:50*. Translated by Christine M. Thomas. Hermeneia. Minneapolis: Fortress, 2002.

Boyle, Robert. *Some Considerations Touching the Style of the Holy Scriptures*. London: Printed for Henry Herringman, 1661.

Brown, Raymond E. *The Birth of the Messiah: A Commentary on the Infancy Narratives in the Gospels of Matthew and Luke*. New York: Doubleday, updated 1993.

Bruce, F. F. *The Acts of the Apostles*. London: Tyndale, 1951.

Brueggemann, Walter. *Israel's Praise: Doxology against Idolatry and Ideology*. Philadelphia: Fortress, 1988.

Bultmann, Rudolf. *Die Geschichte der synoptischen Tradition*. Göttingen: Vandenhoeck und Ruprecht, 1957.

Burchard, Christoph. "Ein vorläufiger griechischer Text von Joseph und Aseneth." *Dielheimer Blätter zum Alten Testament* 14 (1979): 2–53.

———. "A Note on ῾RHMA in *JosAs* 17:1f.; Luke 2:15, 17; Acts 10:37." *Novum Testamentum* 27 (1985): 281–95.

Calvin, John. *Calvin's Commentaries: The Acts of the Apostles 1–13*. Translated by J. W. Fraser and W. J. G. McDonald. Grand Rapids: Eerdmans, 1965.

Carey, Greg, and L. Gregory Bloomquist, eds. *Vision and Persuasion: Rhetorical Dimensions of Apocalyptic Discourse*. St. Louis: Chalice, 1999.

Charlesworth, J. H. "The Jewish Roots of Christology: The Discovery of the Hypostatic Voice." *Scottish Journal of Theology* 39 (1986): 19–41.

Charpentier, Etienne. *How to Read the Old Testament*. Translated by John Bowden. London: SCM Press, 1985.

Chevallier, Max-Alain. "L'argumentation de Paul dans II Corinthiens 10 à 13." *Revue d'Histoire et de Philosophie Religieuses* 70 (1990): 3–15.

Collins, Adela Yarbro. *The Combat Myth of the Book of Revelation*. Harvard Dissertations in Religion 9. Missoula, MT: Scholars Press, 1976.

———. "Feminine Symbolism in the Book of Revelation." *Biblical Interpretation* 1 (1993): 20–33.

———. "Insiders and Outsiders in the Book of Revelation." In *To See Ourselves as Others See Us: Christians, Jews, and "Others" in Late Antiquity*, edited by Jacob Neusner and Ernest Frerichs, 187–218. Studies in the Humanities. Atlanta: Scholars Press, 1985.

———. "Introduction: Early Christian Apocalypticism." *Semeia* 36 (1986): 1–11.

———. "What the Spirit Says to the Churches: Preaching the Apocalypse." *Quarterly Review* 4, no. 3 (1984): 69–84.

Collins, John J. *The Apocalyptic Imagination: An Introduction to Jewish Apocalyptic Literature*. New York: Crossroad, 1987; 2nd rev. edition, Grand Rapids: Eerdmans, 1998.

———. "Introduction: Towards the Morphology of a Genre." *Semeia* 14 (1979): 1–20.

———. "The Symbolism of Transcendence in Jewish Apocalyptic." *Papers of the Chicago Society of Biblical Research* 19 (1974): 5–22.

Collins, R. F. "Paul's Damascus Experience: Reflections on the Lukan Account." *Louvain Studies* 11 (1986): 99–118.

Czachesz, István. "Socio-Rhetorical Exegesis of Acts 9:11–30." *Communio Viatorum* 37, no. 1 (1995): 5–32.

De Vaux, Roland. *Ancient Israel: Its Life and Institutions.* Translated by John McHugh. London: Darton, Longman and Todd, 1961.

Dibelius, Martin. *Studies in the Acts of the Apostles.* Edited by H. Greeven. Translated by Mary Ling and Paul Schubert. London: SCM, 1956.

Dimant, D., and J. Strugnell. "The Merkabah Vision in Second Ezekiel (4Q385 3)." *Revue de Qumran* 14 (1990): 331–48.

Dupont, Jacques. "La structure oratoire du discours d'Etienne (Actes 7)." *Biblica* 66 (1985): 153–67.

Ellul, Jacques. *Apocalypse: The Book of Revelation.* New York: Seabury, 1977.

Fekkes, Jan. *Isaiah and Prophetic Traditions in the Book of Revelation.* Journal for the Study of the New Testament: Supplement Series 33. Sheffield: JSOT Press, 1994.

Fischer, Walter R. "A Motive View of Communication." *Quarterly Journal of Speech* 56 (1970): 131–39.

Florovsky, Georges. *Collected Works of Georges Florovsky.* Vol. 1, *Bible, Church, Tradition: An Eastern Orthodox View.* Belmont: Nordland, 1972.

———. "Ethos of the Orthodox Church." In *Orthodoxy: A Faith and Order Dialogue,* edited by Keith R. Bridston, 36–51. Geneva: World Council of Churches, 1960.

Ford, David F., and Frances Young. *Meaning and Truth in 2 Corinthians.* Grand Rapids: Eerdmans, 1987.

Frye, Northrop. *The Great Code: The Bible and Literature.* Toronto: Academic Press Canada, 1981.

Gager, J. G. "The Attainment of Millennial Bliss through Myth and the Book of Revelation." In *Visionaries and Their Apocalypses,* edited by P. D. Hanson, 146–55. Philadelphia: Fortress, 1982.

Gaventa, Beverly Roberts. *From Darkness to Light: Aspects of Conversion in the New Testament.* Philadelphia: Fortress, 1986.

Gitay, Yehoshua. *Prophecy and Persuasion: A Study of Isaiah 40–48.* Forum Theologiae Linguisticae 14. Bonn: Linguistica Biblica, 1981.

Goulder, Michael. "Vision and Knowledge." *Journal for the Study of the New Testament* 17 (1995): 53–71.

Gruenwald, Ithamar. *Apocalyptic and Merkavah Mysticism.* Leiden: Brill, 1980.

Guenther, Heinz O. "Early Christianity, Q, and Jesus." *Semeia* 55 (1991): 41–76.

Haenchen, Ernst. *The Acts of the Apostles: A Commentary.* Translated by Bernard Noble and Gerald Shinn. Philadelphia: Westminster, 1971.

Hall, Robert. "Living Creatures in the Midst of the Throne." *New Testament Studies* 36 (1990): 606–13.

Hamm, D. "Paul's Blindness and Its Healing: Clues to Symbolic Intent (Acts 9, 22, and 26)." *Biblica* 71 (1990): 63–72.

Hanson, John S. "Dreams and Visions in the Greco-Roman World and Early Christianity." In *Aufstieg und Niedergang der römischen Welt* 2.23.2, edited by Wolfgang Haase, 1395–1427. Berlin: de Gruyter, 1980.

Hase, Karl von. *Geschichte Jesu, nach akademischen Vorlesungen.* 2te Aufl. Leipzig: Breitkopft u. Haertel, 1891.

Hedrick, Charles W. "Paul's Conversion/Call: A Comparative Analysis of the Three Reports in Acts." *Journal of Biblical Literature* 100 (1981): 415–32.

Heil, John Paul. *The Transfiguration of Jesus: The Narrative Meaning and Function of Mark 9:2–8, Matthew 17:1–8, and Luke 9:28–36.* Rome: Editrice Pontificio Instituto Biblico, 2000.

Hellholm, D. "The Problem of Apocalyptic Genre and the Apocalypse of John." In *1982 Seminar Papers*, edited by Kent Harold Richards, 157–98. Society of Biblical Literature Seminar Papers Series 21. Chico, CA: Scholars Press, 1982.

Hemer, Colin J. *The Letters to the Seven Churches of Asia in Their Local Setting.* Journal for the Study of the New Testament: Supplement Series 11. Sheffield: JSOT Press, 1986.

Hills, Julian V. "Luke 10:18—Who Saw Satan Fall?" *Journal for the Study of the New Testament* 46 (1992): 25–40.

Hoffmann, P. *Studien zur Theologie der Logienquelle.* Neutestamentliche Abhandlungen 8. Neue Folge. 2nd ed. Munster: Aschendorff, 1972.

Hubbard, Benjamin J. "The Role of the Commissioning Accounts in Acts." In *Perspectives in Luke-Acts*, edited by Charles H. Talbert, 187–98. Edinburgh: T&T Clark, 1978.

Humphrey, Edith M. "Collision of Modes?—Vision and Determining Argument in Acts 10:1–11:18." *Semeia* 71 (1995): 65–84.

———. *Ecstasy and Intimacy: When the Holy Spirit Meets the Human Spirit.* Grand Rapids: Eerdmans, 2006.

———. "The Hegemony of Liberation" (Society of Biblical Literature 2000 Paper), http://www.edithhumphrey.net/response_to_elizabeth_schussler_fiorenza.htm. Accessed July 18, 2006.

———. "In Search of a Voice: Rhetoric through Sight and Sound in Revelation 11:15–12:17." In *Vision and Persuasion: Rhetorical Dimensions of Apocalyptic Discourse*, edited by Greg Carey and L. Gregory Bloomquist, 141–60. St. Louis: Chalice, 1999.

———. "'I Saw Satan Fall . . .'—The Rhetoric of Vision." *ARC: The Journal of the Faculty of Religious Studies, McGill University* 21 (1993): 75–88.

———. *Joseph and Aseneth.* Guide to Apocrypha and Pseudepigrapha 8. Sheffield: Sheffield Academic Press, 2000.

———. *The Ladies and the Cities: Transformation and Apocalyptic Identity in Joseph and Aseneth, 4 Ezra, the Apocalypse, and The Shepherd of Hermas.* Journal for the Study of the Pseudepigrapha: Supplement Series 17. Sheffield: Sheffield Academic Press, 1995.

———. "A Tale of Two Cities and (at least) Three Women: Transformation, Continuity, and Contrast in the Apocalypse." In *Reading the Book of Reve-*

lation: A Resource for Students, edited by David L. Barr, 81–96. Atlanta: Society of Biblical Literature, 2003.

———. "Which Way Is Up? Revival, Resurrection, Assumption, and Ascension in the Rhetoric of Paul and John the Seer." *ARC: The Journal of the Faculty of Religious Studies, McGill University* 33 (2005): 328–39.

———. "Why Bring the Word Down? The Rhetoric of Demonstration and Disclosure in Romans 9:30–10:21." In *Romans and the People of God*, edited by S. Soderlund and N. T. Wright, 129–48. Grand Rapids: Eerdmans, 1999.

Ingham, Michael. *Mansions of the Spirit: The Bible in a Multi-Faith World*. Toronto: Anglican Book Centre, 1997.

Janzen, Ernest P. "The Jesus of the Apocalypse Wears Emperor's Clothes." In *1994 Seminar Papers*, edited by Eugene H. Lovering Jr., 637–61. Society of Biblical Literature Seminar Papers Series 33. Atlanta: Scholars Press, 1994.

Jervell, Jacob. "The Center of Scripture in Luke." In *The Unknown Paul: Essays on Luke-Acts and Early Christian History*, 122–37. Minneapolis: Augsburg, 1984.

Johnson, Luke Timothy. *The Acts of the Apostles*. Sacra Pagina Series 5. Collegeville, MN: Liturgical Press, 1992.

Jörns, Klaus Peter. *Das hymnischen Evangelium: Untersuchungen zu Aufbau, Funktion und Herkunft der hymnischen Stücke in der Johannesoffenbarung*. Studien zum Neuen Testament 5. Gütersloh: Gerd Mohr, 1971.

Just, Arthur, ed. *Luke*. Ancient Christian Commentary on Scripture. Downers Grove, IL: InterVarsity, 2003.

Keller, Catherine, "Die Frau in der Wuste: Ein feministlisch-theologischer Midrasch 1 zur Offbarung 12," *Evangelische Theologie* 50 (1990): 414–32.

Kennedy, George A. *New Testament Interpretation through Rhetorical Criticism*. Chapel Hill: University of North Carolina Press, 1984.

Kern, Philip H. *Rhetoric and Galatians: Assessing an Approach to Paul's Epistle*. Society for New Testament Studies Monograph Series 101. Cambridge: Cambridge University Press, 1998.

Kilgallen, John J. "The Function of Stephen's Speech (Acts 7:2–53)." *Biblica* 70 (1989): 173–93.

Koresh, David. "An Unfinished Manuscript by David Koresh on the Seven Seals of the Book of Revelation." Appendix in James D. Tabor and Eugene V. Gallagher, *Why Waco? Cults and the Battle for Religious Freedom in America*, 187–211. Berkeley: University of California Press, 1995.

Kreitzer, Larry. "Sibylline Oracles 8, The Roman Imperial Adventus Coinage of Hadrian, and the Apocalypse of John." *Journal for the Study of the Pseudepigrapha* 4 (1989): 69–84.

Kurz, W. "Hellenistic Rhetoric in the Christological Proof of Luke-Acts." *Catholic Biblical Quarterly* 42 (1980): 171–95.

Léglasse, S. "Encore ἑστῶτα en Actes 7,55–56." *Filologia Neotestamentaria* 3 (1990): 63–66.

Lewis, C. S. *The Weight of Glory.* New York: Macmillan, 1949.

Longenecker, Richard. *The Acts of the Apostles.* The Expositor's Bible Commentary 9. Grand Rapids: Zondervan, 1981.

Lund, N. W. *Chiasmus in the New Testament.* Chapel Hill: University of North Carolina Press, 1942.

MacCormack, Sabine. *Art and Ceremony in Late Antiquity.* Berkeley: University of California Press, 1981.

Mack, Burton L. "Elaboration of the Chreia in the Hellenistic School." In *Patterns of Persuasion in the Gospels,* edited by Burton L. Mack and Vernon K. Robbins, 31–67. Sonoma, CA: Polebridge, 1989.

———. *A Myth of Innocence: Mark and Christian Origins.* Philadelphia: Fortress, 1988.

———. *Rhetoric and the New Testament.* Minneapolis: Fortress, 1990.

Mack, Burton L., and Vernon K. Robbins. *Patterns of Persuasion in the Gospels.* Sonoma, CA: Polebridge, 1989.

Maier, Harry O. *Apocalypse Recalled: The Book of Revelation after Christendom.* Minneapolis: Fortress, 2002.

Malbon, Elizabeth Struthers. "Text and Contexts: Interpreting the Disciples in Mark." *Semeia* 62 (1993): 81–101.

Marshall, I. Howard, Stephen Travis, and Ian Paul. *Exploring the New Testament.* Vol. 2, *A Guide to the Letters and Revelation.* Downers Grove, IL: InterVarsity, 2002.

McCant, Jerry W. "Paul's Thorn of Rejected Apostleship." *New Testament Studies* 34 (1988): 550–72.

McGuckin, John Anthony. *The Transfiguration of Christ in Scripture and Tradition.* Lewiston: Edwin Mellon, 1986.

Meyers, Carol L., and Eric M. Meyers. *Haggai, Zechariah 1–8.* Anchor Bible 25B. Garden City, NY: Doubleday, 1987.

Michaels, J. Ramsey. "Revelation 1:19 and the Narrative Voices of the Apocalypse." *New Testament Studies* 37 (1991): 604–20.

Muilenburg, J. "Form Criticism and Beyond." *Journal of Biblical Literature* 88 (1969): 1–18.

O'Rourke, John J. "The Hymns of the Apocalypse." *Catholic Biblical Quarterly* 30 (1968): 400–422.

Perelman, Chaim, and L. Olbrechts-Tyteca. *The New Rhetoric: A Treatise on Argumentation.* Translated by John Wilkinson and Percell Weaver. Notre Dame, IN: University of Notre Dame Press, 1969.

———. *La Nouvelle Rhétorique: Traité l'argumentation.* 2 vols. Paris: J. Vrin, 1958.

Perrin, Norman. "Eschatology and Hermeneutics: Reflections on Method in the Interpretation of the New Testament." *Journal of Biblical Literature* 93 (1974): 3–14.

Pervo, Richard. *Profit with Delight: The Literary Genre of the Acts of the Apostles.* Philadelphia: Fortress, 1987.

Peterson, Erik. *The Angels and the Liturgy*. Translated by Ronald Wells. New York: Herder, 1964.

Pettem, Michael. "Luke's Great Omission and His View of the Law." *New Testament Studies* 42 (1996): 35–54.

Pippin, Tina. *Death and Desire: The Rhetoric of Gender in the Apocalypse of John*. Literary Currents in Biblical Interpretation. Louisville: Westminster John Knox, 1992.

Plank, Karl A. *Paul and the Irony of Affliction*. Atlanta: Scholars Press, 1987.

Porter, Stanley E., and Thomas H. Olbricht, eds. *Rhetoric and the New Testament: Essays from the 1992 Heidelberg Conference*. Journal for the Study of the New Testament: Supplement Series 90. Sheffield: JSOT Press, 1993.

———. *The Rhetorical Analysis of Scripture: Essays from the 1995 London Conference*. Journal for the Study of the New Testament: Supplement Series 146. Sheffield: Sheffield Academic Press, 1997.

Pregeant, Russell. *Christology beyond Dogma: Matthew's Christ in Process Hermeneutic*. Semeia Supplements 7. Missoula, MT: Scholars Press; Philadelphia: Fortress, 1978.

Preminger, Alex, and L. Greenstein, eds. *The Hebrew Bible in Literary Criticism*. New York: Ungar, 1986.

Robbins, Vernon K. *Exploring the Texture of Texts: A Guide to Socio-Rhetorical Interpretation*. Valley Forge, PA: Trinity Press International, 1996.

———. "From Enthymeme to Theology in Luke 11:1–13." In *Literary Studies in Luke-Acts: A Collection of Essays in Honor of Joseph B. Tyson*, edited by R. P. Thompson and T. E. Phillips, 191–214. Macon, GA: Mercer University Press, 1998.

———. *Jesus the Teacher: A Socio-Rhetorical Interpretation of Mark*. Philadelphia: Fortress, 1984.

———. "The Present and Future of Rhetorical Analysis." In *The Rhetorical Analysis of Scripture: Essays from the 1995 London Conference*, ed. Stanley E. Porter and Thomas H. Olbricht, 24–52. Journal for the Study of the New Testament: Supplement Series 146. Sheffield: Sheffield Academic Press, 1997.

———. "Socio-Rhetorical Criticism: Mary, Elizabeth, and the Magnificat as a Test Case." In *The New Literary Criticism and the New Testament*, edited by Edgar V. McKnight and Elizabeth Struthers Malbon, 164–209. Valley Forge, PA: Trinity Press International, 1994.

———. "Using a Socio-Rhetorical Poetics to Develop a Unified Method: The Woman Who Anointed Jesus as a Test Case." In *1992 Seminar Papers*, edited by Eugene Lovering, 302–19. Society of Biblical Literature Seminar Papers Series 31. Atlanta: Scholars Press, 1992.

Rogers, Eugene F. *Sexuality and the Christian Body: Their Way into the Triune God*. Oxford: Blackwell, 1999.

Rosenblatt, Marie Eloise. *Recurrent Narrative as a Lukan Literary Convention in Acts: Paul's Jerusalem Speech in Acts 22:1–21.* Collegeville, MN: Glazier, 1990.

Rowland, Christopher. *The Book of Revelation.* London: Epworth, 1993.

Rudberg, Gunnar. "Zu den Sendschreiben der Johannes-Apokalypse." *Eranos* 11 (1911): 170–79.

Schaberg, Jane. *The Illegitimacy of Jesus: A Feminist Theological Interpretation of the Infancy Narratives.* New York: Crossroads, 1987.

Schüssler Fiorenza, Elisabeth. "The Composition and Structure of the Book of Revelation." In *The Book of Revelation: Justice and Judgment,* 159–80. Philadelphia: Fortress, 1985.

———. "The Ethics of Biblical Interpretation: Decentering Biblical Scholarship." *Journal of Biblical Literature* 107 (1988): 3–17.

———. *Revelation: Vision of a Just World.* Proclamation Commentaries. Minneapolis: Fortress, 1991.

———. *Rhetoric and Ethic: The Politics of Biblical Studies.* Minneapolis: Augsburg, 1999.

Scott, J. M. "The Triumph of God in 2 Cor 2:14." *New Testament Studies* 42 (1996): 260–81.

Segal, Alan. *Two Powers in Heaven: Rabbinic Reports about Christianity and Gnosticism.* Leiden: Brill, 1977.

Shaw, Graham. *The Cost of Authority: Manipulation and Freedom in the New Testament.* Philadelphia: Fortress, 1983.

Siew, Antoninus King Wai. *The War between the Two Beasts and the Two Witnesses: A Literary-Structural Analysis of Revelation 12.1–14.5.* Library of New Testament Studies 283. New York: T&T Clark, 2005.

Soards, Marion L. *The Speeches in Acts: Their Content, Context, and Concerns.* Louisville: Westminster John Knox, 1994.

Spong, John Shelby. *Why Christianity Must Change or Die: A Bishop Speaks to Believers in Exile.* New York: HarperCollins, 1998.

Stamps, D. L. "Rhetorical Criticism and the Rhetoric of New Testament Criticism." *Literature and Theology* 6 (1992): 268–79.

Stanley, David M. "Paul's Conversion in Acts: Why the 3 Accounts?" *Catholic Biblical Quarterly* 15 (1953): 315–38.

Stendahl, K. *Paul among Jews and Gentiles.* Philadelphia: Fortress, 1976.

Steuernagel, G. "AKOYONTES MEN TES PHONES (Apg. 9.7): Ein Genitiv in der Apostelgeschichte." *New Testament Studies* 35 (1989): 619–24.

Stylianopoulos, Theodore G. *The New Testament: An Orthodox Perspective.* Vol. 1, *Scripture, Tradition, Hermeneutic.* Brookline, MA: Holy Cross Orthodox Press, 1999.

Swanton, Michael, ed. *The Dream of the Rood.* Manchester Old and Middle English Texts. New York: Barnes, 1970.

Swete, Henry Barclay. *The Apocalypse of John.* London: MacMillan, 1906.

———. *The Apocalypse of St. John.* 2nd ed. London: MacMillan, 1907.

Tabor, James D. *Things Unutterable: Paul's Ascent to Paradise in Its Greco-Roman, Judaic, and Early Christian Contexts*. Lanham, MD: University Press of America, 1986.

Talbert, Charles. *Literary Patterns, Theological Themes, and the Genre of Luke-Acts*. Missoula: University of Montana Press, 1974.

Tannehill, Robert C. "The Functions of Peter's Mission Speeches in the Narrative of Acts." *New Testament Studies* 37 (1991): 400–414.

———. *The Narrative Unity of Luke-Acts: A Literary Interpretation*. Philadelphia: Fortress, 1986.

Thompson, Leonard. *The Book of Revelation*. London: Epworth, 1993.

———. *The Book of Revelation—Apocalypse and Empire*. Oxford: Oxford University Press, 1990.

Thompson, Richard P., and Thomas E. Phillips, eds. *Literary Studies in Luke-Acts: Essays in Honor of Joseph B. Tyson*. Macon, GA: Mercer University Press, 1998.

Tkacz, Catherine Brown. *The Key to the Brescia Casket: Typology and the Early Christian Imagination*. Paris: University of Notre Dame Press, 2002.

Tolkien, J. R. R. "On Fairy-Stories." In *Essays Presented to Charles Williams*, 33–89. Oxford: Oxford University Press, 1947.

Townsend, John T. "Acts 9:1–29 and Early Church Tradition." In *1988 Seminar Papers*, edited by David J. Lull, 119–31. Society of Biblical Literature Seminar Papers Series 27. Atlanta: Scholars Press, 1988.

Tuell, Steven Shawn. "Haggai-Zechariah: Prophecy after the Manner of Ezekiel." In *Thematic Threads in the Book of the Twelve*, edited by Aaron Schart and Paul L. Redditt, 263–86. Beiheft zur Zeitschrift für die altentestamentliche Wissenschaft 325. Berlin: de Gruyter, 2003.

Turner, Max. "The Spirit of Prophecy and the Power of Authoritative Preaching in Luke-Acts: A Question of Origins." *New Testament Studies* 38 (1992): 66–88.

Vollenweider, Samuel. "'Ich sah den Satan wie einen Blitz vom Himmel fallen' (Lk 10:18)." *Zeitschrift für die neutestamentliche Wissenschaft und die Kund der alteren Kirche* 79 (1988): 187–203.

Watson, Duane F. *The Intertexture of Apocalyptic Discourse in the New Testament*. Society of Biblical Literature Symposium Series 14. Atlanta: Society of Biblical Literature, 2002.

Watson, Duane F., and Alan J. Hauser. *Rhetorical Criticism of the Bible: A Comprehensive Bibliography with Notes on History and Method*. Leiden: Brill, 1994.

Webb, Robert. "'Apocalyptic': Observations on a Slippery Term." *Journal of Near Eastern Studies* 49 (1990): 115–26.

Wheelwright, Philip. *Metaphor and Reality*. Bloomington: Indiana University Press, 1962.

Wilson, Robert R. "Early Israelite Prophecy." *Interpretation* 32 (1978): 3–16.

Witherup, R. D. "Functional Redundancy in the Acts of the Apostles: A Case Study." *Journal for the Study of the New Testament* 48 (1992): 67–86.

Wuellner, Wilhelm. "Jesus' Sermon in Luke 12:1–13:9." In *Persuasive Artistry: Studies in New Testament Rhetoric in Honor of George A. Kennedy*, edited by Duane F. Watson, 93–110. Journal for the Study of the New Testament: Supplement Series 30. Sheffield: JSOT Press, 1991.

———."Rhetorical Criticism and Its Theory in Culture-Critical Perspective: The Narrative Rhetoric of John 11." In *Text and Interpretation: New Approaches in the Criticism of the New Testament*, edited by P. J. Hartin and J. H. Petzer, 170–85. Leiden: Brill, 1991.

———. "Where Is Rhetorical Criticism Taking Us?" *Catholic Biblical Quarterly* 49 (1987): 448–63.

Index of Authors

219

Index of Scripture and Other Ancient Writings

John

Acts

Old Testament Pseudepigrapha

1 Enoch

SUBJECT INDEX